Worlds of Literacy

THE LANGUAGE AND EDUCATION LIBRARY
Series Editor

Professor David Corson, *The Ontario Institute for Studies in Education,*
252 Bloor St. West, Toronto, Ontario, Canada M5S 1V6.

Other Books in the Series

Critical Theory and Classroom Talk
    ROBERT YOUNG
Language Policy Across the Curriculum
    DAVID CORSON
School to Work Transition in Japan
    KAORI OKANO
Reading Acquisition Processes
    G. B. THOMPSON, W. E. TUNMER and T. NICHOLSON (eds)

Other Books of Interest

Attitudes and Language
    COLIN BAKER
Education of Chinese Children in Britain and USA
    LORNITA YUEN-FAN WONG
European Models of Bilingual Education
    HUGO BAETENS BEARDSMORE (ed.)
Language Education for Intercultural Communication
    D. AGER, G. MUSKENS and S. WRIGHT (eds)
Life in Language Immersion Classrooms
    ELIZABETH B. BERNHARDT (ed.)
Psychology, Spelling and Education
    C. STERLING and C. ROBSON (eds)
Teaching Composition Around the Pacific Rim
    M. N. BROCK and L. WALTERS (eds)
World in a Classroom
    V. EDWARDS and A. REDFERN

Please contact us for the latest book information:
Multilingual Matters Ltd,
Frankfurt Lodge, Clevedon Hall, Victoria Road
Clevedon, Avon BS21 7SJ, England

THE LANGUAGE AND EDUCATION LIBRARY 5

Worlds of Literacy

Edited by

Mary Hamilton, David Barton and Roz Ivanic

MULTILINGUAL MATTERS LTD
Clevedon • Philadelphia • Adelaide

ONTARIO INSTITUTE FOR STUDIES IN EDUCATION
Toronto

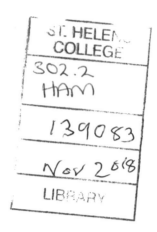
Library of Congress Cataloging in Publication Data

Worlds of Literacy/Edited by Mary Hamilton, David Barton and Roz Ivanic.
p. cm (The Language and Education Library: 5)
ISBN 1-85359-196-3 (hbk). ISBN 1-85359-195-5 (pbk)
1. Literacy. 2. Literacy programs. 3. Literacy–Social aspects.
I. Hamilton, Mary, 1949- . II. Barton, David, 1950- . III. Ivanic, Roz. IV. Series.
LC149.W65   1993   93-13326
302.2'244–dc20

British Library Cataloguing in Publication Data

A CIP catalogue record for this book is available from the British Library.

Canadian Cataloguing in Publication Data

Main entry under title: Worlds of Literacy
(The Language and Education Library: 5)
Includes index.
ISBN 0-7744-0413-2
1. Literacy. 2. Literacy programs. 3. Literacy–Social aspects.
I. Hamilton, Mary, 1949- . II. Barton, David, 1950- . III. Ivanic, Roz. IV. Series.
LC149.W67 1994   302.2'244   C94-930355-0

Multilingual Matters Ltd

UK: Frankfurt Lodge, Clevedon Hall, Victoria Road, Clevedon, Avon BS21 7SJ.
USA: 1900 Frost Road, Suite 101, Bristol, PA 19007, USA.
Australia: P.O. Box 6025, 83 Gilles Street, Adelaide, SA 5000, Australia.

Ontario Institute for Studies in Education
252 Bloor Street West, Toronto, Ontario, Canada M5S 1V6.

Index compiled by Meg Davies (Society of Indexers).
Typeset by Severn Graphics, Clevedon, Avon.
Printed and bound in Great Britain by WBC Print, Bridgend.

Contents

DAVID BARTON

Preface: Literacy Events and Literacy Practices

Roz Ivanic and I sat in the sun lounge of the Midland Hotel overlooking the wide expanse of Morecambe Bay, with the slight worry of knowing that the roof of the room we had booked for the conference had fallen in. The young manager, Grant, swept in, in shirt sleeves, a waistcoat, friendly: 'No problem, don't worry, nothing to worry about, you're free to use the whole hotel'. He went away and returned a few minutes later with a book in his hand. We all shuffled chairs and formed a triangle around a low table. 'Right", he said, "Right, fire away'.

Roz and I had come to make the arrangements for the Worlds of Literacy conference, one of the steps in the preparation of this book. So far we had contacted the hotel by letter, along with two telephone conversations and a fax. Now we had to meet to finalise the details. Negotiating with a hotel manager was something neither Roz nor I had ever done before. I had come with a few notes on a piece of paper: 'Where hold meetings? When meals? Cost of reception?. . .' But we had no idea where to start the discussion, nor how to start it. Uppermost in my mind was the fact that we had sent out two hundred invitations for local people to attend a reception with drink and food on the Thursday night, but we had not explained this to Grant nor worked out the cost for it. Obviously not a place to start the discussion.

Grant placed his large black book on the table, a diary with two days to a page. He opened it to Thursday 21st June, a clean blank day, and wrote with a black ball-point pen 'Worlds of Literacy'. I found it comforting to watch someone writing, the book and the pen making a strange situation more familiar. Sitting opposite someone, reading upside down what they were writing also brought back distant memories. 'What time will you arrive?' Suddenly the diary structured the whole event. We could discuss it chronologically. Everything became straightforward and simple. Between the three of us we talked, and constructed possibilities. He wrote. He wrote agreements, such as that breakfast would be at eight o'clock, and he wrote instructions, such as to the night porter to move some chairs. When we got up and walked round the hotel, Grant took the diary and stopped and wrote in it whenever something was decided.

This whole meeting was a literacy event, constructed out of our literacy practices, our accepted ways of doing things, and revolving around some writing, the diary. Literacy events are the particular activities where reading and writing have a role; literacy practices are the general cultural ways of using reading and writing which people draw upon in a literacy event.

Later, we talked to Grant about the diary. He described a whole cluster of practices associated with the diary, including where it is kept, who looks at it. When people arrive for work each day, one of their first tasks is to check in the diary. He joked that the diary holds the hotel together, stressing that 'the hotel' is as much the social action as the physical building. The fallen roof is not that important, but if the diary went missing then the hotel would fall to bits.

Phil Baber

There are several things to note about this literacy event, and about literacy events more generally. Firstly there were several people involved. There were three of us and we had particular roles. Power was spread between us differently. We were customers and, despite 'you can have everything you want', he was in charge. He held the book and did the writing. Each of us had our purposes and we had to come to agreements; the writing served to confirm those agreements. He held the book in a way that we could always see what he was writing, and we could ask him to change something after he had written it.

Secondly, reading, writing, listening, speaking were all totally inter-twined. The oral and written aspects of it cannot easily be separated. We spoke, we glanced at pieces of paper. Someone said something and someone else wrote it down.

The literacy practices are social practices, accepted ways of doing things. For each of us there were appropriate ways of acting, and ways which would have been inappropriate. At one point Roz, who was sitting nearer to Grant than me, peered into Saturday's entry and asked 'Two weddings on Saturday, does it matter?' 'No.' As I watched her leaning over I wondered if you are allowed to read other entries in the diary. There were definitely limitations created by the situation: only he could write in the diary, for example.

There were bits of the literacy which were new to me: new literacy practices which I learned during the event. There were other parts I did not understand: instructions for moving the chairs were written in a code and there were special names for certain arrangements of tables and chairs. Similarly, the different possibilities of food for the reception had their own names peculiar to the hotel trade. It is worth pointing out that Grant apologised for 'not being very good at spelling': he struck us as being highly literate, in that he was able to make literacy do what he wanted.

This example could be explored further, using it to understand a particular world of literacy in great detail. However, there are broader connections to be made, situating this example as part of a more social view of literacy. Up till now, people developing social views of literacy have demonstrated how literacy is situated in its specific environment and dependent on its context. In this book we want to develop beyond this, showing how there are links and parallels between these different contexts. Our idea is that there are different *worlds of literacy:* in a country like Britain there are distinct literacies which exist alongside each other; that individual people have different experiences and different demands made upon them; and that different people have distinct experiences of and hopes and purposes for reading and writing. There are the separate worlds of adults and children, of people speaking different languages, of men and women. There are also various public worlds of literacy, defined by the social institutions we participate in – including school, work and official bureaucracies.

In this book we explore some of these different worlds of literacy with their own literacy practices and events. By placing them next to each other we can begin to see how they differ and what they have in common. This can help identify the ways in which literacy is shaped and patterned by wider social practices and values in society.

MARY HAMILTON

Introduction: Signposts

This introduction provides a guide for using the book, both in terms of the theoretical ideas that lie behind it and in 'signposting' the various themes and issues that the articles deal with. We hope this will help readers to move between articles and to find new connections for themselves. We also hope it will enable you to move between this book and the many others recently published which are exploring new views and worlds of literacy. We begin by describing briefly who we are, the variety of people and voices in the book and how we came to produce it.

Who We Are and How We Made This Book

The three overall editors of this book have worked closely together for a number of years. At Lancaster University, where we are based, we work in the Literacy Research Group. We are also founder members of a national network linking practitioners and researchers in Adult Basic Education, Research and Practice in Adult Literacy (RaPAL). Our starting point for this book was to bring together people we knew from different worlds of literacy, including those working in adult basic education, schools and higher education, researchers, adult students of writing, community publishers – people who do not often get the opportunity to meet together to discuss their concerns.

This book contains a wide variety of topics, styles and voices: we have gone to great lengths both to retain this diversity and to ensure overall coherence. There has been a remarkable amount of collaboration between contributors: in June 1990 all contributors met at a conference to present their case studies and begin work on the common theme chapters. Since then we have kept in touch with all contributors, circulating and commenting on drafts. Several collaborative articles have resulted from groups that formed at the conference.

The different voices in the book speak through very different styles, depending on the world of the author. For example, we all draw on ideas in books: sometimes these references get written down formally, sometimes they do not. In traditional academic style, some contributors refer to other written articles outside this book, while others do not. The ideas in this book are sometimes expressed in formalised, impersonal academic language. Sometimes these conventions are challenged. Some authors speak in the first person to describe personal experience. Still others have written in the style of research reports. There are accounts of teachers' professional experience and of students reactions to being taught. We encouraged people to include pictures, diagrams and other ways of getting their ideas over in the belief that creative communication has many dimensions.

We believe the diversity of styles strengthens the message of this book and also its accessibility: different readers will find different articles easy to read, depending on their own background and familiar world of literacy. As you read and perhaps feel an outsider to some styles, it is worth reflecting that others will be reacting differently.......

The New Views of Literacy

The idea that reading and writing are embedded in a social context, that there are different literacies rather than one monolithic literacy is now beginning to be accepted. We can make several links between current literacy theory and the work described in this book. This literature is briefly described here so that readers can key into our writing from their own starting point.

In many ways the idea of many literacies parallels the insights from recent work on spoken language. Contemporary debates recognise the diversity of language varieties, all linguistically valid but valued differently within our societies. They also recognise that some 'standard' forms of language are privileged and others marginalised because of historical circumstance and power struggles between different social groups (Fairclough, 1989; Afro Caribbean Language & Literacy Project, 1990). Literacy has often been one important means of strengthening standard language forms and so is central to issues of language and power, intimately connected to our notions of identity and social value.

Taking a new look at reading and writing has also raised questions about the relationship between oral and written discourse, and about how people move from one to the other as they communicate. We now see that becoming literate involves complex translations between the many styles of spoken language and the many forms and purposes that written language may take. Old assumptions that writing is simply a mirror of spoken language or that it is a totally different, separate world should have been laid to rest (Finnegan, 1988).

An important approach advocated in this book is to put the insights and perspectives of literacy learners and users at the centre of research about literacy. This strongly complements the work of researchers such as Flower (forth-coming) and Bereiter & Scardamalia (1987), who have documented through 'protocols' people's own perceptions, understandings and decision-making processes as they read and write. It also grows from the traditions of adult literacy work in the UK and elsewhere that literacy programmes should start from the insights and experience of learners themselves (see for example, Mace, 1992; Frost & Hoy, 1986; Gardener, 1985; Gatehouse Community Publishing Project, 1983).

A second important link is with the large and growing literature documenting the variety of communicative styles and cultural values that people bring to literacy. Michaels (1981), for example, has described different styles of story-telling in infant classrooms; Scollon & Scollon (1981) investigated inter-ethnic communication working with Athabascan children. Heath (1983) produced an influential ethnography of 'the ways with words' of two contrasting communities in the Southern United States. Scribner & Cole (1981) looked at three parallel literacies existing side-by-side in a single community in West Africa: these were associated with the different domains of school, religion and personal communication. Hornberger (1989) has looked more generally at the issues of bi-literacy.

One of the strengths of this new literature is the variety of research methods it draws on, including ethnographic, comparative and historical research. This is especially true of work which looks at literacy in its broader social context. This work does not take education as its central focus but instead asks the questions 'what role does literacy play in society, in this person's life, for this social group?'. Historians such as Graff (1981) and Clanchy (1979) have looked at the development of literacy over time; writers such as Street (1984), Wagner (1987) and Lankshear & Lawler (1987) have taken a cross-cultural perspective. A growing number of research studies use an ethnographic approach to literacy within their own familiar societies and cultures: Schiefflin & Gilmore (1986) and Barton & Ivanic (1991) are two recent examples. The field of gender and language has been extremely influential (see Coates, 1987 and Graddol & Swann, 1989) and we are now beginning to see analysis of gender and basic literacy (Rockhill, 1987; Horsman, 1990). The literacy issues facing cultural and ethnolinguistic minorities have been explored by Philips (1983) , Fishman (1988) and Wagner (1991). Some studies have concentrated particularly on the private and personal sphere of literacy in family life (e.g. Taylor, 1985). All of this work takes a questioning look at the role of formal schooling itself and literacy learning within it (Cook-Gumperz, 1986; De Castell et al., 1986), a theme that is prominent in this book too.

The idea of many literacies is developed from the point of view of the text itself, by those working on genre theory (see Halliday, 1989 and Kress, 1989). Hammond (1990) and McCormack (1990) have looked at genre in relation to adult literacy, and Martin (1989) has discussed it in relation to schooling.

The notion of emergent literacy in young children is another related theme: this moves away from the 'blank slate' approach to teaching reading and writing by recognising that beginning readers and writers bring their own, pre-existing knowledge and purposes to literacy learning which can be effectively built on by teachers (Hall, 1987; Well, 1986; Goelman *et al.*, 1984; Teale & Sulzby, 1986).

The new views of literacy are relevant to teachers at all levels of the education system. Corson (1990), Ivanic (1990), Ivanic & Hamilton (1991) and Schwab (1990) have all shown how these new understandings can inform a coherent approach to language across the curriculum. The new views of literacy demonstrate in detail how the purposes, effects and type of literacy for a given social group may be very different from those given recognition in schools and how this may result in children progressing unequally toward schooled literacy. They also show how other important social institutions such as those dealing with employment or religion make different demands on people's literacy. The school's understanding and treatment of such differences is crucial in helping all children progress towards literacy, in building on the variety of sociocultural backgrounds that form the reality of peoples lives and in informing notions of what contemporary literacy really means.

The work outlined above has explored the ways in which literacy acquisition connects with sociocultural background. This book joins that exploration, contributing both *detail* in the form of new case studies and *coherence* in the way it draws out themes.

How The Book Is Organised

In this book our strategy is to identify some of the different worlds of literacy with their distinct literacy practices and events by means of a series of case studies. We go further to make connections between them, discussing their uniqueness and points of communality, by means of section themes, signposts and collaboratively written articles.

In thinking about how to organise the contributions, we began with section headings like gender, childhood literacy, academic literacy, bilingual literacy – areas of interest that readers would easily recognise and that were our own starting point. The aim of this book, though, is to not only explore our different experiences of literacy but to move further on by drawing together some common threads from this diversity. In order to draw attention to common themes in these different areas of interest, we finally settled on sections which cut across them. To a large extent, these themes grew out of our discussions and reflections as we made the book together.

In **Section 1** we present two overview chapters, which draw out common themes. Brian Street identifies themes related to literacy and personal and national identity, and relates the case studies to his theoretical framework. Jane Mace has related the case studies to issues in adult education and current literacy practice.

Section 2 illustrates the diversity of literacies in our society and in the experience of individuals. The articles in this section were not chosen to be comprehensive, but to raise questions about diversity and the limited assumptions we often make about the forms and purposes of literacy.

Tricia Hartley describes the different voices within one community of minority language speakers. She shows how the complexity of this bilingual, bicultural world is increased by gender patterning and by changes across generations. She reminds us that 'worlds' of literacy are not fixed, but dynamic.

Paul Davies reports on research which documents the everyday collision between the world of bureaucratic literacy, with its special purposes of literacy as evidence, accountability, record-keeping and the needs, goals, resources and interpretations of individual citizens. This is another important aspect of the world's perspective, that there are dominant, sanctioned literacy world-views enshrined within public institutions. School is a powerful one of these. Official agencies are others, as are religions and workplaces.

Nichola Benson, Sarah Gurney, Judith Harrison and Rachel Rimmershaw show the leaps that students have to make in learning the demands of academic literacy in higher education, which are different from the other literacies common to their lives. They outline some of the struggles and conflicts involved in this transition which are echoed many times in other parts of this book.

Two of the articles deal with cultures within Britain that are still primarily oral and therefore outsiders to the literacy club. Agnes King describes her work with travelling communities in the North of England, whose identity rests on remaining outside of settled society and its institutions and does not want to be absorbed by them. Hubisi Nwenmely deals with the world of Kweyol (French Creole) speakers, a language that until very recently has had no written form.

Finally, we have an article on home-school communication which reveals (from the parents' point of view) how limited a school's strategies may be in dealing with parents needs for information and contact, and how written communication can even have a harmful 'distancing' effect on communication in and out of school. Here, as in the other articles in this section we are reminded that the functions of written and oral communication are closely intertwined in people's everyday lives and balanced differently for different groups and different purposes.

Section 3 moves on to articles which illustrate that people's uses of literacy and their sense of themselves as readers or writers is closely tied up with their feelings of social and personal identity.

Nigel Hall and Anne Robinson demonstrate that the process of literacy learning for very young children signals important messages about identity and control in school.

Irene Schwab introduces a case study which raises the issue of how to represent the language of black writers in writing, and how the decisions that are made around this are tied up with identity.

Sarah Padmore shows how our identity is formed by the people surrounding us who love and respect us. In childhood, these people may act as role models and mentors who take a particular interest in us, giving advice that is carried through into adulthood. These guiding lights shape our achievements and attitudes towards literacy.

Paul Davies *et al.*, in a collaboratively written article, offer us some telling metaphors – of literacy as robber, of living simultaneously in two worlds: World I (the private, personal) and World II (the public, social). They show how literacy (and especially writing) can function powerfully to decrease or promote our sense of self-worth.

Section 4 contains examples of the changes people experience and the choices that face them when learning and using new literacies. Two of these articles deal mainly with choices in literacy and literacy learning: Margaret Herrington discusses the advantages and disadvantages of learning literacy at home or in an educational centre. Mukul Saxena describes the complex choices available in a multilingual community and the social significance of these, mirroring wider choices and values.

Two of the articles deal mainly with the changes associated with becoming literate: Jenny Horsman describes how we may have unreal expectations of the power of literacy to change women's lives which are disorganised by other social pressures and roles. Jean Hudson carefully charts the change in a young child's emergent writing, as seen from a teacher's perspective.

The final article brings choice and change together to explore the implications of moving between private and public literacies for women. Through words and images it exposes the whole cultural baggage that is part of the definition of these separate worlds. Choices are tricky and change is difficult to achieve but its implications are far reaching in redefining the way we see ourselves and are valued by others for what we do.

The final section, **Section 5**, contains strong statements from people who have worked with others to create new ways of communicating through the written word. In different ways they all emphasise the power of collaboration in making change happen and in enabling us to take hold of literacy for ourselves. They are all collaboratively written articles.

Peter Goode, Joe Flannagan and Gillian Frost are part of an adult basic education collective. They are working to take control of their education, using literacy to shape (and finance) a dream. They describe the different sorts of collaborations that they use in their work. They also reflect on what is lost when people move towards the accepted world of literacy, as well as what is gained.

Angela Karach and Denise Roach write about the important role of collaboration in writing and other activities for mature women in transition to academic student life. They see collaborating to create and express new ideas as one way of putting into practice their feminist ideals and subverting the strong patriarchal, individualist, elitist culture that permeates academic institutions.

Victor Grenko and Stella Fitzpatrick write about their experience of defining and communicating the taboo: bridging the world of mental illness and everyday life, the worlds of thought and feeling. An important issue is brought up here as they describe moving from the private world of the amateur cartoonist to the public world of published author having to deal with the response of readers, with the additional challenge and risk that this involves (a theme that is echoed in other articles too).

Finally, a short collaborative piece makes the point again that worlds of literacy are not permanently fixed but have to be challenged and re-created to meet the changing needs of individuals. Literacy practices can be seen as a game of rules that can be negotiated and changed to shift the balance of power between the players.

Signposts

These are the **THEMES** which are signposted:

Gender
3, 9, 12,
14, 18, 20

GENDER AND LITERACY The implications of becoming literate are different for women and for men because their lives and roles are structured differently. There are distinctive gendered uses and meanings for literacy and several articles here concentrate on women's worlds of literacy. These discussions are rooted in the large field of gender and language. Much has been written on the silencing of women's voice in literature, and in the processes of creating knowledge, whereby certain types of knowing are privileged or excluded. Within the feminist movement there has been an emphasis on women's writing as an enabling tool for creating our own stories and as a key to personal and social transformation.

There has been some focus on gender and basic literacy and the articles in this book take up this exploration and make links with other silenced voices.

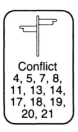

Conflict
4, 5, 7, 8,
11, 13, 14,
17, 18, 19,
20, 21

CONFLICTS BETWEEN WORLDS OF LITERACY The formal education system is the most powerful world of literacy in our society. It dictates what counts as real knowledge or proper language. The normative, standardising function of the education system ensures that some forms of language and written expression are judged to be superior to others and are required for success within academic life. Other forms are devalued. That gives rise to conflicts for those of us entering formal education but resisting these norms. Redefining, negotiating worlds of literacy, not just adapting to existing ones, pressing for the validity of the different, devalued forms to be recognised – this is an insistent theme that runs throughout the book and intimately connected with issue of identity.

Bilingual
3, 7, 11, 17

BILINGUAL/MULTILINGUAL LITERACY People who read and write more than one language have clear uses for the different languages and scripts. These different cultures of literacy are easily identified, linked as they are to different languages and scripts. Varieties of Black English is a more ambiguous area and provides an important link into considering the whole range of 'acceptable' and 'unacceptable' (proper/bad) varieties of English that exist in the different regions of the UK and beyond, and which implicate and position everyone of us.

ORAL AND WRITTEN LANGUAGE are interwoven in communication patterns. Making choices between them, moving from one to the other in developing a personal style of expression – this is the reality of people's experiences even in a print-saturated culture like our own. We also make use of many other communication technologies. How can we give recognition to all these modes of expression within education, encouraging creative and flexible translation between them?

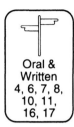

Oral & Written
4, 6, 7, 8, 10, 11, 16, 17

CHILDREN AND SCHOOL LITERACY Young children entering school encounter a new world of literacy which may or may not have similarities with their familiar home world. This theme is less well-represented in this book than others – redressing the balance in the literature as a whole which is strongly focused on children.

Children
5, 6, 8, 10, 12, 16

ADULT LEARNER WRITERS Adults entering education are encountering a new world of literacy, whether they are an adult going to a local group for help with basic English or a mature student entering university. This theme is strongly represented and points up common dilemmas facing mature students at all levels of the education system. Adults' experiences of entering formal learning situations also throw a new light on the adjustments and dilemmas faced by children in the course of their initial schooling.

Adults
5, 6, 7, 9, 12, 14, 15, 19, 20, 21

INSIDE AND OUTSIDE OF EDUCATION Uses of reading and writing in our everyday domestic life are often not counted, but they are a distinct world of literacy, the one in which most of us feel at home. There are many descriptions in this book of the distinct cultures of literacy that exist in people's home surroundings and in particular the different ways of passing on literacy values and skills that they embody. There are many 'teachers' who are not in schools.

Inside/ Outside
5, 6, 7, 8, 14, 19, 20, 21

Where the culture of home differs significantly from school it is easy to feel excluded from the 'literacy club', to feel an outsider to the culture of educational institutions. Many articles touch on this theme, describing the difficulties in communicating that arise. They emphasise the importance of teachers taking these issues of difference on board and encouraging students to reflect on them as part of the educational process.

Public/
Private
4, 6, 9,
13, 14, 15,
18, 21

THE SEPARATION OF PUBLIC AND PRIVATE WORLDS is a recurring theme. This is not the same as isolation, but more to do with the different significance of literacy when used for personal expression and the confirmation of ideas, intimate social relationships as opposed to the public world of mass media, work, official and legal purposes. The power dynamics, the exposure to public opinion and response, the valuing of certain styles of communication, all are totally different in the two realms. This may cause problems when an individual tries to cross from one world into the other without adequate awareness or skills to operate under a different set of rules.

References

Afro-Caribbean Language & Literacy Project in Further & Adult Education (1990) *Language & Power*. Harcourt Brace Jovanovich.

Barton, D. and Ivanic, R. (1991) *Writing in the Community*. London: Sage.

Bereiter, C. and Scardamalia, M. (1987) *The Psychology of Written Communication*. Hillsdale, NJ: Elrbaum.

Clanchy, M. (1979) *From Memory to Written Record*. Cambridge, MA: Harvard University Press.

Coates, J. (1987) *Women, Men and Language*. London: Longman.

Cook-Gumperz, J. (1986) *The Social Construction of Literacy*. Cambridge: Cambridge University Press.

Corson, D. (1990) *Language Policy Across the Curriculum*. Clevedon: Multilingual Matters.

De Castell, S. Luke, A. and Egan, K. (eds) (1986) *Literacy, Society and Schooling*. Cambridge: Cambridge University Press.

Fairclough, N. (1989) *Language and Power*. London: Longman.

Finnegan, R. (1988) *Literacy and Orality*. Oxford: Blackwell.

Fishman, A. (1988) *Amish Literacy: What and How it Means*. Portsmouth, NH: Heinemann.

Flower, L. in press. Studying cognition in context: Introduction to the study. In L. Flower, V. Stein, J. Ackerman, M. Kantz, K. McCormick and W. Peck (eds). *Reading-to-Write: Exploring a Cognitive and Social Process*. Oxford: Oxford University Press.

Frost, G. and Hoy, C. (1986) *Opening Time*. Manchester: Gatehouse Books.

Gardener, S.S. (1985) *Conversations with Strangers: Ideas about Writing for Adult Students*. London: Adult Literacy and Basic Skills Unit.

Gatehouse Community Publishing Project (1983) *Where Do We Go From Here? Adult Lives without Literacy*. Manchester: Gatehouse.

Goelman, H. Oberg, A. and Smith, F. (eds) (1984) *Awakening to Literacy*. London: Heinemann Educational.

Graddol, D. and Swann, J. (1989) *Gender Voices*. Oxford: Blackwell.

Graff, H. (ed.) (1981) *Literacy and Social Development in the West*. Cambridge: Cambridge University Press.

Hall, N. (1987) *Emergent Literacy*. London: Edward Arnold.

Halliday, M.K. (1989) *Spoken and Written Language*. Oxford: Oxford University Press.

Hammond, J. (1990) Choice and genre in adult literacy. *Prospect* 5(2), 42-53.

Heath, S.B. (1983) *Ways with Words*. Cambridge: Cambridge University Press.

Hornberger, N. (1989) Continua of bi-literacy. *Review of Educational Research* 59(3), 271-296.

Horsman, J. (1990) *Something on My Mind Besides the Everyday*. Toronto: Womens Press.

Ivanic, R. (1990) Critical language awareness in action. In R. Carter (ed.) *Knowledge about Language and the Curriculum*. London: Hodder and Stoughton.

Kress, G. (1989) *Linguistic Processes in Sociocultural Practice* (2nd edn). Oxford: Oxford University Press.

Lankshear, C. and Lawler, M. (1987) *Literacy, Schooling and the Revolution*. London: Falmer Press.

Levine, K. (1985) *The Social Context of Literacy*. London: Routledge and Kegan Paul.

Mace, J. (1992) *Talking about Literacy*. London: Routledge.

Martin, J.R. (1989) *Factual Writing: Exploring and Challenging Social Reality*. Oxford: Oxford University Press.

McCormack, R. (1990) *Genre and Process*. Adult Literacy and Basic Skills, Unit Newsletter No. 37. London.

Michaels, S. (1981) 'Sharing Time': Children's narrative style and differential access to Literacy. *Language in Society* 10, 423-442.

Philips, S.U. (1983) *The Invisible Culture: Communication in Classroom and Community on the Warm Springs Indian Reservation*. New York: Longman.

Rockhill, K. (1987) Gender, language and the politics of literacy. *British Journal of Sociology of Education* 8(2).

Schiefflin, B. and Gilmore, P. 1986, *The Acquisition of Literacy: Ethnographic Perspectives* Vol XXI in the series *Advances in Discourse Processes*. New Jersey: Ablex.

Scollon, R. and Scollon, S.B.K. (1981) *Narrative, Literacy and Face in Inter-Ethnic Communication*. Norwood, NJ: Ablex.

Scribner, S. and Cole, M. (1981) *The Psychology of Literacy*. Boston: Harvard University Press.

Street, B. (1985) *Literacy in Theory and Practice*. Cambridge: Cambridge University Press.

Tannen, D. (ed.) (1992) *Spoken and Written Discourse: Exploring Orality and Literacy*. Norwood, NJ: Ablex.

Taylor, D. (1985) *Family Literacy*. London: Heinemann.

Teale, W.H. and Sulzby, E. (eds) (1986) *Emergent Literacy: Writing and Reading*. Norwood N.J: Ablex.

Wagner, D. (1987) *The Future of Literacy in a Changing World*. Oxford: Pergamon Press.

Wagner, S. (1990) *Analphabetisme de minorité et Alphabetisation d'affirmation nationale*. Ottawa, Canada: Mutual Press.

Wells, G. (1986) *The Meaning Makers*. London: Hodder and Stoughton.

Section 1:

Bringing Together Our
Worlds of Literacy

BRIAN V. STREET

1: Struggles Over the Meaning(s) of Literacy

This was written as a reflection on the papers in this volume when they were presented at the 'Worlds of Literacy' conference. We have kept the references to the conference in here, since they throw light on the process of generating ideas together — the sense of excitement and exploration that is at the root of this book.

In reflecting on the stimulating and productive discussions of the conference, I would like to focus on the language we use and the questions we ask in considering literacy issues. The organisers encouraged a tendency towards creative anarchy, with a great deal of brain storming and breaking of boundaries: I would like to subvert this process in turn by proposing ways of bringing order in. I shall consider the 'working weekend' in terms of five active headings that stress process and action rather than fixed or static meanings. Some of the headings and discussions are new to me too and I am struggling to make sense of them: the ideas are therefore not always easy to understand at first but I would argue that we need challenge and difficulty if we are to make progress. It is not worth coming all this way and making all this effort just to repeat to each other platitudes that we already know and are comfortable with.

Constituting Identities and Being Positioned Through Literacy Practices

In learning specific literacy practices we are not just acquiring a technical skill but are taking on particular identities associated with them. Different literacy practices position us differently in social space. Using her extensive collection of photos, Fie van Dijk, for instance, showed how visual images of readers tended to literally position men and women differently: men were often at a table or desk in a studious pose, whilst women were depicted lying back on sofas or reclining in the grass, with their texts part of the landscape, a decorative addition to the picture rather than hinting at serious

See
Chap. 18

See
Chap. 14

See
Chap. 20

See
Chap. 17

See
Chap. 9

See
Chap. 19

attention. Jenny Horsman described how women in the Canadian Maritimes saw literacy as a way of changing their lives, a way out of oppressed situations, yet sometimes the organisers of literacy tuition re-positioned them back in domestic space, either by taking classes to the home or by teaching only those skills associated with domestic-type employment. Angela Karach and Denise Roach discuss the problems women have of maintaining their *own* identities within formal education. They describe the complexities and sense of dislocation women feel when pressures to conform to male values and identities do not fit with their own values and identities in higher education.

Such positioning through literacy is not always determined from above, however: there may be resistance and challenge to the dominant ideology of literacy. Mukul Saxena, for instance, described debate amongst Punjabi families in London about which literacy, language and script it was appropriate for children to acquire. Hindi written in Devnagri was associated with nationalism and the creation of respect and identity, in contrast with the demeaning self-image generated by Punjabi children's experience of British schooling. Punjabi, written in Gumurkhi, was associated for some with religious learning and for others with a secular, socialist identity. The Punjabi community was creating their own literacy market, choosing amongst a multiplicity of languages and literacies as a response to their minority situation in a racist culture. Here literacy practices did not simply position learners but provided a choice of identities. Shirley Cornes similarly included in her list of questions to literacy students not just 'how I have been' but 'how I would like to be'. Literacy practices can be a way of effecting personal as well as social change: of re-positioning oneself, constituting new identities. Peter Goode talked powerfully from personal experience of 'becoming a new person' through the particular literacy practices developed at Pecket Well.

Work on gender, ethnicity, and class as they relate to literacy practices can help reveal the richness and complexity of such identities. This is all a long way from simplistic notions of 'functional illiteracy' or 'work-oriented' literacy programmes that dominate popular and media representations of the 'Worlds of Literacy'.

Defining and Negotiating What Literacy Means

The meanings of literacy are not fixed but can be contested. Debates over the meanings are not just academic issues but part of empowerment: the power to name and define is crucial to real practices, to policy making and to design of educational programmes. Popular representations tend to define 'literacy' in relation to the concept of 'illiteracy': the word literacy in phrases like 'International Literacy Year', I suspect, tends to be taken as meaning 'illiteracy': it has a negative connotation that refers to a problem, often couched in terms of a 'disease' or pathology, as a lack in certain individuals. The Brazilian educator Paulo Freire had tried to rehabilitate the word and give it a positive, creative and empowering meaning. But a glance at the newspaper coverage of International Literacy Year suggests that he had only succeeded inside his own circles. David Barton at the beginning of the weekend said that he preferred to talk about literacy practices and literacy events, terms that are not just jargon but which can help us to focus on the real activities involved in reading and writing and get us away from some of the stereotypes carried in the current language in which literacy is discussed. In many circles now we talk of literacies rather than a single monolithic literacy and that also helps avoid some of the stereotypes. Similarly, the headings I have chosen here all signal active practices of literacy rather than passive or fixed meanings.

See Preface

Part of the struggle over the meanings of literacy has already been fought out in relation to language differences. For instance, it is now more common to talk of 'dominant' languages rather than standard languages, precisely to draw attention to the fact that what is taken as 'standard' is only one version amongst many and the question of how it comes to dominate others has still to be asked: it is not a fact of nature that certain dialects or registers are assumed to be the proper ones to talk. Exposing how they come to have and perpetuate their power position is a crucial part of language politics. I would like to propose that we similarly adopt the notion of 'dominant' literacies to signal that we always need to question how one comes to be dominant and to marginalise others rather than just accept it as 'standard'. In some ways it is harder to do this with literacies than with languages, since it appears more self-evident that there are different languages around us, whereas the success of the dominant literacy is demonstrated by the very fact that it presents itself as the only option. If the society does refer to other literacies they tend to be seen as failed attempts at the real thing, as inadequate and impoverished usages that need to be remediated by proper, mainstream teaching. Mukul Saxena and Irene Schwab have begun to show us how alternative literacies may be identified and how they may come into conflict with the dominant versions, but in both cases they are dealing with multi language as well as multi literacy situations: it is harder to identify alternative literacies within the same language, but once the concept is clear and the notion of 'dominant' literacy becomes familiar, we should be able to recognise and give credit to the rich range of alternatives that have until now been ruled off the agenda. Adult literacy tutors, especially those involved in community writing and publishing are in a good position to do this and there is scope for important research projects and collaboration with academics in this area.

See Chap. 17, 11

See Chap. 21

See Chap. 9

See Chap. 5

See Chap. 20

Being Isolated

Victor Grenko and Stella Fitzpatrick provide a moving and powerful account of how literacy practices can be used to help overcome isolation, both physical and mental. The monsters of mental illness were curiously similar to what Shirley Cornes described as the 'stigma' of illiteracy: in this society mental fears and pressures often take concrete form and this is evident in popular ways of talking both about mental problems and about the literacy difficulties that we all face to various degrees. Victor has used writing as a way of sorting out some problems, of communicating with others and of challenging the positioning that society had determined for him. Collaborative writing groups and social interactions around literacy may provide similar ways of breaking the isolating, 'brahmin' model of learning that predominates in much of our education system. Nichola Benson, Sarah Gurney and Judith Harrison – students at Lancaster University – described how the same isolation and stigma may operate at university. Angela Karach and Denise Roach from a feminist perspective indicated ways in which collaborative literacy practices can help provide an alternative to the competitive and isolating pressures of student life.

Handling Multiplicity of Languages and Literacies

See Chap. 17

See Chap. 5

All societies involve multiple uses of language, dialect, register and of literacy practices and historical accounts suggest this has long been the case. And yet some societies such as the UK still operate on a monolingual and monoliterate model: despite the evident variety of linguistic uses around us, we act as though there is only one proper usage. The advent of European integration in 1992 might help break this peculiar isolation down and some of the evidence at this weekend suggests literacy practitioners on the ground are well aware of it. As Mukul Saxena showed, having a range of languages to choose between need not be a 'problem', as some sectors of education and the media have represented it, but a rich resource. His work highlights the processes of choice or what linguists call 'codeswitching' that we are all involved in but which are apparently more apparent when the switches are between languages. In this case people were codeswitching between Persian/Arabic, Roman/Devnagri and Gumurki scripts. Rachel Rimmershaw and her Lancaster University students demonstrated that similar switching, of both code and mode (between oral and written) are required of students but here the different genres are less apparent and the rules for switching are frequently obscured. University lecturers tend to assume that writing an 'essay' or talking in a seminar or to notes are 'natural' and straightforward and give students little instruction or advice on the complex linguistic functions involved in these processes. Students often do not know what to expect, they find tutors have different expectations according to discipline and personal taste. The situation in itself, it is assumed, will make clear the appropriate genre to use and no other clues are provided. First year students, particularly mature students who don't bring immediate school experience with them, can find these linguistic assumptions the most difficult to cope with, partly because they are not made explicit. And yet much 'failure' may be the product of such genre confusions rather than an indicator of lack of ability. The role of different literacies in these processes is even less understood or researched than of different spoken language styles.

Irene Schwab described in detail the difficult choices about language and script that faced some Afro-Caribbean students on the Centerprise community literacy project in Hackney. The main contribution of the teachers was to make explicit just what the choices were, in a way that according to Rachel Kimmershaw is not done at universities. One of the students, writing an account of his own life, used a mix of Jamaican and standard English forms in his writing and the tutors opened up for him discussion of the implications of choosing a particular variety in which to publish. Their conclusions were not so much to prescribe a single choice as to develop awareness of what is involved: of how language works, of the social and political factors that underlie 'standard' or dominant forms and to develop knowledge and respect for speakers' own Creoles. The politics of language and power in the broadest sense evidently lie behind decisions about writing in such contexts. I would argue that this is true of most everyday contexts too, but it is usually more hidden and harder to bring to the surface than in the situation we have heard about here.

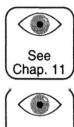

See Chap. 11

See Chap. 5

Indeed, the rich examples provided this weekend demonstrate how little we generally know about language variety in our own society. We need research on language and literacy variation in the UK and we need to share our current knowledge of practice on the ground: literacy practitioners have a key role to play in this as they are often involved in precisely these situations.

Learning Literacies

The predominance of adult literacy practitioners at the weekend raised the issue of how the learning of literacy as an adult relates to child learning. Nigel Hall and Anne Robinson showed that there are new ways of teaching literacy in school and that the kinds of schooling that often generated the literacy problems suffered by the current generation of adult literacy students have not always continued into the present day. Their account of the emphasis on students' own writing, on interactive and creative uses of writing, on process rather than product, had many similarities with current

See Chap. 10

See
Chap. 15

See
Chap. 9

adult literacy practice. In both cases the emphasis is on treating students as people – something that teachers seem to have found harder with young people – and in seeing literacy practices as more than mere technical skills. Joe Flanagan and Peter Goode described how at Pecket Well too, they had learned to write and express themselves as people before worrying too much about the technicalities of spelling and grammar. Could school be like this, was an inevitable question, to which the answer appeared to be yes in the case of Nigel and Anne's example: but people were suspicious of how widespread such cases were and felt that a new generation of adults with learning and literacy difficulties was still being produced. Margaret Herrington gave a moving account of the importance of confidence building in literacy tuition: even in the context of distance learning it was important first to establish personal contact and build a real relationship before a person could get on with the learning process at a distance.

Successful literacy learning was, therefore, connected with much deeper cultural values about identity, personhood and relationships. As we had learnt through all the talks and as all the headings above bring out, literacy is not simply a technical and neutral skill but is imbued with relations of power and ideology and with deep cultural meanings about identity both personal and collective. The richness of people's literacy practices that such an insight opens up was probably the main positive memory that I took away from the weekend. The main negative feeling was how little we currently know and how many misconceptions and misleading notions of literacy have to be cleared away in this society before we can begin to learn. Weekends such as this provide an important and refreshing start by clarifying the language we use and the questions we ask about literacy.

JANE MACE

2: Reflections and Revisits

Before the book, the conference. Before the conference, the original circular. In the circular, the health warning: this will be hard work. No passive listening in the back row to lengthy perorations from Important Speakers specially imported for the event. No loose and wandering discussions. Participants will need to anticipate that this is a weekend designed to make something. And it *was* hard work, both for those who prepared it and those who participated. Everyone who came was expected to be both an Important Speaker and Attentive Listener. There were no elites – and no back rows.

The effort required of this book's editors and contributors, in the subsequent eighteen months, has also been considerable. What is striking, from Mary Hamilton's summary of the work method, is how the same principles of democratic participation have been at work in compiling this as were evident in the conference. It would have been so much easier for one or two people to be the editor, bully conference members to send in their papers, and write an introduction. Instead, the book is an illustration of a more complex and egalitarian literacy practice, in which writers and readers change places and authors also act, at different points, as editors.

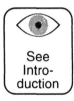

See Introduction

Publications have been made from conferences before. It is a familiar academic convention to publish the 'proceedings' of conferences, and numerous textbooks are the result of an edited collection of conference papers.[1] Equally, many readers will be familiar with the idea of the writing weekend: designed and organised as a creative event, in which literacy students (sometimes from one project, sometimes from a number all over the country) gather together to discuss, draft and edit their own and each other's writing, and (usually later) design and order a resulting collection for publication.[2]

'Worlds of Literacy' weekend organisers asked participants to draft and prepare before, draft and discuss during, and further draft and edit afterwards, a range of individual and group presentations. The event combined the advance preparation of the academic conference with the risky and creative work of the writing weekend; this publication is the highly unusual result.

My own contribution here is short, as it was then. I was asked, with Brian Street, to pick out some themes from the workshops to reflect back to participants on the Saturday. I wrote some notes, spoke from them, and later, tidied them up as a draft to go on in this book. They are here to offer a glimpse, not so much of the book to come, but of the social event from which it originated.

I picked out five themes that had struck me as interesting, which I summarised like this:

- Choice and change are difficult;
- Literacy is oral;
- Literacy is academic;
- Writing is revisiting;
- Collaboration.

Choice and Change are Difficult

At the first evening workshop, Roz Ivanic had invited us to indicate our interests in and questions about literacy on slips of paper and then to group ourselves with others for syndicate work on the basis of these indications. This, I suggested, had revealed several problems of choice:

- choosing which, of many questions, to put down;
- choosing how to express the question in writing;
- choosing which, of the other slips of paper, seemed related to mine;
- recognising that by this choice, I was committing myself to a grouping of interest I was only partially clear about;
- knowing I was thus being asked to take responsibility for the 'curriculum' of my own learning in the conference programme.

All this had been hard for me; and I suggested from my observations, hard for others, too.

See
Chap. 17

See
Chap. 9

Mukul Saxena had spoken of difficult choices made in a Punjabi-Hindi family in Southall, trying to decide whether the children should learn Hindi or Punjabi as the mother tongue, and having to make different literacy choices for different purposes. (At the temple, for example, he reported that there was no choice about how to write the Hindi notices; they had to be handwritten, as the only typewriter they could get was an English one.)

Shirley Cornes, speaking of women students in Dorset had described how women both want and fear the change which educational experience might imply. Angela Karach and Denise Roach had given us a vivid account of how choosing to make such change by engaging in academic study meant having to make difficult choices about when and how to change either their own literacy practice or that of the institution.

See Chap. 20

Literacy, we say, offers us *choice* and *control* (words, incidentally, which feature in the rhetoric of both the political right and left.) These moments at the conference struck me as a sharp reminder that neither of these are easy gifts to use; and that both are highly relative terms.

Literacy is Oral

At an event with much discussion about written literacy, Fie Van Dijk's reminder that literacy is about listening and talking too had felt important. Denise Roach had spoken about the value of women in academic courses gain from 'talking together'. The mother in Mukul Saxena's study, trying to decide what to say in a letter in Hindi to a relative in Delhi had spoken to her mother about it in Punjabi. Shirley Cornes had suggested that the discussion about the task of writing CV's was as important as the written CV itself in the Dorset women's return to study courses.

See Chap. 18

See Chap. 20

See Chap. 17

See Chap. 9

In short, I suggested that there were a number of moments at the conference which underlined the unequal status given by our culture to oral forms of literacy, illustrated vividly by the contrast (offered by Paul Davies) between the tradition on the stock exchange that 'the gentleman's word is his bond' and the obligation by the state on unemployed people to give written evidence of 'actively seeking work'.

See Chap. 4

Literacy is Academic

Sarah Gurney, Judith Harris, Nichola Benson and Rachel Rimmershaw had told us about the 'in' and 'out' of learning to read and write in a university setting. (People who 'master' academic writing have got 'in', independently of what they use it for, Rachel suggested). A central issue in academic study, as they put it to us, was how academic students can make a relationship between book knowledge and their personal experience.

See Chap. 5

For literacy students, as Joe Flanagan put it, the issue is being able to ask for and be given the meaning of words like 'mythology', without fear of being put down for not already knowing their meaning. (Don't deny me those words', he said; 'that's my journey forward'.)

See Chap. 19

Jenny Horsman spoke of women in Nova Scotia feeling 'shut off from the world' while looking after the children (one told her that she felt others thought you needed to be literate in order to have children). Denise Roach and Angela Karach felt 'shut off from the world' of an academic institution

See Chap. 14

dominated by male values. Both examples, I said, suggested that different worlds of literacy give us a feeling that there are different entrance tests before we feel eligible to be part of them.

Writing is Revisiting

See Chap. 20

Isaac Gordon's return to Jamaica meant that, on his return to Hackney, he also wanted to revisit the story he had written of the upbringing he had had there. Irene Schwab's account of the two parts of his autobiographical writing suggested how a new view of an experience can result in a desire to change the written account of it.

See Chap. 11

Victor Grenko and Stella Fitzpatrick told us of the year and a half they have worked together on Victor's pictorial and written work on *A Guide to the Monsters of the Mind*. Victor spoke of experience as a mental patient: 'You're like a man searching for his identity – going through his papers' and this search, in his writing, seemed to be a kind of visiting and revisiting of his imagination.

See Chap. 21

Nigel Eall and Anne Robinson told us of the children with whom Nigel has been corresponding; this, I suggested, was in part a story of how personal letters represent a revisiting by the writer to the reader.

See Chap. 10

I also suggested, in my presentation, that the process of writing and reporting back from notes such as these was a process of revisiting the quality of talk during an event, and a means of giving it one kind of shape and emphasis.

Collaboration and Resistance

This was the most memorable theme for me in the whole event. The two group sessions on writing essays in the academic institutions were the most obvious examples: they told of collaborative methods of resisting low spirits and low confidence in the face of the apparently all-powerful literacies of 'logical argument', 'objective evidence' and unfamiliar theoretical language. Angela Karach, in her paper, quoted another degree student saying that gathering with other women students to give each other support in this had given her the sense that they were 'in the same boat'. Like other literacy educators, I had heard this precise expression used many times by literacy students, expressing the value they felt from learning in a group with equals, and was struck by the common ground between the two worlds of literacy that its use in this session suggested.

See Chap. 20

It is usual to expect that a writer for a known reader may feel free in how she writes. However, these two discussions made clear that although the reader for an academic essay may be known and familiar, as was Rachel

Rimmershaw, course tutor, the essay writers still worked to constraints. The tutor represents something larger; and the writer, her student, knows this. The theme of resistance – strategies for challenging the conventions of the larger literacy culture she represents – concerned questions of how to reverse the structural inequality in the writer-reader relationship.

See
Chap. 5

Those were my comments at the time; and the last one returns me to the discussion with which I began – on the literacy process of gathering both a conference and a book. Fortunately, it is impossible to predict the range of debates and themes that will grow from this one.

Notes
1. Two examples, from conferences I attended in the same year as 'Worlds of Literacy' are:
   Haffenden, Ian *et al.* (1990) *Towards 1992: Education of Adults in the New Europe: Proceedings of the 20th Annual Conference 1990.* Sheffield: Standing Conference on University Teaching and Research in Education of Adults (SCUTREA).
   Freeland, Jane (1990) *Literacy and Liberation: World University Service Annual Conference 1990.* London: World University Service.
2. Two recent collections of writing from writing weekends:
   Buckley, Anne *et al.* (eds) (1989) *Given the Chance We Can Do It.* Dublin: National Literacy Agency.
   NFVES (1991) *If It Wasn't for the Second Chance* . . . National Federation of Voluntary Education Schemes (available from Avanti Books, Stevenage, Herts.)
   Earlier examples, now out of print, but both available in the Write First Time Archive at Ruskin College Library, Oxford are:
   Cambridge House Literacy Scheme (1979) *Listening Ears.*
   Write First Time (1978) *Let Loose.* Write First Time.

Section 2:

Different Voices:
Handling Multiplicities
of Literacy

There are many purposes and ways of communicating in our society and many varieties of reading and writing which correspond to these. The contributions in this section illustrate these literacies and the different voices that give rise to them. An important theme is the perspective of people who are outsiders to the literacy 'club' — where literacy is seen as being tied to the use of standard English, to success in school and to academic pursuits.

TRICIA HARTLEY

3: Generations of Literacy Among Women in a Bilingual Community

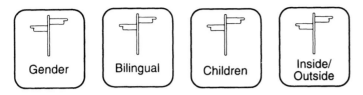

The Town and the Community

Brierfield is a small town of around 10,000 people situated between Nelson and Burnley in North-East Lancashire. Pakistani Muslim people, mainly from the Gujrat/Jhelum area in the north of Pakistan, began settling here some thirty years ago, and there is now a tightly-knit Muslim community of approaching 2,000 people linked by family networks, intermarriage and shared employment patterns, as well as by common cultural and religious backgrounds.

The language spoken by members of the community is Panjabi, which as used in Pakistan does not have a written form. For written communication, therefore, people use Urdu, the national language of Pakistan, a much-venerated literary language and the language of much formal schooling in Pakistan. While some of the words and certain of the grammatical forms of Urdu and Panjabi are similar, they are distinct languages, and some members of the Brierfield community who speak Panjabi as a first language know no Urdu. (These are often people who had only limited opportunities for schooling in Pakistan, including a substantial number of women.) Many younger members of the community, born and brought up in the UK, have their opportunity to learn Urdu at after-school classes run by community members in Brierfield.

See Chap. 7

It is at other after-school classes that many of Brierfield's Muslim children have their introduction to a further written language – the Arabic needed to read the Koran, instruction on which is an essential feature of the

29

See
Chap. 17

life of every young Muslim. Add to these community and religious languages the command of English (both standard written and Lancashire spoken variants!) required to function in Brierfield, and it becomes clear that the background against which members of this community make choices about what they say, read and write is very complex.

The Research Study

The dozen or so women I talked to during the course of this small study were all Muslim women of Pakistani origin attending, or with close relatives who were attending, women-only classes in English and Urdu in Brierfield, run by Nelson and Colne College of Further Education whose main site is only a few miles away. As one of the tutors of the English classes, I was fortunate to have had the chance to get to know most of the women I eventually interviewed over several years before I began this research.

See
Chap. 11

However, I must add the note of caution that I am not bilingual, nor am I Muslim. I was therefore documenting the literacy practices of the community to a great extent 'from the outside', and so unavoidably bringing my own interpretations to bear on what I was told. Although many previous students of minority ethnic communities in Britain have been researched in this way (for example, Shaw's 1988 study of the Muslim community in Oxford, and Ballard & Ballard's on the Sikh community in Leeds, 1977), their authors recognise the far-from-ideal nature of 'outsider' ethnography. All my interviews took place of necessity in English, or in one case with the interpreting help of another of the interviewees, as my command of Panjabi would have taken us no further than introductions and enquiries after each other's health! In an attempt to minimise the impact of my own interpretations of what I was told, I have quoted the exact words of my interviewees directly from my tape transcripts, thus representing some of my interviewees as expressing themselves, at times, with some difficulty in English, whereas with the advantage of a bilingual interviewer they would have had the chance to make these points much more fully and confidently. I feel it is important that the reader bears in mind these limitations, and the small-scale nature of the research, when reading this outline account.

I began the research almost by accident, as discussion about the British education system within the group I was working with led on to comparisons with Pakistan and comparisons between individual women's educational experiences. Several sharp contrasts emerged – between young women educated in Pakistan and those wholly or partly educated here, between older and younger women's experiences of schooling, and amongst the older women, between those who had attended school and those who had had no formal education at all. This naturally led on to a discussion of literacy practices – what, if any, reading and writing went on in each of our homes, who did it, who shared it, what languages and written scripts were involved and so on. Within the group, we ranged from women who spoke Panjabi and some English but did not read and write in any language, through those who only read and wrote in English, although it was their second or third language, through to one young woman who put my British university education to shame with her command of five spoken languages and four different written scripts, gained during her 'good, but not unusual' secondary schooling in Pakistan!

The brief British school experience of Amina, the youngest woman in the group, who had come to Britain in her early teens with very little spoken English, reminded us just how little our monolingual culture values the rich linguistic backgrounds of newcomers from outside Europe. Amina's linguistic education in the UK had been firmly based on the 'deficiency model', with her fluent Panjabi, basic Urdu and modicum of written English counting for very little in the face of the overwhelming pressure to learn to 'speak English' in order to be allowed to progress onto anything else. Jane Miller, looking at the issue of language in multi-ethnic British schools, points out the irony that '(w)hereas learning a foreign language or even one or two dead ones as well has always been the *sine qua non* of a 'good' education, . . . a child with two or three non-European languages, in some of which he may be literate, could be regarded as quite literally languageless when he arrives in an English school, where 'not a word of English' can often imply 'not a word' . . . ' (1983: 5).

I decided to try to follow up the discussions of the whole group, and the questionnaire about literacy practices that we all completed during our discussions, with some more in-depth interviews with six of the women I had talked to. I had become particularly interested in the place of literacies in family life, and in the varying experiences of women from different generations, so I asked three pairs of women from the same families (two pairs of mothers and daughters and one pair of sisters) if I could interview them at home. They all agreed to the interviews and to the use of a tape-recorder to record them, which their unskilled interviewer managed with variable success (for instance, the occasion when I turned the tape over in the middle of fascinating discussion and somehow managed not to press the 'start' button again properly. . .) In the account I hope to pick out a few of the issues which emerged in the group discussions and the individual interviews. (In all cases, the names used are not the real names of the participants, in order to preserve their privacy.)

Shared Experience

Perhaps the most striking feature of the study for me was the way that reading and writing were seen by the women I talked to as shared experiences within the family or wider community, rather than things that were done by individuals separately. The written word, whether in English or Urdu, was often something to be discussed amongst the whole family, while the need for a written communication might call for a joint effort. This approach had arisen perhaps to some extent from necessity, since in many families some members had had extensive opportunities to develop their skills in reading and writing while others had had no such chances. Literacy skills, whether in English or Urdu, were skills to be made available to family and community in the same way as skills in dressmaking or building: individual literacy skills did not assume the paramount importance they had done in my upbringing, for instance. Those with literate skills were seen as having a responsibility to use these for the benefit of all, in exactly the same way as community members with a particularly good command of spoken English were naturally relied on by others as unofficial interpreters and accepted this role without hesitation.

See Chap. 17

See Chap. 13

In such a community, as Brian Street points out: 'Lack of literacy skills . . . need not be represented as though people are suffering from some . . . handicap . . . (C)ommunities develop networks of exchange and interdependence in which literacy is just one skill amongst many being bartered . . . In this situation, the acquisition of literacy skills is not a first order priority at the individual level, so long as it is available at the community level' (1990: 3). All my informants' families had one or more members on whom others tended to rely for help in coping with the reading and writing tasks that arose in daily life. This approach perhaps mirrors the shared nature of experience in general in this community, in which events, whether happy or sad, are shared, in which money and property are often regarded as being held in common, and in which nothing is too much trouble to help a friend or relation in need.

Oral Traditions

See Chap. 14

However, a further noticeable feature in the accounts of the women I talked to was the apparent *lack of need* for reading and writing in the everyday lives of some women. In particular, the lives of many older women who had not had the opportunity of schooling seemed structured in such a way that literacy skills which I had always seen as being significant appeared of minor importance. Brought up with a wealth of oral tradition, these women had an apparently inexhaustible fund of children's stories, songs, family histories, descriptions and instructions stored in their minds, – without my constant need for a written aide-memoire!

When I was discussing this with Sughra, a mother of grown-up children in her late forties, she described learning how to cook particular dishes as a young bride by watching her sister-in-law – something of a late crash-course, since in a relatively privileged upbringing in which her family had always had a cook, she had never done any cooking until she married and found she was expected to take her turn at cooking the family meal with other female relations! Sughra contrasted this with the opportunities open to her own children, who could learn to cook in the traditional way by watching her, or by opening a recipe book and following the instructions – an option not available to their mother. Asked whether she thought having to rely on her memory for such things as recipes had improved her memory powers, she agreed that it had – but admitted that every time she made a particular recipe she did it a little differently . . .

Family Roles

In Brierfield, where more than one person in a family had literacy skills, age and gender seemed to play an important part in who did what. Thus, the husbands of all married women I talked to took a daily paper – usually the 'Daily Jang' or another Urdu newspaper, with the younger men also taking English local or national papers. However, in contrast to the proprietorial attitude sometimes to be found amongst European 'heads of the household' about *'their'* newspapers (I remember one Irish informant in a previous study describing her father's papers as *'sacrosanct, like his place at the table*) the women I talked to described their husbands as regularly reading out important news or interesting snippets to the rest of the family, involving other members of the family in the reading rather than shutting them out. It was not the case, as in the communities studied by Klassen (1991) and by Rockhill (1987) in Canada and the US, respectively, that women took charge of most of the family paperwork: in Brierfield, each sex and age-group had its own area of responsibility. 'Official' communications in Urdu were usually dealt with by husbands, and contents passed on to other family members as appropriate. The shared nature of such experiences of written media echoes that reported by Shirley Brice Heath in the US black working-class community of Trackton, in which 'reading is a social activity . . . The evening newspaper is read on the front porch for most months of the year . . . Circulars or letters to individuals . . . are read aloud and their meaning jointly negotiated by those who have had experience with such activities . . . ' (1983: 196).

See
Chap. 18

When it came to formal communications in English, these were often entrusted to teenage children to read and translate or explain, since in several families they had a better command of written English than their parents.

See
Chap. 8

Contrary to Klassen's finding that children were regarded as unreliable informers, in the Brierfield community children's developing skills in English were respected and admired, and the translation of English communications, particularly from schools and nurseries, was their allotted task in many households.

The position with regard to letters to and from family and friends was different again, however. In most families, letters in Urdu were exchanged regularly with relatives in Pakistan, and such letters tended to be written by one *family* to another *family,* with each family member passing on messages and news. The person who physically *wrote* such letters tended therefore to be simply the scribe, following others' instructions and including his/her own news rather than taking over the content of the letter. In general, women were seen as 'in charge' of what went into such family communications – unless the letter was to a close relative or friend of the husband – even when, as in many cases, they were not able to write the letter physically themselves. Women who were literate in Urdu often found themselves in great demand as scribes and helpers for friends and neighbours who had not had the same educational opportunities, particularly for more personal communications where their tact and discretion were demanded.

Sughra described graphically how she had relied on such help in Pakistan when her husband first came to England alone many years ago: her education, after her mother's death when she was small, had been very patchy and left her with some ability to read Urdu but very little command of writing. 'I reading is . . . little bit, and letter is . . . read. No writing . . . I think. If I am go to school, I read, I write letter.' She described how her sister-in-law helped her to read the letters she had difficulty with, and a friend wrote her replies down for her. For Sughra, the experience, although common to many women of her generation, was frustrating, and she determined that her daughters would not suffer in the same way for lack of educational opportunities. The result is that her older daughter, Alia, an articulate woman in her early thirties who had a good traditional secondary education in Pakistan before returning to England, is literate in both English and Urdu. She tends to do not only much of the scribing for her mother and other family members but also for many of her neighbours and friends as well – a duty which she is happy to perform *most* of the time, she told me – apart from when a neighbour turns up intent on a long missive just when Alia is particularly busy!

See
Chap. 20,
Chap. 22

Where only one member of a household had literacy skills, this tended to be the husband, and if he was unable to cope alone with written communications – reading a letter which had arrived from the children's nursery, for example – a friend or neighbour with the necessary skills could always be relied upon to help. Some husbands needed no such help, however. For example, Kaneez, a woman in her thirties with four children, told me that her husband Younis, a successful small businessman who reads both English and Urdu with ease, dealt with almost all the communications to and from their household, since she herself had only three years' schooling in Pakistan and lacked confidence in her command of basic reading and writing in English and Urdu. Their children were as yet too young to be very actively involved in the literate activities of the household, although both they and Kaneez contributed to family letters.

In our discussions on uses of literacy, Kaneez identified writing down phone messages as the main use to which she put her growing writing ability in English, since she acted as unofficial receptionist for her husband's business, taking an assortment of phone calls every day in both Panjabi and English. She felt she could rely on her memory when the message was left in Panjabi, remembering details of names and addresses and only needing to write down phone numbers, whereas she worried about having to remember English names and other details from messages in English:

> Phone calls . . . a lot of English people . . . Sometimes (a caller) is asking me, 'My message . . . giving Younis . . . and I writing name, and address . . . (I ask) 'Please get . . . spellings' . . . and names and writing, telephone numbers . . . My husband (comes home), and give him that, and . . . giving ring . . .

Aspirations for Children

All but one of the six women I interviewed in detail had children, and all had definite aspirations for them to develop their communication skills as fully as possible. Like Sughra, the other women who had had little chance of education themselves felt strongly about its importance for the next generation, echoing the apparently contradictory feelings of Rockhill's informants, who 'asserted that learning to read and write English was crucial to getting ahead, *and* . . . said that it was unnecessary, for one could get by without it . . .' (1987: 167). Even Alia, however, the most highly-educated of the women I spoke to with twelve or more years of full-time schooling and further part-time adult classes behind her, felt in some sense cheated of the opportunities that might have been hers if she had not given up the chance of going to college in favour of marriage at nineteen, and spoke of encouraging both sons and daughters to reach their full potential in education while they still had the opportunity.

See
Chap. 14

See
Chap. 12

As far as literacies were concerned, all the women were keen for their children to become literate in both English and Urdu: English in order to

See
Chap. 17

succeed in British society in which they all envisaged their children remaining, and Urdu primarily in order to keep in touch with relatives, particularly grandparents, in Pakistan. Most of the women ranked the two languages as equally important for their children, but Kaneez came down heavily on the side of English being more important because her children were living in England: 'English, first important, Urdu second.' This did not stop her from insisting that her children attended classes in Urdu held at the local mosque at weekends, despite their protests: 'My one boy no likes weekends mosque ... (But) I say, 'You going ... to mosque! And after mosque, you playing all days.'

One mother, however, had already met with some disappointment in this undertaking. Sughra had succeeded in encouraging her two daughters, Alia, who was educated in Pakistan, and her young sister Rukhsana, who attended extra Urdu classes after school in Brierfield, to perfect their Urdu. Over her two sons, however, she did not have so much influence, and the boys had rebelled in their teens, refusing to go to after-school Urdu classes, with the result that both now speak, read and write English virtually perfectly but have almost no literacy in Urdu. When I asked how they communicated with relations in Pakistan, Sughra replied that they sometimes wrote their own letters in English to those relatives, mainly younger ones, who could read them, asking them to translate them for the benefit of older relations. Alia, their older sister, however, painted a rather less rosy picture of her brothers coming to her for help in writing, in Urdu, their none-too-frequent letters to older relatives in Pakistan. Her voice held a mixture of annoyance, affection and wry amusement as she described how she, who had always worked hard to do well at school, and who now had enough to do with five children, a part-time job and a husband working and studying long hours, was required at intervals to put aside whatever she was doing to write letters on behalf of brothers who had, in her opinion, been simply too preoccupied with enjoying themselves to learn the necessary skills themselves ... Ironically, the fact that Alia was, in this sense at least, better educated than her brothers, provided not a liberating influence, opening up new horizons for her, but a further aspect of the traditional female role of carer, transmitter of communication and selfless helper of others. As Kathleen Rockhill comments, '(b)ecause it is caught up in the power dynamic between men and women, literacy is lived as women's work but not as women's right' (1987: 153).

See
Chap. 18

Reading for Pleasure

Most of the women with children encouraged them to read widely, and spoke with pride of their children's enthusiasm for reading: Sughra's teenage daughter Rukhsana, for example, 'plenty read the book, in the school library . . . Thirty books finish . . . (She likes getting) two-fifty vouchers: plenty time she buy book.' Sughra, however, felt cut off by her lack of reading skills from sharing this source of enjoyment fully with her children: she did not know *what* Rukhsana read, and rarely asked. She knew that her sons bought a lot of English newspapers to read while they were waiting for customers in the family shop, but had no idea whether these were local or national papers or what types of news her sons were particularly interested in reading: in fact, her contact with her sons' choice of reading matter was largely confined to piling up yesterday's discarded papers and taking them out to the dustbin.

Of the women who had had little education, Sughra was the one who felt most strongly that she would have liked to be able to read, and the only one who echoed Klassen's informants' feeling of exclusion and frustration because of her limited literacy skills. Most adults who *had* reading skills, however, complained of frustration because they never had enough time to read anything simply for enjoyment. Kaneez described her husband as a keen reader, enjoying books but with a particular enthusiasm for the papers:

> Urdu newspapers . . . (three days a week) . . . and English every day. Friday morning my husband wake up about seven o'clock . . . after wash face and change clothes, go back in the shop, buy some newspapers . . . Lots of things, all newspapers . . . First times, newspapers, buy newspapers . . .

Frequently, however, the papers, piled up, unread, because Younis was too busy to read them. The children were now showing signs of following his interest, supported by both their parents, who regarded any sort of reading as beneficial to the children's education. Younis would also have like to see Kaneez herself adopt this route to improving her education, but she was confident in her defence of her own leisure pursuits:

> My husband asking . . . 'Spare times . . . reading and writing . . . Wasting time is watching film and television!' . . . He is asking me, 'No all times you watching films!' I (say), 'Stay home, and spare times watching films, - it doesn't matter!'

One young woman who was able to combine an interest in films and television with her enjoyment of reading was Razia. As a single childless woman of nineteen, working and studying part-time, she had more time to spare than most of the other women I talked to, and spent her spare time and most of her spare money indulging her passion for Indian and Pakistani films and film magazines.

Two popular magazines were available locally - a weekly magazine in Urdu about the Pakistani film industry, and monthly one about Indian films, published in India but written in Englis, – and it had become normal practice for Razia and a group of friends to take turns in buying these for the group to share. The magazines contained all the news on the latest film releases, photos of the stars and lengthy interviews with actors and actresses. Once read and discussed by the group, each magazine was

Cineblitz, Feb '93

divided up between the group members according to their interests, with each taking the sections about her favourite films and actors. Razia kept a scrapbook of cuttings about particular actors and actresses, including pictures and interviews, liberally laced with her own written comments. Woe betide the actor who contradicts in this month's interview what he said last month while there are fans like Razia about!

> His good point, I write it . . . what did he say he like, films, or what he said about serial roles and everything . . . because I write those points, and next month I find new magazine, so I say, 'What Mithun say now?' You know . . . it change.

Razia is insistent that these magazines in no way correspond to the magazines aimed at young women in the Western market: firstly, for example, film magazines have just as many male as female readers, and both her and her brother's bedrooms display posters of actors and actresses from film magazines. (Razia also read occasional TV magazines, and Kylie Minogue and Jason Donovan rub shoulders with Govinder and Mithun on her walls . . .) Film magazines from Pakistan do fulfil one of the functions of Western women's magazines, however, in giving Razia and her women friends, and sometimes her mother too, ideas of the most fashionable clothes designs in Pakistan - ideas which, in consultation between themselves, then can adapt in their own dressmaking:

> My friends, we all talking about it . . . I'll see one design: I'll say I like and my friend say, 'No, that's not good'. You know, sometimes is . . . the arms, just over here, close, I think. 'Oh, we cut here and over here!' You know, we talking about it!

'Talking about it' remains the most obvious and consistent feature of the responses to reading and writing made by the women I talked to in the course of this study. Like the residents of Heath's Trackton, members of the Muslim community in Brierfield have 'a variety of literate traditions, and . . . these are interwoven in different ways with oral uses of language, ways of negotiating meaning, deciding on action, and achieving status . . .' (1983: 234). Literate activities are constantly shared, negotiated, shaped by members of the family and the wider community, and those who have no direct access to the written word are guaranteed access through family members or friends. However, the women I talked to, particularly those who had never had direct access to reading and writing for themselves, were well aware of the power of literacy: their own lives may have been structured so as to minimise its importance, but their children's would not be, and they were determined to give their children the opportunity to read and write fluently themselves. At the same time, the powerful position of these

See Chap. 9

women as communicators – with relatives and friends far away, with children and the differing expectations of the next generation, with me across a cultural and language gap – in no way depended on technical reading and writing abilities, and underlined for me the meaninglessness of any one individual describing herself as *more* or *less* 'literate' than any other.

References

Ballard, R. and Ballard, C. (1977) The Sikhs: The development of South Asian culture on Britain. In J.L. Watson (ed.) *Between Two Cultures*. Oxford: Basil Blackwell.

Heath, S.B. (1983) *Ways with Words*. Cambridge: Cambridge University Press.

Klassen, C. (1991) Bilingual written language use by low-education Latin American newcomers. In D. Barton and R. Ivanic (eds.) *Writing in the Community*. Newbury Park: Sage.

Miller, J. (1983) *Many Voices*. London: Routledge Kegan Paul.

Rockhill, K. (1987) Gender, language and the politics of literacy. *British Journal of the Sociology of Education* 8 (2), 153-67.

Shaw, A. (1988) *A Pakistani Community in Britain*. Oxford: Basil Blackwell.

Street, B. (1990) Putting literacies on the political agenda. *Research & Practice in Adult Literacy* 13, 2-7.

| Conflict | Oral & Written | Public/ Private |

PAUL DAVIES

4: Long Term Unemployment and Literacy: A Case Study of the Restart Interview

Between August 1989 and May 1990 researchers at Lancaster University carried out a study of 100 long term unemployed people commissioned by the Employment Service (Hamilton & Davies, 1990). The aim of the study was to explore the written communication barriers experienced by these long term unemployed people in relation to searching for, and obtaining, jobs. Eighty men and twenty women were interviewed in five clusters of sites across the country. They covered a range of ages and experiences of unemployment and had been identified by staff at Jobcentres and unemployment benefit offices as having difficulties with written communication.

People included in the sample came from a wide range of ethnic and cultural backgrounds, although the vast majority – 85 – were 'white' and mono-lingual. Of those who mentioned a different ethnic cultural background, four described themselves as Asian, four as Afro-Caribbean, four as Travellers, one as Vietnamese, one as Greek-Cypriot, and one as Italian. Those of Asian, Vietnamese, Greek-Cypriot and Italian background were multilingual. Data on the other languages spoken, in addition to English, by those in the Travellers and Afro-Caribbean groups was not obtained.

The research set out to investigate the seemingly straightforward question of whether people with literacy difficulties have problems in getting jobs. But as with many seemingly straightforward questions, not only did the answer turn out to be more complex, but the question itself was far too simplistic. For it was apparent from previous research undertaken by members of the Literacy Research Group at Lancaster University (for example, Hamilton, 1987) that it is not the case that people can either read or write or they cannot. They have found that people's performance in reading and writing varies from setting to setting depending on how familiar and confident they are with a particular activity. Furthermore, a

41

person's performance may be patchy as a result of uneven use and the fluctuating need for literacy skills in daily life.

As expected, a substantial number of interviewees considered themselves to have difficulty with reading and writing. However, the extent and nature of these difficulties varied enormously, ranging from some who stated that they could not read and write at all, to others who mentioned occasional problems, particularly when they were faced with long words and complex sentence structures or stressful situations. However, only half of the respondents thought that their literacy difficulty was a barrier to getting a job, and of these many thought literacy was less of a barrier than their health, age or lack of qualifications, training and experience. The vast majority of those who considered written communication to be the most important barrier were those who were interviewed in specialist literacy provision such as those jobs clubs which catered specifically for those with literacy difficulties. This was not surprising, for by agreeing to participate in such programmes, they had acknowledged that their reading and writing problems caused them difficulties in their search for work.

Many of the people interviewed could not understand why they needed to be more skilled in reading and writing when the jobs for which they were applying had very little reading or writing involved in them. Many seemed particularly concerned by the number of forms which Jobcentres and unemployment benefit offices expected them to complete in their search for work. Consequently, some saw the Employment Service, the organisation equipped to act as a channel between unemployment and employment, not so much as an aid to finding work but more as an additional barrier. At the very least this was a source of irritation for some people, whilst for others it was a cause of great anxiety and tension, as their relationship with Employment Service staff, at least at the formal level, was based on forms, a medium of communication about which they felt anxious. For a few it was a severe problem and they claimed that their problems with completing forms had prevented them from looking for work. One man said he had very little time to give to job hunting as he felt 'all wrapped up in red tape'.

In one sense the relationship between the Employment Service and this particular group of unemployed people represents a clash of different literacies. On the one side is the formal, bureaucratic literacy of large and complex organisations, whilst on the other is the informal, casual literacy of a group of people for whom written communication is unfamiliar and uncomfortable. For many it is almost a different way of life. Several mentioned that they were more confident talking about themselves than writing about themselves. It was apparent that in their lives as a whole, they would attempt to resolve problems with their electricity, their poll tax, their children's education or their income support by visiting the electricity showroom, the council office, the school or the Department of Social Security. They would be unlikely to send a letter. Susan Benton's article on home–school communication which appears elsewhere in this section also deals with the problems which arise when an organisation communicates in writing to people who prefer to communicate through face-to-face meetings.

See
Chap. 8

The Literacy Demands of Looking for Work

Not all jobs are obtained by filling out application forms. People in our sample commented on the times they had obtained jobs in the past by informal methods such as a recommendation by a relative or friend or by simply turning up at a factory or building site and being hired on the spot following a short and casual chat with the supervisor or foreman because 'the gaffer liked the look of me'. However, most acknowledged that form filling had become an increasingly common part of job hunting, especially if one was registered at the benefit office or Jobcentre.

There appear to be three main literacy demands in looking for work:
  (i) Reading and understanding: interpreting the intent behind written questions and statements.
  (ii) Form filling: not just the technical skills of writing, but also deciding what information should be written.
  (iii) Organising written information: maintaining records of qualifications, previous jobs, dates attended, etc.

In the following case study, the difficulties associated with each of these elements will be discussed by referring to one particular employment related event experienced by the majority of those in our sample – the letter and form associated with the Restart interview.

The Restart Interview

The Restart interview has been chosen to illustrate the literacy difficulties experienced by many of the people we interviewed for three reasons. Firstly, it illustrates the practical literacy demands of reading, writing and organising written information. Secondly, it highlights how literacy difficulties were related to how people perceived the Restart interview, and why it caused them particular anxiety. For instance, many of the questions they were expected to answer on the Restart form were almost identical to questions asked on another Employment Service form which had created few problems for them. However, many saw the Restart form as serving a different purpose and their problems stemmed directly from this. This suggests that the purpose and context of a form is an important factor in determining whether people have problems with completing it. This point is discussed in more detail below. Finally, although the Restart interview is primarily a spoken conversation between counsellor and client, it is the literacy demands placed upon the client prior to the interview which create a background of stress against which the conversation is conducted.

People who have been unemployed for six months are invited by the Employment Service to have a Restart interview where their situation and their efforts to find work are reviewed by a Restart counsellor. The intended purpose of the Restart interview is to offer help and assistance with the search for work, and to suggest a series of options to be considered by an unemployed person as steps that might be taken to increase their chances of successfully finding employment, for example, by undertaking training or by joining a job club to receive advice and assistance in identifying and applying for job vacancies. However, rightly or wrongly, Restart is considered by some, including large numbers of those in our sample, as primarily a 'checking up on you' interview intended to encourage the unemployed to seek work more actively by considering less attractive employment and training opportunities such as low paid jobs and Employment Training.

To illustrate the literacy difficulties met during the Restart process one person's account of Restart is examined in depth. This case study is based on an interview with a man in his late thirties who lived in the North West of England. Like many in the sample, his previous work experience had been obtained from a series of unskilled manual jobs, and it was this type of employment to which he wished to return. His first language was English, and from his interview with the Lancaster University fieldworker it was clear that he was extremely skilled in spoken communication, much more so than he was in reading and writing. This particular account has been selected because it sheds light on the main issues connected with the Restart interview, and although people do not have identical Restart experiences, the account given here is broadly representative of those people in our sample who found this interview a stressful experience. In addition to the views and experiences of this person, generalised statements based on accounts of other people in the sample are also given to provide a fuller picture of people's Restart experiences.

Reading the letter

An unemployed person is invited to attend a Restart interview by letter. This gives details of the date and place of the interview and is accompanied by a Restart interview form which the unemployed person is asked to complete prior to the interview, although help in filling out the form can be offered at the interview.

The Restart interview is intended to be helpful, although the letter contains a sentence which states:

> The rules for receiving benefit and credit of National Insurance contributions means that people who do not attend interviews at the Jobcentre or the Unemployment Benefit Office without giving a good reason may lose their benefit and/or credits. If you cannot come at the time we have given you, it is very important to tell us straight away. You can do so by ringing this number . . .

So there is an element of 'carrot and stick' about the letter. But for this person, who was anxious about his ability to read and understand the meaning of letters, it was the 'stick' which had the greater impact.

> It always says how it's free (he means voluntary), but if you don't attend you may lose benefits or credits. I mean you're not going to turn round and say 'Oh maybe they won't'. You've got to go, you know, so I think its just a form of blackmail, that's the way I look at it, turn up or else.

This an example of a man trying to make sense of a complex sentence. Because he cannot be sure what it means, his tendency is to fear the worst and assume that the threat to his benefit will actually be carried out. His lack of confidence with reading means he focuses on this aspect of the letter rather than on the fact that the interview is described as voluntary. So he begins his participation in the Restart process feeling concerned and threatened.

Filling out the form

The Restart interview form in use at the time the research was undertaken was made up of four sections. Section 1 asked for personal details such as name, address, age, qualifications, etc. Section 2 asked for such information as 'What type of job are you looking for?', 'Are you looking for permanent work?', 'How far are you prepared to travel daily to get to work?'. Section 3 asked questions about 'What have you been doing to find work?', for example, 'Have you applied for jobs in the last four weeks?' and 'Have you had a job interview in the last four weeks?'. Finally, Section 4 which was entitled 'Looking Forward' asked people to answer such questions as 'Do you need help to get back to work?'.

At the end of the form the unemployed person has to sign a statement saying 'The information given on this form is true and complete'. As such, in the eyes of many unemployed people, the form assumes the status of a legal document in much the same way as a Tax Return does, and although there is no statement which explicitly says that giving false information

Section 6 - Declaration

The information given on this form is
true and complete.

Signature

Date

Please tick this box if someone else
has filled this form in for you.

could lead to prosecution, mention is made on the front of the form that
unemployment benefit is linked to being available for work and may not be
paid if you

> unreasonably restrict your chances of getting work because of the
> type of job you are looking for, the hours you can work, the rate of pay
> you want, or the places where you are prepared to go to work.

Many are careful, therefore, to complete the form as accurately and
truthfully as possible to avoid any potential financial consequences. However, this often proved a problem because they were unsure about the
meaning of particular words and phrases in some questions and were
anxious as to how their answers might be interpreted by the Restart
counsellor. For example, there were questions on the form asking people
whether they were seeking permanent or temporary work, and some
people wondered whether this meant that reduced or no benefit would be
given to those only looking for temporary work. Furthermore, they were
unsure what the exact difference between the two was. For instance, if they
took contract work, after what length of time did temporary become
permanent and vice versa?

Another question which caused concern was one that asked, 'How far are
you prepared to travel daily to work?'. They were confused as to whether

this implied that the Restart counsellor would understand if, for example, more than two bus rides away was too far to travel, or whether they should be prepared to make quite difficult and time consuming journeys to demonstrate that they were actively seeking work.

In the individual example I am focusing on, the man was perplexed by what he was told was a suitable answer to the question 'What type of work are you looking for?':

> Usually, just put general labourer. I used to always put general labourer, but was told last week that I can't put that down anymore because it narrows the field down. I've got to put the 'ing' down to give it a bigger scope or something. I don't know what that means, I mean general labourer or general labouring, it seems the same to me either way, but she (Restart counsellor) crossed it out and I had to do it again. She wouldn't even fill it in, she just crossed it out and said 'put general labouring'.

What is the difference between general labourer and general labouring? Does the former refer specially to jobs in the construction industry, whilst the latter could include all physical work no matter in what industry it was undertaken? Perhaps this is what the Restart counsellor meant by giving it 'a bigger scope'.

Although it is obviously a sensible piece of advice to advise an unemployed person to consider a wider range of possible jobs, why insist on making him cross out his original idea to replace it with the new one? And why did she insist that he wrote it himself? This particular person was unable to answer these questions and was worried

Section 2 - The type of job you want

8. What type of job are you looking for?

9. What other jobs would you consider?

If none, please say why:

10. Are you looking for permanent work?

YES ☐   NO ☐

11. Are you looking for temporary work?

YES ☐   NO ☐

If **YES**, how long do you want to work for?

12. If you are offered a job can you start right away?

YES ☐   NO ☐

15. How far are you prepared to travel daily to get to work?

that he had signed a statement containing information about himself which he did not fully understand. He was concerned that what he had written on the form might be used in evidence against him if, for instance, it was decided to suspend his benefit because he turned down labouring jobs in an industry in which he was not keen to work. Perhaps this is why the Restart counsellor wanted the words to be in his handwriting, to provide more watertight evidence?

Of course, this might be a case of reading too much into a situation which is in fact much more straightforward. Moreover, we have only been given one side of the incident, and it would be interesting to have been able to discuss it with the Restart counsellor, but interviews with such people were outside of the scope of the research. However, from the perspective of this person, it was an incident which caused him great concern. As was mentioned above, he embarked on this Restart journey with feelings of trepidation, not completely understanding its implications, but fearing the worst. Then he was asked to cross out the job title he had always used, and with which he was familiar, and replace it with a word whose meaning was unclear. He was then asked to sign the form stating that his answers were 'true and complete', even though in his mind this was no longer the case.

See
Chap. 13

Providing the proof

During the period in which the research took place, there was a change in the regulations for unemployed people. Instead of having to declare that they were 'available for work', they were required to prove that they were 'actively seeking work'. This tightening of the definition of unemployment was interpreted by some in our study as an example of the government putting pressure on the Employment Service to reduce the number of those officially registered as unemployed. This change had not gone unnoticed by the man on whom we are focusing, who commented on the new forms which had been introduced to administer this change, and which the Restart counsellor might ask to see at the interview:

> They've got a new one, its like half the size, just with a bit more telling you, you've got to bring proof . . . firm that you go to, either ask them to sign it or stamp it. Pressure that's what I thought, straight away. She said 'We'll send for you again in 3 weeks and keep sending for you every 3 weeks, and then we'll give you a bit of a break.' At the end of 3 weeks you've got to give them this card and they turn round and say, 'Well alright you tried there', and they give you another card, but you can't go to the same place, it's got to be different ones again.

Providing written proof that you have been actively seeking work is not a major headache for some groups of people who are used to applying for white collar jobs with major companies. It is simply a matter of compiling a portfolio of job adverts, photocopies of letters of application and employer responses. For others, however, matters are not that simple. Many of those in our sample applied for work in a less formal and more verbal way, by asking friends and family to 'keep an eye out for them', casually turning up at factories for 'spec applications', and so forth. It is harder for those who are used to applying for jobs in this fashion to gather written evidence. As is evident from the quotation above, it has been suggested by the Employment Service that unemployed people keep a record of these informal application, by asking employers to give them a written note or by stamping a card. This presents problems, however. First, it is rare for casual job callers to actually meet 'the boss'. Often they get no further than a gatekeeper, receptionist or secretary, and these people are reluctant to sign anything on behalf of the company as they seldom have the authority to do so. Second, even if a casual caller does get to talk with 'the boss', she/he may not provide written evidence of the meeting, especially if they receive lots of casual callers. We were told of an incident where a large group of unemployed people, protesting against the new 'actively seeking work' regulations, enquired at their local unemployment benefit office about vacancies in the Civil Service. The manager of the office referred them elsewhere and was then faced with the request from each member of the group to provide written evidence that they had called at his office looking for work in the Civil Service. Obviously their intention was to make the point that such written evidence can sometimes be difficult to obtain.

Another factor that makes providing written evidence difficult is that many of those we interviewed were unfamiliar with the practice of maintaining records in a manageable form. As was stated earlier, one of the three literacy elements in looking for work is the maintenance of written records. We would argue that whilst certain groups in our society are part of a 'paper work culture', there are others, including many of those in our sample, who are not. Their practice of maintaining and retrieving information about themselves, which appears to be based on their own memories and those of their families and friends, contrasts starkly with that of a large organisation such as the Employment Service where considerable emphasis is attached to recording written information in files and record cards.

Conclusions

The motto of the Stock Exchange (at least before the 'Big Bang' transformed it from an actual place into a system of inter-connecting computer terminals) is 'My Word is My Bond'. This simple statement says a lot about the ethos of the institutions and the people who trade there. The stockbrokers and jobbers who bought and sold stocks and shares did not give each other written receipts, for it was expected that a verbal agreement made between 'honourable men' was an absolute guarantee. Indeed to ask for a written record of a transaction would appear vulgar and an insult to the reputation of the people who worked there.

It is clear from the new 'actively seeking work' regulations with which unemployed people have to comply that their word is no longer regarded as sufficient evidence of job hunting and written proof is required.

Restart tends to have a low reputation amongst many of those we interviewed. It was launched as a major initiative to provide support and guidance to unemployed people, to 'restart' them on the road to employment. Many in our sample did not see it in that light. Of the 100 we spoke to, 40 could not recall their experiences of their Restart interview in any detail. It did not appear to stand out in their minds as an identifiable event, distinguishable from other interviews in the Jobcentre. 30 were dissatisfied with their experience, 15 had mixed memories of it and 15 were satisfied. Thus only 15% were able to say that their Restart interview had enabled them to move closer to a particular occupational goal.

Some people saw Restart as primarily an interrogation. Others saw it as a chance to be offered something new by the Employment Service. On both counts, it was seen as unsatisfactory. There was little evidence that people got satisfactory job leads from Restart. The only jobs people recalled being offered were of low paid and dangerous work which they would not consider. One man was offered a job working with chemicals and was warned that he 'had to wear special clothes, and had to have a bath because it would be dangerous to children.' His wife insisted that he did not take the job for fear of putting their children's health at risk.

Comments on good experience emphasised counsellors who did not pressurise but appeared to understand the client's situation. They recalled the Restart Counsellor being 'helpful', 'good',

> a nice friendly person, put alternatives to you, jobs that may be going. She rung somebody up as we were talking . . . that is helpful you know.

Whatever the good and bad features of Restart are for unemployed people as a whole, for those who are concerned about their ability at reading and writing, Restart poses particular problems, because of the difficulties they experience understanding and interpreting questions, writing the answers down and obtaining and organising the written material to prove that they are actively seeking work. Many stated that the Restart form had 'trick questions' on it which could be 'used against you'. The Restart counsellors appeared to interview from the written answers on the form, and people talked about 'double meanings' and 'words being twisted'. People were not certain about Employment Service definitions of certain words and phrases and felt anxious that a wrong interpretation could lose them benefit. Thus people tended to experience more literacy difficulties with the letters and forms associated with Restart than they did with other Employment Service forms which they completed in less stressful circumstances.

It is important that any organisation such as the Employment Service whose purpose is to serve the needs of a particular group of people should be aware of the differing requirements of the sub-groups within the larger population. It is evident from the willingness of the Employment Service to fund research into literacy and unemployment that they recognise this need. Because significant numbers of long term unemployed people have literacy problems and find official forms and letters difficult to manage, steps might be taken by the Employment Service to eliminate, or at least alleviate, their difficulties by reducing the amount of written communication between unemployed people and themselves. There was evidence that in some Jobcentres, Restart counsellors did offer considerable help to those who could not cope with completing the form. This in itself does not remove all the problems Restart poses for this group, but at least it lifts some of the pressure and anxiety off those who do not find reading and writing an easy form of communication, and increases their chances of finding the Restart interview a positive and supportive experience.

Acknowledgement

The extracts used in this article were taken from the Restart Interview Letter and Restart Interview Questionnaire used by the Employment Service at the time the research was undertaken in 1989/1990, and are reproduced with the permission of the Controller of Her Majesty's Stationery Office.
   It is the policy of the Employment Service to update and renew forms continuously and the present version of the letter and form may differ from that quoted.

References

Hamilton, M. (1987) *Literacy, Numeracy and Adults: Evidence from the National Child Development Study.* Adult Literacy and Basic Skills Unit.

Hamilton, M. and Davies, P. (1990) *Written Communication Barriers to Employment.* Lancaster University: Final Report to the Employment Service.

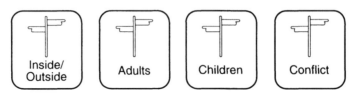

Inside/Outside   Adults   Children   Conflict

NICHOLA BENSON, SARAH GURNEY,
JUDITH HARRISON AND RACHEL RIMMERSHAW

5: The Place of Academic Writing in Whole Life Writing

Introduction

This case study shows how three students see their experience of learning to write in the academic community, in relation to their previous uses of writing. It arose from work done by Nichola, Sarah and Judith on a course led by Rachel in the academic year of 1989-1990. The three students were enrolled in degree courses which included substantial study of Education, but also of Mathematics (Sarah), Linguistics (Judith) and Visual Arts (Nichola). Nichola and Sarah were young students just turned twenty, who were in their final year of study at the time, and Judith was a mature student who still had a year of her degree course to come. What they have in common is that they all chose to tackle an assignment for Rachel's course on Schooling and Language which asked them to reflect on their experience of learning to write at university. Offering this assignment was one of a range of strategies Rachel was using (including the encouragement to write collaboratively) to get students to make personal sense of the ideas and reading offered on the course. This is how the task was defined:

> How well has your previous experience prepared you for writing academic essays at university? Draw on whatever sources seem relevant* to discuss the transitions you have had to make and how they could have been supported.
>
> *(This could include your own and others' experience, published or unpublished research on writing, prescriptions for writing or the teaching of writing, and so on.)

Their responses included many fascinating insights into the experience of writing as students which are beyond the scope of this case study. What was clear from what all of them wrote, however, was that they had a strong sense of writing essays at university as another 'world of literacy' into which with some difficulty and less than optimum support they had had to initiate themselves. At the same time what was striking was the kind of relationships they saw between this new 'world of literacy' and ones with which they were already familiar. In describing the transitions they had to make, only Sarah confined her account to her earlier experiences in school. Both Nichola and Judith wrote about their wider lives of family, friends and work to tell the story.

The data for this case study are a set of short extracts from the original essays chosen to give a flavour of the stories they told, and the reflections they prompted, about learning to write. These were presented as an interactive poster at the Worlds of Literacy Conference at Morecambe in June 1990. The comments of all four authors on these quotations, together with those of other participants at the conference (some anonymous), form a second level of data. All the quotations and 'highlights' of the reactions form Part 1 of this chapter. In Part 2 we have identified three 'themes' which emerge from this data which we are calling 'membership', 'initiation', and 'experience'.

Part 1: The Poster and Some Reactions

The three students' writing formed subsections in the poster entitled 'Sarah's Story', Judith's Journey' and 'Nichola's Networks'.

Two Way Mirrors:
Reflections On The Place Of Academic Writing In The Whole-life Writing Experiences of Three University Students

Rachel's Refraction

The writing on these posters was not written for this occasion. It is all taken from essays written as part of these students' coursework for an Educational Studies course I teach. The assignment these three chose asked them to write about how well their previous experience prepared them for writing academic essays at university, and what transitions they had to make. What struck me about what they wrote was that although they were thinking about writing in an academic context, only Sarah told a story which confined itself to earlier academic experiences. All three gave me the privilege of a glimpse into their lives, and they have agreed to share a little bit of them with you too. There were many fascinating experiences and insights in the stories they told me, but we have picked out a few here which illustrate some connections between different worlds of literacy. We hope you will start a dialogue with us by reacting to anything which strikes a chord with you.

Sarah's Story

Readers' Reactions

There was a general feeling among the **infant school** teachers that we should be allowed to read as often as we liked. I think that this was in the belief that we would be influenced by the styles and language used in these books.

I suppose academic conventions are learned by this "blotting paper" process to a large extent too. Perhaps we should use these models of academic writing more explicitly, so that learning writers can consciously take on board (or reject) the styles and language of the academy.

Rachel

I can't remember being open to any resources other than Janet and John sort of literature.

Nichola

Upon reaching **junior school,** so the timetabled lesson of English appeared. I remember using the SRA exercises but since answer cards were readily available many pupils, myself included, cheated. The reason for this is that the teacher recorded our scores and marked them on a chart on the wall. Not only did the marks become more important than the learning experience but it also became classroom knowledge as to who was excelling or who was falling behind.

At my junior school we also had our marks up on the wall, and two children got caught giving false marks. We were moved to certain tables, and places around that table, depending on our exam scores that week. The scores were definitely more important than actually learning.

Nichola

Word bloody power!
Anon

All this was probably so important that you scarcely knew what was in the cards themselves. My criticisms of the cards as "tests" rather than "real reading" become irrelevant when "playing the game" overrides everything.

Roz Ivanic

Moving to the local comprehensive school involved many changes. The five English periods were split up into 2 x reading, library, comprehension and punctuation / grammar. The library session took place once a week and consisted of students choosing a project which could be on a subject of their choice. Although I remember enjoying such an activity the writing consisted of copying rather than composing, an exercise in repeating facts.

Did this have the same function as the infant school reading, I wonder, helping you to become saturated with the style?
Roz Ivanic

And so from such a leisurely exercise to the periods of comprehension and grammar. At junior school I had only touched on punctuation and grammar when using SRA but now I was forced to learn rules which "told" me how to write properly. I began to believe that the writing I had so enjoyed in primary school was incorrect.

HORROR, ABSOLUTE BOREDOM !!! when the "Comprehension / Grammar" English books came out. (And fear!)
Nichola

I wonder what use you make of those "rules" now.
Rachel

For 'O'-level English we were to put all these theories into practice and the essay-writing began. In the factual essay a student took an argument, discussed the pros and cons and came to a conclusion. I always decided my conclusion after seeing how much information I could obtain for both sides. Information was gleaned from books and I remember lacking confidence in expressing my own point of view.

It would be interesting to know how you made the transition from a quantitatlive to a qualitative view of information.
Rachel

I don't recall the sophistication of reading prior to writing on a topic - my essays came straight off the top of my head! . . . The idea of researching to write has only figured since my return to education in middle age.
Judith

I actually did no essay writing throughout the **sixth form**. The writing whch I was required to produce was in the form of experimental reports for Physics or a structured proof for Maths. Both of these were of a predetermined format with no scope for individual expansion to include a student's thoughts on such an exercise.

My O-level English teacher strongly advised us not to do that "sort of essay" as she did not think we could do them very well.
Nichola

And so to University.

University struck me as containing highly intelligent professors who really were not interested in my own thoughts on a subject. My early essays were along the lines of my Library lessons at secondary school in as much as I would copy information and authors' opinions from suggested reading and then rearrange them so that I was not actually committing plagiarism. *Not surprisingly my essays were disjointed and often ambiguous in their meaning due to the wide variety of views I had used.*

Since starting university there have been two main activities which have revolutionized my essay writing.

The **first** was reading V. Zamel's paper "The Composing Processes of Advanced ESL Students". This paper introduced me to the process of composing and how the students interviewed would draft, redraft, revise, discard information which did not say what they really meant, and generally write to discover and make meaning. The whole idea suggested to me that an essay was my own piece of work and I began to question just how much of my own thoughts had gone into past compositions.

The **second** activity which reinforced my new attitude towards composition was discussing the essay-writing process in a workshop. It was most instructional discussing how other people carried out the activity of essay writing. All students had difficulties and apprehensions about different parts of the process and each had their own means of getting around the problem. This activity suggested even more avenues to explore when composing, and being totally honest I thought from this point on I was going to enjoy writing. My only regret is that such enlightenment did not happen at the start of my University life.

Some students come without a sense of plagiarism. They think that rearranging other people's texts is what they're supposed to do. I guess it's not surprising when so much time in schooling has been spent copying out other people's words.
Rachel

How can we show we know the stuff and still sound interesting and original?
Anon

I find I was so concerned with "getting the facts in" that my essays contained no style at all - it was only in the third year that I began to bring this "style" into my essays.
Nichola

I think this is a very important insight. It underlines the importance of the writer making their own voice heard for the coherence of what they write.
Rachel

I still feel my essay writing has a long way to go - I wish we had been helped more in the first year.
Nichola

I was delighted to read this, because it told me that you had really engaged with what you'd read - that reading in this case was not a separate "academic" activity, but one which made a difference to you in practice.
Rachel

Couldn't this begin in the infants school?
Anon

I'm envious of this conviction that some things have been pivotal - I feel as if I've missed some revelations and truths that would make my academic career, if not easier, smoother.
Judith

I do agree that this was a very useful experience especially in seeing how others coped with some of the problems I had.   *Judith*

Some people seem to have such a boring, methodical method of writing essays - at least I enjoy and get deeply involved in my writing, even if "technically" my essays aren't very good.
Nichola

Tell the authorities!
Roz Ivanic

Nichola's Networks

Reader's Reactions

Presumably the arrival of GCSE has changed this.
Judith

I got very high coursework marks since I was neat! That was little use to me in the exams. It will be interesting to see what difference the GCSE will make. Will there be even more emphasis on neatness and presentation rather than content and ideas? I'd like to think not.
Sarah

This is exactly the kind of academic teaching I received.
Sarah

Why is it that teachers seem to think the work is less valuable if it is the product of two people's ideas? Why . . . where more jobs require cooperation between people . . . are schools locked in this traditional attitude?
Sarah

I'm interested that in spite of this good experience of collaborating you were the one who didn't choose to write collaboratively on the course. I wonder if it had something to do with the confidence you talk about here - the confidence in yourself as having something unique and individual to say.
Rachel

Confidence in SELF through collaboration. Do read Angela and Denise's "collaboration" paper, Nichola.
Roz Ivanic

Influences

School

Of the nine O-levels I took only one, art, gave any weight to coursework. Thus I began A-levels with a determined faith in this last exam and a less than reverential attitude to coursework.

Via neat paragraphs, none of which began with an "and" or "but" we learnt how to write correct English. We also learnt however, that we must never be so bold as to suggest something ourselves without rigorous "academic" backup. In short, our own opinions mattered very little.

Possibly one would consider that doing an art 'A'-level would contribute little in my preparation for academic essay writing, but in some ways I think it contributed the most. Left without a teacher, myself and a friend completed our art 'A'-level. We worked together, often helping and advising and once or twice collaborating. (When "caught" we were severely reprimanded.) The experience prepared me for academic essay writing in particular because due to the lack of teacher contact we often wrote very personal reports and comments to our art teacher about our work, aims and achievements. We learned to set our own goals and work to a great extent on our own. Thus we gained confidence in our own thoughts and opinions, in ourselves. This confidence is an essential element in essay writing.

Folk

My family helped to prepare me for academic essay writing by setting the goal to attend university. Coming from a working class background they pushed me quite hard to achieve academic success. Possibly being an only child helped this desire. My parents' lack of knowledge concerning education meant that they never complained when I did my school work in the front room, in front of both the television and fire. This in itself has prepared me for writing academic essays as I find it virtually impossible to work at a desk quietly. I feel that I would have been supported more if my parents had read a quality paper rather than the Daily Mirror, although the left-wing attitude I think has made me more aware, and a more considerate person.

Perhaps one would consider **friends** to be of little consequence when debating preparing for writing. However with my friends I learned how to discuss a topic, and what to aim for. My best friend in particular taught me to relax when considering an essay and look at it from a different angle. She gave me confidence and support and taught me how to trust. I think that such "trust" occurs between an essay-writer and the marker.

All in all, my experience before university made me a confident individual, ready to express her thoughts and views, possibly a little too readily, . . . I was prepared in all of this to communicate well, to write good academic essays of interest.

Fascinating because the dominant image of study is serious and solitary, separated from everyday life - obviously this is a professional-class culture-determined image.
Roz Ivanic

I always wanted music and company at that stage. Now I need quiet and isolation, and my children seek the reverse!
Judith

Is there a proper place to do homework? . . My parents had no idea on things I was learning in Maths, but despite reading the Sun they still had opinions and ideas which would benefit my written assignments. My English teacher felt that we should read a good quality paper and watch documentaries on TV. At 15 I wasn't interested. I still got to university but I learned to swim and sail instead of reading and watching TV. So what makes a truly academic person?
Sarah

Maybe we use friends and fellow students more than we realise because we don't always identify all conversational exchanges as conferring . . . knocking ideas about.
Judith

If you're lucky!
Roz Ivanic
Trust between essay-writer and marker is very rarely evident in my own opinion. The marker always has the upper hand. Only through collaboration throughout the writing process can such "trust" occur.
Sarah
I find this a remarkable statement. As a marker of students' work I have often felt very uncomfortable, that I am in a way betraying a trust. My roles as "arbiter of standards" and "supplier of constructive feedback for writing development" don't sit too easily together. Perhaps it's because the criteria on which the mark is based are mine rather than worked out with the students.
Rachel

It seems significant that the support you got at this stage which helped your confidence was from a friend rather than a tutor. Perhaps you were thinking more of trusting yourself, your own judgment about what and how to write.
Rachel

An enviable confidence - it would be interesting to know if she still felt this confidence after a term or a year at university. I thought I had it to begin with but have found it somewhat shaken, particularly in the second year.
Judith

Doing it

Writing for individual tutors can be a puzzling experience. That is why collaborative sessions are an essential ingredient. Perhaps halving the number of coursework essays and introducing collaborative sessions would be most beneficial to tutor - student relations and students' writing experiences.
Sarah

Different tutors taught me different, often opposing things. For example while one advised an introductory paragraph, another denied the right of one to appear in academic work. . . .
At eighteen I found I had to begin to support myself, but I still had some questions. . . . All of these transitions I think I made bit by bit, discovering a little at a time, from second or third years, tutors and friends. . . . I began to value the importance of coursework

I have yet to find a collaborative writer who has not found the experience beneficial - there must be quite a strong argument for making it part of the undergraduate experience, even if it did not form part of the overall assessment of students.
Judith

I was also introduced to the concept of collaborative writing. This has a number of uses such as distinguishing different styles of writing, approaches to the question posed, and an idea that other language can be used effectively. This could mean that students would learn from each other, particularly from mature students, who quite possibly have had a wider access to knowledge and vocabulary.

I found working with a mature student beneficial. . . . Working with another person certainly introduced double the amount of ideas in a constructive and demanding way. . . . Demanding in that the information had to be sorted, understood, re-expressed and each idea explained clearly so both people understood . . .
Sarah

Reflections

As 'A'-level students we wrote what we thought we should think. No one told us that at university 'personality' was injected. How to deal with such an injection involves a change in essay writing, a personal belief in ideas. In such a way, I would introduce assertiveness training into an undergraduate degree.

This statement dramatises the sense of lack of commitment to the ideas very strikingly.
Rachel

What experiences at university have led you to believe "personality" will be valued?
Roz Ivanic

Great idea! I'm interested in this connection between assertiveness training and image / identity in writing.
Roz Ivanic

I'm glad you think *we* have something to learn from *your* experience.
Rachel

I like to think that all academics are learning all the time from their contact with students as well as from their own academic pursuits!
Judith

The university could also help re-educate the academics it employs about all of these ideas. Still today, when one department advocates writing as individual learning, on very strict terms, another pushes collaborative work. Whilst one department advises us to write in a concise, determined and accepted manner, another advises us to use sub-headings and to be more adventurous. With such differing views, perhaps it is no wonder that we as students feel stretched as to what style to use to please the reader.

Tutors are individuals and their styles and wants should be considered. A set standard is an ideal which may not be possible - however better communications are. I wish every tutor asked us to entertain them.
Sarah

This is not so different from the "outside world" where different kinds of writing are required or appreciated in different contexts. I guess two things are important: 1 that people know what the expectations are so that 2 they can make more conscious decisions about whether and how far to comply with them or renegotiate them.
Rachel

How do YOU find out which tutor wants what? It's the strategies for sussing out expectations that study skills teachers need to teach.
Roz Ivanic

I've never thought of "academic" as pointless - instead I doubt the academic validity (whatever that is) of my own work, but recognise the benefits to me of trying to organise my thoughts and knowledge into a structure and presentation that might make sense to someone else. I value the process but am doubtful about the value of the product to anyone but myself.
Judith

"Academic" might no longer mean "pointless". Our essays, our work are a part of us as students. We must learn to regard them as useful.

This expression of "ownership" has a lot of resonances with things you've said before about confidence and personal development. I like the way you connect that "ownership" here with "usefulness.
Rachel

Wonderful comment on the everyday use of the word "academic"!
Roz Ivanic
Excellent. What more can be said?
Sarah

Judith's Journey

For various reasons that I have never fully explored, [essays] hang heavily over my head like a dark cloud.

So true.
Nichola

The dark cloud perhaps represents helplessness . . knowing 60% of what you read will be irrelevant . . realising you have a deadline to meet but you don't know where to start . . knowing that at the end of all your research and effort your pages of writing will be assessed by one single mark which will probably not represent your efforts or the writing *process* itself. The final mark is felt to be a personal comment (or even attack) on your own worth as a writer. The idea of a "dark cloud" sums all this up.
Sarah

School

I have no clear memories of the early stages of acquiring literacy, other than dim recollections of repetitive exercises in letter formation and one humiliating occasion when, at the stage of being introduced to 'joined-up' writing, I laboriously produced a piece of work in which all the words were joined together. My not very sensitive teacher chose to make it a matter of great mirth for the rest of the class, especially when I, tearfully, claimed that that was how my mother wrote! Apart from that rather painful memory I cannot recall not being able to read and write usefully enough for my own needs.

I remember being forced to write with a pencil because my writing wasn't good enough to use a pen.
Nichola

In previous years other students have talked movingly of the painful experience of literacy problems in primary school. I guess acquiring literacy in the university in an unsupportive context could give rise to similar misery.
Rachel

My education in English included a strong element of syntax and spelling, with an emphasis on the values of these in communicating accurately. . . . In relation to my own writing I feel, sometimes, that I devote so much of my mental energy to ensuring syntactical and lexical accuracy and trying to find well-turned phrases that fine language may, often, screen nebulous ideas and dubious academic content.

Spelling was, and still is. a millstone for me. Even in my 3rd year I have been held up for it. I have a lot of trouble and feel that if it was better, with some tutors I might have gained more marks in essays.
Nichola

One of our classroom activities was to take ten "advanced" words from the dictionary and use them in our daily piece of writing . . . I have found that a carefully laid out, neat, correctly spelt piece of writing will gain just as many marks as a creative but perhaps academically untidy piece.
Sarah

A real danger I'm sure, though a bit of me feels that paying attention to lexical accuracy is part of the business of avoiding nebulous ideas. It's where language is used carelessly that the "academic content" may be in question.
Rachel

I do not recall that using language [differently] for communicating with a remote audience ever seemd a problem for me. The idea of two distinct styles seemed quite logical, and still does, although I am now conscious that there is a danger of too much emphasis on the conventions at the expense of the content and that a certain elitism attaches to the use of academic language.

Take this commentary - I'm sure there are spelling mistakes and incorrect usage of English in places, but I'm not being judged, I'm writing what I feel about each quote rather than what I feel I'm expected to write.
Sarah

Motherhood

At the stage when my son was beginning to try to put his own thoughts into words on paper his mental abilities far outstripped his dexterity, complicated by being left-handed, with the pencil. This, and a teacher who was more interested in draughtsmanship and spelling than he was in words and ideas, effectively quenched my son's enthusiasm for writing. ... So, a child who was vocally very articulate and interested in subtleties of word meaning became very resistant to producing written work. ... His experiences have also been instrumental in tempering some of the attitudes I acquired at school regarding the supposed importance of written language conventions. Only when I witnessed his problem did I realize what the cost might be in terms of creativity and originality of ideas.

Work

I feel that my ten years' working experience in a varied library system has been enormously beneficial in allowing me to take advantage of all the bibliographic resources in the University's library. Whether I make best use of these resources is quite another matter and leads me to an aspect of studying in which my previous experiences and certainly my schooling, have not been of much service. I find no problem in unearthing reading material to provide the basis for my essays but I find great problems in trying to read selectively and in extracting relevant and rejecting irrelevant information.

One great learning experience for me during the period when I was occupied in raising children was my involvement with a large voluntary organisation, the Pre-school Playgroups Association, and subsequently in the local Social Services department. ... [I needed to] produce reports for committees, to carry out surveys and research on aspects of the associations work and influence, to negotiate and justify funding applications , ... Much of this required a clear and coherent writing style that conveyed ideas, evaluated situations, drew conclusions, and persuaded without confusing or alienating.

Suffered for my own son's similar experience, though I believe he learned a lot about how *not* to treat other people as a result.
Anon.

How writers handle the responses to their writing is interesting. I always appreciated detailed responses when I was student, so tend to give them, but maybe some students find them dispiriting.
Rachel

See the film "Dead Poets Society".
Sarah

I feel that I did not learn to use the library correctly until the second term in my third year - I believe this is a very common experience.
Nichola

You are lucky that the library was not a dense jungle for you when you first arrived at university. . ... As for extracting and rejecting information, this is particularly difficult when you don't know in which direction you are going.
Sarah

The implication is that students may not get enough support for either of these senses of "information handling". not just the "using the library" kind.
Rachel

In student writing relevance is often determined by a given title. Perhaps if students owned the questions more, selective reading, and critical reading, might come more naturally.
Rachel
I think this must connect up with Nichola's growing confidence, trust in self, idea of studying as growing as a person. THAT must be the key to selective reading, just as she sees it as the key to writing essays.
Roz Ivanic

I often find I am frustrated at my writing because I want to write what my mind is thinking, but I keep going off in tangents and getting mixed up.
Nichola

I agree a clear coherent writing style is needed . . . but formal teaching in the classroom didn't help you, it was the learning experience of the job.
Sarah

Reflections

Although the purposes of my writing at work were not academic they often required an academic approach, where appropriate sources were acknowledged, substantiated evidence was presented, valid parallels drawn and acceptable conclusions submitted. . . . Prior to this it had not occurred to me to think of these experiences and skills as being of any particular relevance outside the purposes for which I was using them at the time.

Several of my fellow mature students are experiencing similar problems. Few amongst us have acquired the confidence of judgement to be able to predict, reasonably accurately, the level of marks that will be attained or to know whether a piece of writing is as good, or less good, than any other piece that we have produced.

It is impossible to say with certainty that some experiences are more influential than others in forming attitudes and approaches to essay writing. . . . In reality, I think it is likely that some of the negative experiences, not only in relation to writing, have been just as influential as the more positive ones I have recalled. Maybe criticism, whether justified or not, effected some sort of reappraisal in me; perhaps my early humiliation over 'joined-up' writing has enabled me to be more sympathetic to the problems of misunderstanding tasks and to be more careful to establish exactly what I am supposed to be doing. . . . Even the process of writing this essay, having forced me to look at many issues relating to it, is already modifying my attitudes and techniques for subsequent writings.

We talk so much of discipline-specific conventions, we forget those requirements which probably are common to most, and . . . to several non-academic endeavours too.
Roz Ivanic

That's great that everything became useful eventually. But many children (and older students) may never get the opportunity to see these skills pulled together for day to day usage.
Sarah

I don't know if this is peculiar to mature students. It's interpretable as a reflection on how poorly the criteria for assessing academic writing are communicated.
Rachel

This encourages me to continue experimenting with "collaborative assessment" to help students develop this "confidence of judgement".
Roz Ivanic

I think a mature student is much more prepared to argue the mark out.
Nichola

Most of us tend to write for the tutor rather than for our own self-satisfaction. Last year I discovered that if I was happy with the piece then that was good enough reward. . . . . If I received a lower mark I could go to them and say "I liked this piece, why didn't you?", rather than accept the mark and think that perhaps I hadn't quite understood what the tutor had wanted. I may be no better a writer but I have a confidence that what I am saying is my own. School did little to foster that confidence.
Sarah

Yes writing this essay did modify my attitude to essay writing. To say I felt relieved to discover that the discomfort I had experienced in past essay writing exercises was not part and parcel of all writing would be an understatement.
Sarah

To quote Nichola: "maybe *academic* doesn't have to mean *pointless* "!
Rachel

Part 2: Gaining Entry to the World of Academic Literacy

In the poster and the comments that it provoked we recognised the three themes: 'membership', 'initiation' and 'experience' which we offer to you here. Maybe you have seen others.

Membership

Institutions of higher education are not open to all. One of the conditions of membership is being able to operate in the world of academic literacy. To be a member at all requires *'qualifications'* which include being able to conform to the conventions of academic writing by adopting an impersonal formal language and substantiating all viewpoints and ideas by academic reference. Students may see themselves as second-class members of this club, as ones who don't have the same *'right to speak'* that professional academics do.

See
Chap. 13

The Qualifications

The process of acquiring the qualifications to enter university starts very young. In these data each student refers to an emphasis on rules of language at primary school, and regrets the inhibiting effect this can have on creativity and pleasure in the young child's later use of writing. School pupils learn very early that giving teachers what they want – neatness, correct syntax and spelling – often gets the marks, and that content and individuality can be of lesser importance. Judith sees her son as the victim of a teacher too pre-occupied with handwriting and spelling to be able to recognise an underlying sensitivity to the subtleties of word meaning. His way with words and interest in them were very relevant to becoming educated, whether formally or informally, but they were qualifications that weren't recognised at that academy.

See
Chap. 10

Some of the literacy practices the students had to engage in in pursuit of the qualifications were ones they found hard to see the point of. The practice in Sarah's primary classroom of taking ten 'advanced' words from the dictionary and using them in a daily piece of writing taught her that her own words wouldn't do. This sort of message may have deterred many of her classmates from even trying to qualify.

Gaining qualifications can be a competitive business. Nichola and Sarah both recollect the competitive element in primary school language work and the importance of the mark rather than the learning process that achieved it. The qualifications are also graduated. Nichola recalls difficulties with neat handwriting at primary school and the conventions of spelling are still tripping her up at university, as well as some new and confusing conventions and values.

These students didn't see all the literacy practices in their schooling before university as limiting or pointless, however. Sarah believes that as an infant pupil her teachers wanted her to absorb the styles and language offered to her in the reading materials she was encouraged to use. At comprehensive school she enjoyed activities of copying from reference books in library projects. Perhaps, as Roz suggests, this also had the function of helping her to become saturated with the academic style so that she could use it in her writing.

See
Chap. 16

Judith's experience of the early acquisition of formal language skills at school was even more positive, apart from the indelible memory of misunderstanding the task of joined-up writing. She tells how learning the conventions of syntax and spelling gave her pleasure and a certain confidence in her writing style. This led her to recognise both at the time, and in later working situations, their relevance to effective and unambiguous communication.

The Right to Speak
The question of the academic validity of student writing crops up in all three essays. In different ways the students all talk about their confidence, or lack of it, in their work and in their right to speak. While Judith felt more confident than the others that she had the 'qualifications' in terms of ability to write in a recognisably academic style, she sees that the 'right to speak' should be based on something else. She questions whether her writing style is a screen behind which it is possible to hide 'nebulous ideas and dubious academic content'.

See
Chap. 19

It seems that conforming to academic conventions presents students with a paradox. In theory facility in using academic language should make for effective communication of ideas, but some students find that it depersonalises them and removes their individuality from the text, so that whether or not they have the right to speak, they have nothing to say.

See
Chap. 20

Before reaching university each student has already absorbed the idea that all opinions expressed need to be substantiated by reputable academic reference, and that student identity is not important. This requirement for academic substantiation has the effect of undermining personal confidence since it seems to be saying that the views of the individual students are of no value unless it can be demonstrated that they will coincide with those of an accredited academic. So while academic reference for ideas and opinions is seen as lending validity it can also remove ownership.

See
Chap. 13

At O-level Sarah describes drawing conclusions in argument essays on the basis of the number of sources she could find for each 'side'. Later on she still did not feel that the purpose of studying was to develop her own thinking. But happily she now tells how she has learned at last to claim for herself the right to speak by developing her own view of the value of her writing, saying 'I could go to them and say "I liked this piece, why didn't you?" '

Personal confidence in student writing can be undermined by the fact that the writing is assessed by others using criteria over which the student has little, or no, control. The assessment function of the writing can override the learning function and the personal satisfaction of the writer be too much determined by the grade achieved. So, there is a feeling amongst thoughtful undergraduates that they do not really 'own' their writing because the direction, the ideas and the evaluation all come from elsewhere.

Because formal education, in its institutions, has a certificating function, its members must do what they must to graduate. So giving the tutors what they want may be more important to students than establishing a right to speak. Playing the game of proving you've got the qualifications, a lesson learnt early in primary school, may prevail at least as far as graduation to ensure membership of the academic establishment.

Initiation

Having suggested that the academic world is a world of literacy to which students must struggle to gain entry, we can also see from the remarks in these essays something of how membership of this club is consolidated. The initiation process is one which students largely have to discover for themselves, though some educational practices may also support them in learning the ropes.

Student Strategies: Learning the 'House Rules'

It comes as no surprise to any individual that when entering a new social institution there are rules and regulations set to govern their actions within it. It comes as a surprise though, to the student, that such stringent rules exist, not only in the workplace, but in the educational environment too. Yet somehow these three students have learned the rules of the academic game, and how to play and even profit by them. Sarah, Judith and Nichola have tried to pinpoint how they discovered these rules.

One rule – the precedence of presentation over content, making how students write and present a piece of work more important than what they write – was learned very early, as we have seen. Another, which came much later concerned their coming to understand their relationship to the reader of their official academic writing. They discovered that the work they hand in is judged, in part, by the personal response of the marker, and not just in terms of some objective criteria of academic merit. This is where Nichola's sense of trust in her tutors may have been very important. Having discovered the concepts of 'presentation' and 'personality' they had also to consider the content of the work produced. Sarah and Judith both noted confidence seemed to plummet once their undergraduate course had begun, and yet they gradually gained confidence in their 'own judgement about what and how to write'. What constitutes a piece of academic work? At undergraduate level some help is available in the form of course guidelines, book lists and so on, but it is the interpretation of those guidelines which will eventually determine how successful initiates become at the game.

For many students drawing on resources for writing, including books and libraries, is a process whose complexities defeat them well into higher education. Faced with a reading list of a large number of books, selection becomes a major problem. Judith reveals how her professional experience as a librarian helped her exploit the bibliographic resources of the university library but was no help at all in using reading material selectively. Researching to write hadn't figured in her school essays.

Whatever they managed to discover by themselves was useful, but they needed support too, and found at least some among tutors, friends and fellow-students.

Mentors: Support Students need for Developing Literacy in the University
When one comes to university there is an inbuilt expectation that the student is already 'literate'. But as we have seen these students are acutely aware of literacies they haven't got. They make it clear that they could have had better support for learning to write than they did. Over the period they were at university, one way and another, they came to terms with this new world of literacy, but it happened in a fairly haphazard way.

One of the things they had to deal with was the fact that different departments and different tutors had different expectations concerning literacy practices. Perhaps these differences had something to do with Judith's feeling that she lacked the confidence to predict the mark a piece of writing might gain. How do students suss out these expectations? One of Sarah's comments refers to a deliberate strategy of Rachel's to put tutor's expectations on the agenda. Before receiving students' first essays in their first year course at the university, she told them she wanted to be entertained. The first thing discussed when returning their work to them was whether she had been, and (often) why they hadn't believed she meant it!

University tutors can have a positive role to play as models and mentors, supporting students' writing development where there is a basis of trust and the communication is right. Commentators were all surprised by Nichola's reference to trust between essay writer and marker, but Sarah suggests that while she rarely experienced it, such trust could occur if tutors and students communicate during the writing process. Nichola's suggestion that 'the university could help to re-educate the academics it employs about all of these ideas' prompts Judith to point out that academics have much to learn from their contact with students.

Collaboration: Sharing the Experience of Writing and the Process of Learning

See
Chap. 20

Learning acceptable ways of writing in this new world of literacy can be a lonely and confidence-shaking experience. On Rachel's course the students were encouraged to write assignments collaboratively. In spite of initial misgivings, the students who took advantage of this opportunity valued the insights they gained into writing and learning through this process of collaboration.

Nichola had had an earlier experience of collaboration at school through her attempt to resolve an unsatisfactory teaching situation with a fellow student. It illustrates very well the mutual support and opportunity for self development that can occur through collaboration and Nichola attributes some of her confidence on arrival at university to this earlier collaborative experience.

However, she alludes to being 'caught', with the implication that collaboration is not acceptable and is tantamount to cheating. 'Bad show' if two players join together to defeat the rules. Although collaborative writing is very common amongst academics in universities and research establishments for those who have passed the initiation stage, it is viewed with considerable suspicion if engaged in by those who are not academically qualified.

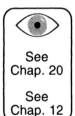
See
Chap. 20

See
Chap. 12

Sarah acknowledged the value of the exchange of experience which happened in a voluntary workshop on writing run in association with Rachel's course. Nichola tells of the supportive contribution of her friends at university, and its role in the development of both her confidence and skill as a writer. Unofficial collaborations of these sorts may be much more common ways in which students learn together how to become initiated into the academic literacy club.

Experience

It is a theme of this book to see literacy not as a unitary 'achievement' but as a range of distinctive and specialised practices associated with particular social institutions. Academic writing itself can be seen as a collection of related literacy practices, of which students' writing in the academy is one. So while few students come to university with 'literacy problems' in the sense used in everyday conversation or the mass media, they almost all come with a great deal to learn about how to participate in the distinctive literacy practices of higher education.

However the reflection of Judith, Nichola and Sarah reveal that these practices are not *so* distinctive or specialised that they make no connection with other writing experiences. In explaining the transitions they had made in their approaches to writing they talked about their wider lives. We learned about Judith's jobs and about her children. We learned what newspaper Nichola's family read, where she used to do her homework, and the importance of her friends and fellow students in getting something out of academic writing.

These spontaneous references to non-academic aspects of their lives when reflecting on academic writing highlight *experience*, both of other 'iteracy practices and of life in general, as an important theme in becoming academically literate'. It shows in two broad ways in the quotations we selected, and the comments they inspired. Firstly there is the issue of the place of personal experience in academic writing – is it appropriate, is it legitimate, is it useful? And secondly there is the converse issue, that of the role of academic knowledge and activities in students' personal development.

The Role of Experience in Academic Writing
There are a number of ways in which common schooling practices downplay or even deny the legitimacy of students bringing their experience into the classroom. Young children eagerly offer anecdotes in classroom discourse in the infants school, and many teachers try to make constructive and thought-provoking use of them. Nevertheless such anecdotes are much less frequent in the later stages of schooling, indicating that students have learned that one of the ground rules of classroom discourse is to keep one's personal experience to oneself.

See
Chap. 20

See
Chap. 16

Another way in which experience is made less personal is through the language conventions that are associated with many kinds of academic writing. When Rachel discussed the messages from her feedback on their first essays with her Year One students they thought approval of the use of the first person was probably an idiosyncrasy of hers, expecting it to be unacceptable to many tutors.

The use of impersonal language in scientific report writing is a well-established convention. The insistence on its use by students reflects a possible mismatch between educational aims and practices. While it *may* be appropriate for communicating to a wide and unknown audience in published journals (though even that could be called into question), that is not what students are writing for in most cases. It may be appropriate to ask students to demonstrate their mastery of the scientific writing conventions as *part* of their scientific education, but it may be counterproductive to expect it all the time. After all an experimental report is an account of what the writer did. Removing all reference to self from the account could discourage reflection and the exploration of personal curiosity or confusion. When Sarah tells us she did no discursive writing in her A-level Maths and Physics courses, we must ask whether giving an account of how *she* had come to a particular belief in physics might not have been intellectually valuable, and whether an account of the process she went through to solve a mathematical problem might not have been useful to her in trying to develop her problem-solving skills and reflect on her own performance.

Judith's response to reading what Nichola had to say was a nice example of how students bring their own experience to academic tasks. She said:

> I am constantly trying to draw parallels with my own experiences. . . . I have more to say about Nichola's essay than Sarah's because I cannot recall too clearly my own experiences as she had done.

It shows how as a *reader* she is processing the text by mapping it onto her own experience.

In discussion at the conference the students realised that, although none of them had experienced collaborative writing for assessment previously, some had collaborated to produce writing in other worlds of literacy, such as lists, notices of events, and letters. So they had viewed the prospect of writing collaboratively as an entirely new experience when in fact the only new thing about it was that it would form part of their assessment. This demonstrates how academic writing is often viewed as being entirely separate from any other writing that people may do in their day to day lives and how little they might recognise the relevance of their experiences elsewhere to the academic world of literacy. The quotations themselves reflect the sense of separation students have between study and life. When Judith said it had not occurred to her to see the writing skills she developed at work as relevant to academic life, many students might say the same sort of thing; that they didn't appreciate the usefulness of certain practices associated with academic writing for writing in other contexts at the time. It makes one question whether students will find the skills they developed in academic writing useful in their later working lives. Moves to widen the

See
Chap. 18

range of types of written work undertaken by students, for example through the *Enterprise in Higher Education* initiative, imply not, or not entirely at least. However Judith's reflection on moving in the other direction between different worlds of literacy reminds us that we should not throw the baby out with the bathwater. For whilst some academic writing conventions can be seen as *merely* conventional, or even downright unhelpful, especially to students, others may be very useful not only in students' learning, but also in their later activities and experiences. If nothing else writing assignments which are more like the writing tasks facing people in the 'world of work' may help students see which of the academic writing conventions appear to have a point in particular kinds of non-academic contexts.

Another way in which the separation of the world of study from the rest of life was reflected in these accounts came from Nichola, who identified herself as coming from a working-class background, and described doing her homework 'in the front room, in front of both the television and fire'. Roz Ivanic, in reacting to this, remarked on the dominant image of study as serious and solitary, a professional-class culture-determined image. It is clearly one of which Nichola was aware when she wrote this, or the details of the circumstances in which she writes would hardly have been worth mentioning. This quotation draws attention to the fact that the academic conventions students come to terms with are not only to do with what the output looks like, but also how it is made.

See
Chap. 14

The Role of Academic Literacy in Personal Development
In spite of statements the three students have made which suggest a sense of divorce between academic and everyday worlds, they have also given a number of revelations about how reading and writing at University can have personal meaning. This perception is most clearly stated by Sarah who explains how reading a particular academic paper made a difference to both her thinking and her actions concerning writing in the future.

Nichola now takes almost for granted the idea that students should find something of personal value in their academic work, and implies that they just need to recognise it, though this is quite a change from the view she says she had in her mid-teens. Her account of how this change of perception came about reveals the importance of a sense of ownership and a purpose for academic writing.

Judith sees the point of academic work in the process of organising her thoughts for communication into a structure and presentation that might make sense to someone else. She values the process but is doubtful about the value of the product to anyone but herself. At the end of her essay she wrote: 'Even the process of writing this essay, having forced me to look at many issues relating to it, is already modifying my attitudes and techniques for subsequent writings', confirming the value of this reflective piece in her own development as a writer, and Sarah claims to have the same feeling.

In very different ways all three students have talked about connecting 'book knowledge' and personal experience. Thank goodness they do – for integrating the student into the whole person has to be the bottom line of education. Setting this assignment was part of Rachel's strategy for doing this. Another was to ask students to review a paper in the exam by saying *what difference* it had made to their thinking. She needs to find more ways.

Was the Struggle Worth It?

A student friend from Newcastle Polytechnic found it helpful to know that students' struggles are recognised when his department gave him this piece by Steven Cahn:

> We must realise that becoming an educated person is a difficult, demanding enterprise. . . . It is painful to have one's ignorance exposed and frustrating to be baffled by intellectual subtleties. Of course there can be joy in learning as there can be joy in sport. But in both cases the joy is a result of overcoming genuine challenges and cannot be experienced without toil.

> It is not easy to read intelligently and think precisely. It is not easy to speak fluently and write clearly. It is not easy to study a subject carefully and know it thoroughly. But these abilities are the foundation of a sound education. [Steven Cahn, New York Times 29th December 1974]

At the time of writing, all three students have now graduated from the university and are beginning to make their different ways in the world. They have learned not merely to 'know their subject' and 'write clearly' about it, but also to reflect on their own learning, to value and understand their own and each other's experience, and to have confidence in their own voices. They have taught their tutor as much as she ever taught them.

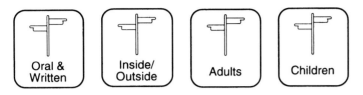

| Oral & Written | Inside/ Outside | Adults | Children |

AGNES KING

6: Literacy and the Travelling Communities

In Britain there are people who travel for their business, taking their homes with them from town to town. As a teacher with a Teaching Support Service I have been involved with two groups of these people.

The first distinct group, Travellers, are considered to be an ethnic minority. David Smith, consultant, Traveller Research and Projects has said:

> The term Traveller refers to all that minority group of people commonly identified as Gypsies, Tinkers or Travellers for whom the travelling life is a significant reference in determining their own lifestyles and attitudes.

Some travel many miles to work. Traditionally many used horses to pull their bow-top wagons, travelling ten to fifteen miles each day. At night they stopped down country lanes, working on farms or in similar occupations. A few continue to travel in this way, in small units.

As towns have sprawled into the surrounding countryside, open spaces have been developed for the needs of town dwellers. Mechanisation had led to a drift of people from agriculture into occupations in towns. The attitude of the settled population had led to pressures on the travelling communities. Many families are having to stop on large council or privately run sites. Others move around unable to find stopping-places.

The Travellers have little history of schooling. Constant movement for jobs and stopping-places prevent the up-take of school places.

For the Showmen a longer season working the Fairs around the country means less time at the winter quarters. Some children only attend school between November and February each year.

In trying to support the children in school, of both groups of travelling people, I realised that different solutions would be required to provide

73

literacy to the unique travelling community. Both groups, Travellers and Showmen, see the greater need for literacy today in their day-to-day lives. Just registering vehicles and filling in forms demand a high level of skill.

To ascertain what the parents wanted for their children I decided to go out and ask them. The following two initiatives resulted.

Traveller Education: A Personal Initiative

Some of the Traveller children in school had parents who had not been in school when children themselves, or only attended spasmodically. The parents either could not read or write, or could only read the printed word. They were unable to read handwritten letters.

I became a Tutor in Adult Basic Education in the hope that some Travellers would attend the class. Despite various forms of advertising the Travellers who were interested in learning to read never arrived at the class.

See
Chap. 15

I realised that the families would not respond to this sort of impersonal advertising; they need a personal approach. I visited the site and did some 'opportunity sampling'. I knocked on the caravan doors and met two families. When I was invited in I talked about education for the children and they brought up the subject of adult education themselves. Hoping they would come along to a class I gave them my personal telephone number. To extend adult education to Traveller families the approach has to be as personal as this.

When there was no telephone call I was disappointed because I believe everyone should be given the opportunity to read and to write. If they have the ability to learn no one should have to depend on others to read their mail. Imagine my delight when I arrived at the next class to find two of the women already there. They had paid a £5 taxi fare from their site to the class.

The aim of the class was to teach adults to read. Some also wanted to learn joined handwriting so that they could read letters and documents. One young girl came along just for one night. Her objective was to learn to write her new surname when she was married.

Some were beginners and they continued to attend until they moved out of the area, firstly to visit a horse fair, then to move permanently to another site on the other side of town.

The Result of Their Initiatives

Not only did the women attend regularly, they brought along others who had never been to school. They progressed in their learning, working diligently for the two-hour session. They began to read the social sight vocabulary needed to shop in town. They had many difficulties to over-come. Unfamiliarity with adult education classes of any kind made the classroom a new environment. Baby sitters were a problem when they all wanted to attend on the same evening. The greatest challenge was in admitting they needed help.

Two Traveller women have made good progress in learning to read, both in class and in practice at home. With the help of their friends they are continuing to learn to read words in the environment. The writing that follows is an example of their achievements.

walk

IT LOVELY in THe summer time you
CAN GO FOR A WALK AND SEE ALL THE
NICE BIRDS AND ANIMELS AND WANE IT
IS SUMMER WE GET READY FOR APPLEBY.
AND ALL THE GIPSY MEET UP AND WE SEE
ALL OUR OLD FRENDS AND REAL ASHINGS IT
IS LIKE OLD TIMES. WE SITE AT THE FIRE
AND SING A SONG AND SUM GIVE A STEP
DANCE.. AND ON A DAY WE GO TO TOWN AND
SEE THE HORSES GETTING WOSHID IN THE
RIVER AND ON THE FEIRE THE OLD WAGGANS
IS THER WATE YOU NEVER SEE AND WANE
MY DAD. WAS A BIT YOUNGER HE WOOD GET
LOTS OF WORK PANTTING SUME OF THEM
AS HE WAS VERY FAMES FOR BILDDING
THE WAGGONS. BUT HE IS OLD NOW AND JUST
GOES FOR TO SEE FRENDS IT IS THE BEST
WEEK OF THE YEAR IT IS NICE TO BEE THE
THINGS FOR SALE THER IS NICE CUPS AND
CUSHINGS ALLSO SHOES AND CLOSE AND
WANE WEN WE COME BACK WE FEEL
AS A PATCHES ON RESAVASHING

BUT WE HAVE NICE FRENDS IN THE SHOPS.
AND AROWND TONN WE ALLSO HAVE NICE
FRENDS IN MEX BRO I SEAN SUME TODAY I
THE ALL CAME TO US TO TORKE ALL THE GIRLS
IN THE SHOPS AND ON THE MARKIT THEY
WAS ALL PLEASED TO SEE US. AGANE AND I
THINK IT. IS VERRY. NICE TO HAVE FRENDS
OTHER THAN JUST TRAVALING PEAPELE. MY
DAD IS VERY WELL LICKET AT YORK.
CASTEL MUSEME FOR PANTTING THE
WAGGAN AND SUM CARTS. HE GETS CARDS
AT XMAS TIME HE AS GOT THEM FOR 27
YEARS NOW THE ALSO OFFERD ME TO GET
MARRID- FROM THER AND LEND ME A DRESS
AND ONE OF THE BUGGYS AND I THORT THAT
WAS LOVELY

In the rest of this article I will describe the second initiative I have been involved in to extend education to travelling people. The 'Postal Lessons' project tried to provide some continuity in the education of the children of Showmen. It made use of written communication to compensate for the face-to-face education the children had to miss, and to keep everyone informed of what others had done.

Postal Lessons

See
Chap. 8

A chance meeting of a concerned mother with a Senior Education Welfare Officer who was looking for a truanting child took place in the local butcher's shop. The welfare officer contacted the Head of the Teaching Support Service who arranged for the mother to take the children to the Teaching Support Service Resource Centre, where the first of the 'Postal Lessons' was provided.

See
Chap. 16

The anomaly of the lessons was that they were never actually posted out to the children. When two support teachers took over the lessons letters were sent to the families with photographs of the teachers. Reading books and materials were prepared for the children. Sometimes the mothers collected the materials from the Teaching Support Centre. They waited

The late Mr. Jimmy Berry painting
an open lot. He made the wagon
which is in York museum.

Teacher Agnes King with grandchildren
of Jimmy Berry, and their living
wagon at Appleby Fair in June 1991.

patiently while workbooks and sheets were corrected and the next lessons
were made ready. A summer booklet was prepared to supplement the
commercial workbooks used. Various worksheets were added for the older
children and notes were added to the pages, encouraging the children to use
the work in an imaginative way. Red plastic folders were used so that the
children could keep their work organised. Later a new Head of the Teaching
Support Service met the Head Teacher of a school in which three of the
families had enrolled their children. It was agreed the literacy and
numeracy work could be supplied from the wintering school. The Support
Teachers visited the school on alternate weeks, on Fridays. They prepared
for the next lessons and collected work from the families and this continued
until one of the Support Teachers took on other responsibilities in the
summer of 1986.

There was a problem when a school gave easy reading books to one of
the children. When the Fair came to town an afternoon was spent assessing

the reading of four of the children. In particular one child had a reading ability about two years above that of the books given to her at a school she had attended for two weeks.

As a result of this discrepancy a file was created to assist teachers when the children attend their schools. A sheet of paper was inserted in the front of the file with the latest details of the child's reading achievements together with notes on other work. Some teachers wrote notes on the work the children did in their school with the result that each successive teacher had notes from the preceding teacher, making continuity of work a reality.

To make transition between schools easier, liaison work with the middle school began in the summer before a child moved up. A mother arranged to bring him back to town specially so that he could join his classmates when they visited the new school. With his friends he met his new teacher, learned the lay-out of the school and what to expect in the next term.

In the autumn teaching took place in the 'wintering' school and the middle school was visited to collect any materials from the teacher so that the child was kept in touch with his class when he was travelling. Parents called occasionally to collect work and to return it for marking at the school. On one occasion a father called at the Teaching Support Service carrying the distinctive red folder.

There were problems of keeping the children up to date with their peer-groups, and we all, class teacher, parents and I looked forward to having the children back in class so that they could work with their peers.

After a few weeks back in class we all realised that weekly lessons would have to be attempted in the spring term to compensate for the times when the school was following different schemes of work which could cause confusion. Files were created with lots of labelled clear sleeves so that work-sheets, work ideas and books could all be kept in one work folder which could be taken to each successive school by the child. Another folder was supplied to be kept at home with completed work which had been marked by a teacher with work to do when the child may miss attending a school.

After discussion with Headteachers, class teachers and myself, it was agreed that the travelling child should be twinned with another child. This meant that the class teacher had to think of a child in the same class who was working at the same rate as the travelling child. Each week when I went into school to collect the lessons to send to the children, the class teacher would give details of the work done or about to be done by the twinned child.

The aims of the lessons
(1) To provide continuity of education for the children when their parents were travelling to the Fairs around the country.
(2) To make it easier for the children when they returned in the winter to their classes in Doncaster.
(3) To provide literacy.

The following approaches/methods were used.

(1) Photocopied pages of work and of text were sent to the travelling child. This meant that:
   (a) the child was only asked to do one week's work at any time;
   (b) the child was not faced by over-large amounts of work;
   (c) work could be returned frequently for marking;
   (d) the children were not left without work while it was being marked.
(2) The lessons were delivered to the butcher's shop or to the grandparents' wagon. They were put into a large, dated envelope with the Teaching Support Service address on it, so that the parents could return it for marking (by post if they wanted) at any time.
(3) The telephone number of the TSS was on the front of the work folder and a map of Doncaster with the location of the TSS marked so that any teacher in a visited school could make contact, if necessary.
(4) Parents, relations and friends who were visiting the families at the Fairs agreed to collect lessons from the butcher's shop.

Sometimes teachers explain lessons to the class before the children do any work or writing. It was proposed that tape recorded lessons of the class teacher would be attempted. However, in practice this was never done. Teachers preferred to either explain the points to me so that I could pass on the information to the parents, or I would write notes to the children or parents, with the explanations. Teacher notes were often used and computer discs were used on a few occasions. Details of radio and television programmes were passed on to the parents. The possibility of using a video camera was never explored. When the class went on a trip when the travelling child could not attend, it could have been useful. Instead every effort was made to have the children back in town when a trip was planned so they could have first hand experience. One boy even managed to be included in a residential weekend.

How did the postal lessons work?
The first family to use the new weekly lessons found that teachers in a Sheffield school did use the folder and the work I had prepared. A telephone call from a mum alerted me to the fact that one child was doing well with his reading and the teacher in his visited school would help him with the next

book if I sent it at the weekend with his grandfather.

What were the advantages of these lessons? .

The children were happy to return to town for one or two days in the summer, knowing they could follow the current curriculum, knew the topic work and were rejoining their own peer group.

See
Chap. 10

Examples of good practice from the class could be photocopied and forwarded to the travelling child. As well as poems and stories, topic work and letters could be sent giving all the pupils real situations for using a different genre of English.

When travelling, the postal lessons helped the children to have a programme relevant to their needs and at appropriate levels.

The parents (and other relatives) were actively involved in the education of the children, not only in the collection and delivery of the packages but in discussions with class and support teachers. The parents always had appropriate work for the children, including travelling days when the children could not attend any school.

Teachers were able to use the work in the folders when appropriate. When a new child started in a class they always had work to do immediately until the teacher could organise other activities. The children always had a collection of literacy materials suitable for their needs and interests, not just a collection of exercise books from each school visited.

A dialogue could be initiated between teachers through the folders. Finally there was more continuity with the weekly lessons due to the help of parents, other relations, teachers and not least of all the butchers at the shop in town.

| Bilingual | Oral & Written | Conflict | Adults | Inside/ Outside |

CAROL MORRIS AND HUBISI NWENMELY

7: The Kwéyòl Language and Literacy Project

Kwéyòl is like a ship ready to go on a voyage and calling everyone aboard. If you do not come, you'll be left behind.

(Constance 1989)

Kwéyòl Speech Communities

French Creoles are spoken in many different parts of the world: Mauritius, Réunion, Seychelles and Rodrigues in the Indian Ocean; Louisiana in the USA; Cayenne in South America; and Haiti, Martinique, Guadeloupe, St. Lucia, Dominica, Grenada, Carriacou and the Grenadines, Trinidad and Tobago, Désirade, Marie Galante, St. Maarten, Les Saintes and St. Barthélemy in the Caribbean.

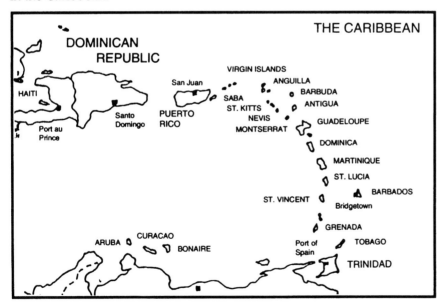

Kwéyòl Speech Communities in the Caribbean

81

The precise circumstances surrounding the development of the various French Creoles vary a great deal. In Mauritius, for example, there are large Indian and Chinese communities, whereas in the Caribbean, the majority of the population was originally transported as slaves from different parts of West Afrika. None the less, the similarities between French Creoles are far more striking than the differences, and we will use the word Kwéyòl to refer to them.

Although there are small Seychellois and Mauritian communities in the UK, by far the largest Kwéyòl speaking population comes from the Eastern Caribbean. Kwéyòl is spoken by small numbers of older speakers in Grenada, Trinidad and the Grenadines. In St. Lucia and Dominica, however, the majority of the population speak Kwéyòl as their mother tongue and the main focus for this section will, therefore, be on these two islands.

The French West Indian Company first established St. Lucia as a French colony in 1642. In the next 150 years the island changed hands between the French and the British some fourteen times, but remained under British control from 1803 until independence in 1979. Dominica has had a similarly chequered history. It was French between 1632 and 1732 and again between 1778 and 1783 when it finally passed to the British. These extended periods of contact with French at a critical period in the history of the Caribbean have had a lasting effect on the linguistic situation in both islands.

For further information, see Nwenmely (1991) which refers, in depth, to the development of the Kwéyòl language.

Acceptance of a distinctive Eastern Caribbean Afro-French identity is becoming increasingly widespread in the Caribbean and is illustrated for instance, by a change in terminology. St. Lucians and Dominicans have traditionally referred to their language as Patwa whereas people from Martinique and Guadeloupe call it Kwéyòl. When the Standing Committee for Creole Studies standardised the orthography in 1982, it was agreed to call the language Kwéyòl, thus bringing it into line with Banzil Kwéyòl – the International Kwéyòl movement.

Educational Status of Kwéyòl

The low status of Kwéyòl in the Caribbean has meant that, until recently, it has received little attention from educators: English is the medium of education; Kwéyòl is the language of the home. In Britain, most people assumed that, because English was the official language of the Eastern Caribbean, St. Lucian and Dominican children would naturally speak English. The low status of Kwéyòl also meant that people from the Eastern Caribbean were slow to volunteer information on their linguistic back-

See
Chap. 11

ground. In the course of their own education, they would have received severe reprimands and, in some cases, beatings from parents for engaging in what was commonly called 'yard talk' or 'that bad language'. For many years following their arrival in Britain, such parents also discouraged their children from talking Kwéyòl. For these reasons, teachers and others often came to learn, only by accident, that Kwéyòl was a fundamental part of the linguistic repertoire of this area of the Caribbean and, indeed, the mother tongue of the majority.

The History of the 'Patwa Project' (Kwéyòl Project) in Tower Hamlets

The National Literacy Campaign in the UK was launched in 1975, to establish classes and courses for English-speaking people who had difficulty in reading and writing (estimated at that time as two million). By 1975, ILEA's Bethnal Green Institute Adult Literacy Scheme had been established for two years and by 1976, many Dominican and St. Lucian people were coming to classes to improve their reading and writing. Carol Morris was the organiser of the scheme at that time and during the next three years, she and the team of tutors became concerned that they could not proj erly meet the learning needs of their Eastern Caribbean students.

The following conversation took place over lunch:

Carol Morris: 'Excuse me, but you speak another language!'
Dominican student: 'Patwa! No, it's not a language, its just whal we speak among ourselves.'
St. Lucian student: 'It's broken French, you can't write it down. No, it's not a language'.

After a number of similar conversations, Carol looked for help and advice regarding a written form of Kwéyòl. These searches led her to visit St. Lucia in 1980. She found the teaching tapes prepared by a Trinidadian, Dr. Lawrence Carrington, which were used for instructing US Peace Corps volunteers working in St. Lucia. Carol also found a number of people involved in the Creole Standing Committee and that, despite what many people had said to the contrary, the people of St. Lucia spoke Kwéyòl, known as Patwa. This visit launched a number of connections which were consolidated in 1983 with a working visit of four months.

In 1982 Carol, working with Stan Emmanuel, a St. Lucian youth leader working in the Saxon Youth Club in Bow, London, sponsored a number of seminars to discuss Kwéyòl language issues and to sound out the views of the local Eastern Caribbean community (estimated at some 17,000 people) regarding establishing a Kwéyòl Literacy Scheme. Additionally, Cynthia Alcindor, a member of this seminar group, approached Carol Morris in 1982 with a problem which epitomised the discrimination faced by Creole speakers. Her nephew's school in Stoke Newington asked all parents to write stories in their own languages, so that these could be produced in the mother tongue and English. These booklets were to be illustrated by the children and to be used as bilingual readers in the classroom. What could the Kwéyòl-speaking parent do? There was no written form for the language. What evolved from the conversation, was the St. Lucian folk tale, *'Pyé Papay-la'* being told by Cynthia. This was written down using the English spelling system and then translated into English. This booklet took its place in Princess May School's set of bilingual readers and also became a popular reader in local adult literacy schemes.

Peeay Papii Pawpaw Tree

1st Edition	2nd Edition

Gobuday koo mar say mootay. Lay weevay deemee peeay papii la buday paytay!

Big Belly started to climb. When he reached halfway in the paw paw tree his belly burst!

Gobouden koumansé mouté. Lè'y wivé a dimi pyé papay-la bouden'y pété.

Big Belly started to climb. When he reached halfway in the paw paw tree his belly burst!

Extract from first edition of *'Pyé Papay-la'* using the English spelling system and second edition using Kwéyòl spelling system.
by Cynthia Noel

The Kwéyòl Project was financed through Tower Hamlets Institute of Adult Education to enable a young St. Lucian medical student, Eugene Frederick, to co-ordinate the launching of the first phase of the (Patwa) Project classes in May 1984. This ran parallel with the development of a Black Studies course. It was felt important to develop the two courses in parallel, in order to enhance and encourage an Afrikan educational and cultural perspective which would in turn facilitate understanding of the historical development of the Kwéyòl language in the Caribbean.

Since May 1984, a number of very exciting developments have taken place. There were no teaching materials apart from 'A Handbook for Writing Creole' (Louisy & Turmel-John, 1983). The classes therefore, have always been run on workshop basis; the experts are the Dominican and St. Lucian Kwéyòl speakers, the tutors guide the workshops by structuring the approach to spelling and grammar, and working with the students to produce teaching and reading materials. A Newssheet and Patwa Primer 1st Edition were published, two short plays written and performed in class to video, and also a full length play, 'Papa Montenez', written by the students. One act of this play was performed at the Tower Hamlets Institute of Adult Education 'Open Curtain Festival' in July 1985. This was the first time that a Kwéyòl play had been performed in Britain and it was very

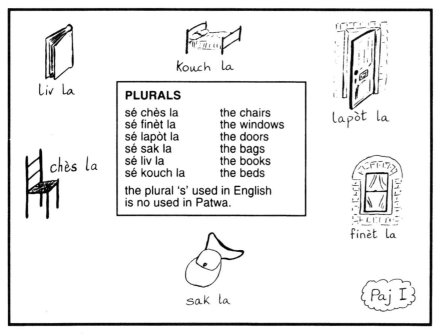

PLURALS

sé chès la	the chairs
sé finèt la	the windows
sé lapòt la	the doors
sé sak la	the bags
sé liv la	the books
sé kouch la	the beds

the plural 's' used in English is no used in Patwa.

liv la · kouch la · lapòt la · chès la · sak la · finèt la · Paj I

Extract from *Newssheet* July 1984

SÉ EGZÉSIS	EXERCISES
FÈMÉ LAPÒT-LA, SOUPLÉ	FÈMÉ KÈTIN-LA, SOUPLÉ
close the door, please	draw/close the curtain, please
OUVÉ LAPÒT-LA, SOUPLÉ	LIMÉ LAMP-LA SOUPLÉ
open the door, please	light the lamp, please
LAKLÉ LAPÒT-LA, SOUPLÉ	MÉTÉ KLÉTÉ-A, SOUPLÉ
lock the door, please	put the (electric) light on, please
OUVÉ FINÈT-LA, SOUPLÉ	BALYÉ KAY-LA, SOUPLÉ
open the window, please	sweep the house, please
FÈMÉ FINÈT-LA, SOUPLÉ	SOUKWÉ SOUPY-A, SOUPLÉ
close the window, please	shake the mat, please

MWEN KA ALÉ PÉNTIWÉ KAY-LA	MWEN LAS
I am going to paint the house	I am tired
MWEN KA ALÉ NÈTWÉ FINÈT-LA	MWEN VLÉ ALÉ DÒMI
I am going to clean the windows	I want to go to sleep
MWEN KA'Y NÈTWÉ TWEZIN-A	MWEN KA ALÉ DÒMI
I will tidy up the kitchen	I am going to sleep
MWEN KA'Y FÈMÉ KÈTIN-LA	YO OSWÉ MWEN PA BIEN DÒMI
I will draw-close the curtain	I didn't sleep well last night
MWEN KA'Y OUVÉ FINÈT-LA	MWEN TÉ NI A MOVÉ WEV
I will open the window	I had a bad dream

Extract from *Patwa* a First Primer, 1985

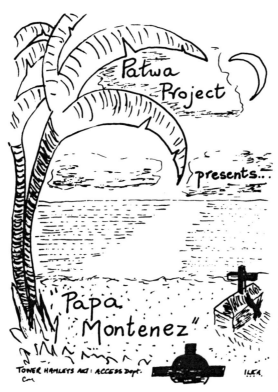

Programme cover for the play *Papa Montenez* at the Curtain Theatre, Tower Hamlets, 1985.

popular with the multiracial audiences at the festival. The second play was *Vòlè an Laplas-la,* written by students, directed by Hubisi Nwenmely and performed by members of the, by now, three Kwéyòl classes, as their contribution to National Caribbean Focus year in July 1986. More recently (1990), the project published *Kalalou Kwéyòl* – a collection of short stories, poems and other works in Kwéyòl and English. Extracts from *Kalalou Kwéyòl* were performed at the East London Festival of languages, prior to publication.

Programme cover for the Caribbean Focus year
performance of *Vòlè an Laplas-la,* 1986.

Extract from the book *Kalalou Kwéyòl*, 1990.

One of the aims of the Kwéyòl Project – from its inception – has been to develop literacy skills amongst St. Lucian and Dominican people and to encourage the development of students to become tutors on the Project. Carol Morris was very pleased to hand over the literacy teaching to Hubisi Nwenmely in February 1986; Hubisi now teaches the language group, whilst a former student, Jackie John-Rose now teaches the literacy group. More students are being prepared for participating on the Kwéyòl Tutor Training Programme, to facilitate the setting up and teaching of additional Kwéyòl classes. Another aspect of the Project has been to develop Kwéyòl language classes, to make them available in the same way that Spanish, French, Urdu, Hindi and other language classes are part of Adult Education provision. These classes appeal to young people whose parents are Kwéyòl speakers and who want to be able to speak the language for social and cultural heritage reasons, especially for when they visit the Caribbean and want to converse with their families and friends back home. They also appeal to people who want to visit the Eastern Caribbean either for holidays or for work.

Other aims of the Kwéyòl Project include:

- developing a GCSE or equivalent for the Kwéyòl language;
- setting up a Tutor Training Programme to facilitate additional classes;
- establishing a Kwéyòl Resource Centre.

Our general aim is to have two tiers within the language provision, i.e. Kwéyòl for cultural and heritage purposes targeted to the children of Kwéyòl speakers and Kwéyòl as a foreign language.

Despite informal evaluation exercises at the end of each year, it became necessary to undertake a rigorous evaluation of the Kwéyòl language and literacy classes for the following reasons:

(i)   To assess the curricula.
(ii)   To assess the teaching methods employed in facilitating language skills and effective oral and written skills.
(iii)   to identify strategies for improvement.

As part of her MA course work, Hubisi jointly produced a Kwéyòl listening, reading, oral and writing test which was submitted to the RSA Examination Board for validation. Further work on the production of the Kwéyòl GCSE test and validation of the language and literacy classes is being pursued as part of her research programme. Members of the project continue to produce a wide range of material which is now starting to be more widely circulated, enjoyed and often used as part of adult literacy work. Take, for instance, *Sent Lisi* by Cindy Marie Augustin which appears in *Kalalou Kwéyòl*.

Sent Lisi	*Saint Lucia*
Sòlèy-la ka bat asou do mwen,	The sun beats down on my back,
Mé Mwen Kontan, mwen wivé,	But I am glad I am here,
Sent Lisi, mi mwen, mwen viwé.	Saint lucia, here I am, I have returned.
Sé pa dé zan dépi mwen té kité,	It is not two years since I have been away,
Mé apwézan mwen vini pou wèsté	But this time around, I am here to stay.
Fwédi-a anlè-a té twò mové	The cold above was just too much,
Mwen vini pu pwan chalè Sòlèy-la	I have come back to taste the sun,
Glo-a anba-a té telman fwèt,	The water below was much too cold,
Mwen vini pou poute lanmè salé.	I have come back to taste the sea.
Sé fèy-la la-ba-a té twò sèk,	The leaves beyond were just too dry,
Mwen vini pou touché zèb séwen.	I have returned to touch the moist grass.
Magwé mwen ja maché otan chimen,	Although I have walked many a street,
Mwen épi Sent Lisi pa sa sépawé.	Saint Lucia and I could never part.

Students of the Kwéyòl Literacy class now write distance learning materials for people in the Bouton District of Soufriere, St. Lucia which have proved very popular in developing Kwéyòl literacy skills in that community.

A recent development is the formation of Mouvman Kwéyòl-London, a body with a wide ranging agenda. The Mouvman see Kwéyòl language and literacy as a tool for cultural maintenance and enhancement within the UK. Although Kwéyòl literacy activities were initiated by English speakers, notably Carol Morris, it is felt that the time has now come for Kwéyòl speakers to play a central role in this process as tutors. Mouvman Kwéyòl also aims to link into the world wide Kwéyòl network through organisations like Banzil Kwéyòl in the Seychelles and the Eastern Caribbean Standing Committee for Creole Studies, which encourage the use of Kwéyòl as a spoken and written language. It also plans to build up an archive of history, music, folk culture and contemporary issues in Kwéyòl for use as resource and research material.

The Kwéyòl issue can sometimes be a very sensitive one. It is a language of social solidarity and as such, suggestions that it should be used in domains which are normally reserved for English, can provoke very defensive reactions. Constance (1988), for instance, records the following comments on the subject of learning to read and write Kwéyòl:

> Kwéyòl is our culture and we have to keep what is left of our culture to ourselves.

> If you want white people to know your business, that is up to you. But let me say, it is trouble that you will get. When the same man you have taught goes and teaches the police all that he knows, on that day, we are all in trouble!

> Do you think I would let these people influence how my language should be spoken? Never!

> Am I stupid or a mad man? Can't I and the other people see what the Government is up to? After all these years they have been saying that Kwéyòl is not a language, now they've changed their minds and want to write it. When they write it they will rename it and call it theirs.

While many people remain defensive about Kwéyòl, there is none the less a growing feeling that the Kwéyòl community in Britain should keep pace with what is happening in the Caribbean. A great many people see the advantages of being able to read and write the mother tongue as a way of affirming cultural pride, roots and increasing self-worth and confidence. It can also rekindle an interest in academic study and fuel Kwéyòl speakers'

BOUTON KWEYOL GROUP

How did this group start? In 1989 a teacher came from London to spend a holiday in Bouton, a Quarter of Soufriere. The teacher, Carol Morris, explained to some of the Bouton people that one of her classes in London was teaching Dominican and St. Lucian adults, whose first language is Kwéyòl (Patwa), to read and write their language and she showed them a little book – 'Pyé Papay-la' – written in Kwéyòl and English by one of the London students.

Some of the Bouton people said: 'Well, teach us too!' So, we sat under the mango tree and started Lékòl Kwéyòl – young and old. The students were enthusiastic and worked very hard, wanting to continue when Carol returned to London.

Back in London, Carol Morris told the Kwéyòl literacy class about the Bouton group and the London students agreed to write lessons and post them to Bouton. This was very successful and the Bouton students did the exercises, posted them back to London for marking and then the London students returned them with another exercise. The Bouton group are now writing exercises for the London Kwéyòl Group.

As all readers know, 1990 is designated International Literacy Year by UNESCO and as the Bouton group were doing so well with their lessons Carol Morris wrote to Embert Charles and Kendel Hippolyte of the Folk Research Centre (FRC), Castries and to the Bouton group with a proposal to come over to Bouton in August to help link up the Bouton group with FRC and to encourage and train the students to run their own Literacy Project with support from FRC.

So, for two and a half weeks in August 1990 classes were held in Bouton on six afternoons per week and there were 14 students divided into two groups – the Senior Group and a Children's Group. All of the Senior Group proved very, very capable and enthusiastic and were soon able to work on their own. The children all worked very enthusiastically and the faster ones helped the less confident children. In all, the group undertook about 25 hours of teaching and learning.

This booklet includes examples of writing done by the students and is something for the Bouton Kwéyòl Group to be proud of and cherish as an example of self-help in advancing St. Lucian language and culture.

October 1990

Extract from *Lékòl Kwéyòl Bouton, Awou,* 1990

The next piece is a poem about Christmas followed by questions
to answer. We hope you enjoy this exercise.

"NWÈL"

Tout lé lanne won lè sa la
Tout moun ka pwé pawé
Pou lè Nwèl wivé.

Dépi Janvye ka fini
Tout moun ka kouwi,
Péyé sa yo ka dwé
Si sé an bonn Nwèl yo vlé pasé.

Pou pasé an bonn Nwel an Sent Lisi
An boutey wom nésésité: Pèlay di
Piti kon gwan ka wiboté
Pou fè Nwèl la an siksé.

Chanté Nwèl tou-pa-tou
Pou mété nou an spiwit Nwèl-la
Pas si ou pa chanjé
Nwèl sé li vennsenk désanm.

Nwèl, Nwèl nou ka atandé'y
Pou nou sa wiboté
Lè sa la nou ka swèté
Tout moun an bonn Nwèl
Pas Nwèl la wivé.

Bonn Nwèl.

KÈSTYON ASOU NWÈL.

1.   Ki lè moun ka swété Nwel?

2.   Pou ki sa chanté Nwèl tou-pa-tou?

3.   Sa ki nésésite pou pasé an bonn Nwèl?

4.   Pou ki sa moun ka pwépawé?

5.   Ki sa ki ka fè'y sav Nwèl opwé?(near)

6.   Sa'w ni pou fè si ou vlé pasé an bonn Nwèl?

7.   An ki mwa moun ka koumansé pwépawé pou Nwèl?

8.   Ki sa moun ka fè lè Nwèl?

9.   Ki lès ki ka wiboté?

10. Ki sa moun ka swété yon a lot lè Nwèl?

Tjebé fò!   Bonn Nwèl!

Distance learning material from the Bouton Kwéyòl Group to the London
Kwéyòl Group, Christmas, 1990.

interest in taking up more educational studies, including Afrikan/Caribbean history and contemporary Black issues.

For some students, learning Kwéyòl language and literacy has renewed interest in returning to the Caribbean to settle on a permanent basis, whilst for others, it has helped re-new contacts with friends and family in Dominica and St. Lucia.

Although activities in the area of Kwéyòl literacy and language teaching are recent, the signs are that they have been built on a solid foundation. It is important to understand, for instance, that any developments in the UK are not taking place in isolation. The growing recognition of Kwéyòl in the Eastern Caribbean inevitably reinforces the efforts of Kwéyòl speakers in Britain; so too, does the awareness of belonging to a world-wide Kwéyòl speaking community. The present situation can perhaps be summed up with a Kwéyòl proverb: *'Sé pou'w mantjé néyé pou ou apwann najé'* (In order to learn to swim, you must survive drowning). The shift of Kwéyòl to English is such that the mother tongue in Britain is in danger of drowning. However, initiatives such as the Kwéyòl classes and 'Mouvman Kwéyòl' mean that for the present at least, a growing number of people are swimming irrespective of the tide.

References
* Access Department, Tower Hamlets Adult Education Institute, (1985) *'Patwa'*
Alladina, S. and Edwards, V. (1991) *Multi-Lingualism in the British Isles*. 2 vols. London: Longman.
* Augustin, C.M. (1990) Sent Lisi. In H. Nwenmely (ed.) *Kalalou Kwéyòl*.
Carrington, L. (1984) *'St. Lucia Creole': A Descriptive Analysis of its Phonology and Morpho-syntax*. Hamburg: Helmut Buske Verlag.
Constance, E. (1990) Pros and Cons of Learning Kwéyòl. In H. Nwenmely (ed.) *Kalalou Kwéyòl* (pp. 2-6).
* Distance Learning Material from the Bouton Kwéyòl Group to the London Kwéyòl Group, Christmas 1990.
* Fontaine, D'Jamala M. (1988) *Lékòl Kwéyòl*. Grand Bay, Dominica: The Author.
Louisy, P. and Turmel-John, P. (1983) *A Handbook for Writing Creole*. Castries, St. Lucia: Research St. Lucia Publications.
* Morris, C. *et al.* (1990) *Lékòl Kwéyòl Bouton*.
* Morris, C. (June 1983) *Newsletter from St. Lucia*.
* Noel, C. (1982) *Pyé Papay-La*.
* Nwenmely, H. (1990) (ed.) *Kalalou Kwéyòl*.
* Nwenmely, H. (1990) An evaluation of the Kwéyòl Project carried out as part of M.A. in Second Language Learning and Teaching, Birkbeck College, University of London.
Nwenmely, H. (1991) The Kwéyòl speech community. In S. Alladina and V. Edwards (eds) *Multilingualism in the British Isles*. 2 vols. London: Longman.
* Tower Hamlets Adult Education Institute (July 1984) *The Patwa Project Newssheet*.

* Available from the Kwéyòl Project, c/o H. Nwenmely, 23 Lister House, Lomas Street, London E1 5BG.

Acknowledgement

We both wish to thank Jennie L. Cooke for her patience and typing of this article.

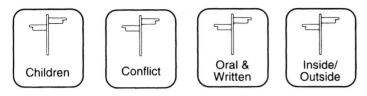

| Children | Conflict | Oral & Written | Inside/ Outside |

SUSAN BENTON

8: Networks of Communication Between Home and School

Introduction

This paper is concerned with communication patterns between home and school, two different worlds of literacy. It was stimulated by my own experience as a teacher and as a parent. My original idea was to look at problems connected with *written* notes from the schools, but it soon became clear that the notes and newsletters were mainly well-received. As I researched, what emerged was that many problems connected with communication between home and school were in fact hidden behind the written notes. I therefore changed my main focus to investigate the wider issues affecting communication.

The schools I studied were two primary schools in Lancaster, which I will refer to as Ashfield and Hillside. For both schools, information was gathered from parents through questionnaires sent via school to every family. At Ashfield, these questionnaires were followed-up by in-depth interviews with parents and teachers and observations of practices in and around the school. A relatively high response was received from both schools: 48% (Ashfield) and 53% (Hillside) although there was not the same contact or follow-up work done in the Hillside school community. I interviewed 21 different parents from Ashfield, including some who had not returned the questionnaire. I contacted these people in the playground, or via the school records, either by telephone or by knocking on their doors. I also spent a lot of time in and around the school and the local area, observing the interactions between all the different groups of people. I compared these experiences with my own, and with those of another five parents whom I interviewed although they were not concerned with the target schools. All this helped me to build up a richer picture of the communication patterns between home and school.

The Communication Networks

Very early in my project it became clear that the networks for commu-

See
Chap. 3

nicating and passing on information orally were of more significance than the written notes and newsletters which came home from school. These networks were often very effective in disseminating significant information about school which could not be obtained through the written letters, but at the same time they perpetuated mistruths and much inaccurate school gossip. Significant also was the fact that groups of parents, whom I first encountered at random in the playground, explained to me that they belonged to distinct social groups, associated with the local area where they lived and their socio-economic status, and that they did not communicate well with each other. One of the first mothers I asked about the communication with school told me, indicating some gatherings, mainly of women, standing in a different part of the playground, that I should also ask 'them over there' because they were 'posher' and so would have a different impression. In other words, they would be better able to communicate with the school. Ironically, the more middle class parents had the impression that *they* were discriminated against when they contacted the school and that the more working class communities were favoured. The class distinctions were mentioned by many parents during the interviews but surprisingly both considered the other group to have better communication channels with the school. In fact with the exception of the very few parents who helped regularly in school, almost *all* the parents expressed feelings of distance or exclusion from the school, and this fitted in with my own experiences.

Regardless of your own educational background, or class, or even the amount of time you invest in your children's education, contacting teachers and finding out what your child is doing in school, or how they are getting on, is problematic. Because teachers are so over-burdened with work, and especially with after-school chores, there are very few opportunities, formal or informal, for parents to talk to them. And yet, without exception, *all* the parents I contacted wanted their children to succeed at school and expressed a desire to know in more detail what was happening in school. This explained why most parents appeared to be quite organised with what they did with notes, the majority taking the time to record school information in diaries or by posting it on pinboards. The *written* information, however tended to be factual, informing about significant school dates and events, and did not give parents the extra information they wanted about what the children were learning and how well they were doing. Some parents are assertive enough to simply approach the teacher regularly for an update, but it was clear that such parents are labelled by the teachers as 'pushy' or a nuisance. Most parents are aware that this direct approach system could not work for the majority because of the time involved so, not wanting to appear to be fussing, resort to other method of finding out what is going on.

See
Chap. 3

They talk to other parents or quiz their children: "What did you do at school today, love?", only to get a less than coherent response, e.g. 'Uh, nothing much' or to find that the information they get is 'half there' or even inaccurate. In such a case the networks of parents become very important because other children may have a different interpretation of the same event. One mother told me she relies on her neighbour's child for information since her own son neither remembers the information from school nor brings home notes.

The 'rich' picture on the following pages is to demonstrate pictorially what I imagine is happening all over the country as parents collect their children from primary school. I should emphasise that many of the parents I spoke to were in close, almost daily, contact with the school. This made a great difference to communication since most could go directly to the teacher if any problem arose, and also had the opportunity for 'comparing notes' with other parents. A minority of teachers indeed made a point of coming out and greeting parents and informing them directly about minor problems which may have occurred. Needless to say reports about communication channels were much more positive for these teachers. There are, however, an increasing number of parents who work and are unable to get into school regularly. Some of these may indeed be prevented, through their other commitments, from attending the infrequent open days or evenings. Some of these people find the notes and newsletters to be very inadequate. The schools tend to keep the information deliberately simple and factual, in order to ensure maximum comprehension, but this can be interpreted by some parents as impersonal, and at worst, as one described some of the notes from Hillside, 'peremptory, even rude'. These working parents are deprived of the personal contact with school and other parents and would like more personal comment in the written communications. The picture attempts to show how easily misunderstandings can arise. For example a teacher's comment that the children 'may bring tracksuits for games' is translated to the parent as an imperative 'we've got to have a tracksuit'.

What the Parents Think: Details from the Questionnaire

In interpreting the results from the parents' questionnaires one must be aware that people filling in the questionnaires tend to answer what they think they should answer and not always the 'truth' (researchers call this 'positive response set'). One indication of this was that on the questionnaire most people reported feeling comfortable in school, yet during interviews talked about hesitance and reluctance to go and contact teachers. One must also remember that there are indications that the questionnaire was returned by the more responsive parents, those who are already in touch with

A 'rich' picture depicting the scene

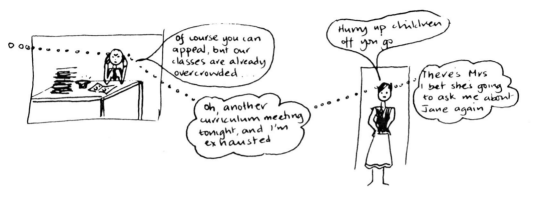

as parents collect their children at the end of school

school things and so the ones who have the *fewest* problems with communication.

Despite certain variations, there are, however, many points which came up in interviews with parents which were confirmed by the questionnaire. On the whole parents reported that they were satisfied with many aspects of communication with school, such as the notes and newsletters, although they did not go far enough. Most people who responded found them to be clearly written and easily understood, but this may not be true of those 'hidden' people I did not manage to contact who experience real difficulties with reading and writing, and who may also have problems dealing with the school at all. These could be a significant group of 'reluctant' parents, who get the majority of information about school through the children, and possibly inefficiently, if not actually 'incorrectly'. Many parents wanted more details about the curriculum, and although they try to keep a constant check on what and how their children are doing, by talking to the children themselves, or by monitoring reading books or any other work which comes home, this is felt to be insufficient by most.

There was a general feeling that parent–teacher meetings were at present not adequate, because they do not allow parents to find out all they would like to know; many said they were too infrequent and too brief. On the other hand, teachers felt that more meetings would either take up valuable 'allocated' time, which they could hardly spare, or would impinge on their free time, and would anyway be wasted because most of the parents they really *need* to talk to (i.e. of the children experiencing most difficulties), do not turn up for meetings. My research indicated that some parents had

See
Chap. 6

childcare restrictions, or other social problems which prevented them from attending and that they might be the 'reluctant' parents already referred to. At the last consultation evening only those parents who were worried about their child's progress were asked to come in for a consultation, but this has the effect of ignoring the interested parents of averagely successful children and is sensed and resented by some parents. There is an additional flaw in this system since, because they have never met the teacher, some parents are not aware that their children are having problems. Despite the system for contacting parents directly, if there is a need to discuss real problems, there is still a possibility that the parents of a child who is 'doing alright, but could

See
Chap. 22

do better', is not invited to discuss the child's progress. A parent who may feel hesitant or inadequate about contacting school is not actively encouraged to come in (it is also likely that the children will adopt a similar reluctance towards school, which may even develop into feelings of failure or inadequacy), while those who come in anyway, simply because they are interested, may feel they are wasting the teacher's time.

Teachers are generally seen to be very helpful and supportive when parents approach them with problems; however, it is very much left up to the parents to make moves towards school. Bearing in mind the difficulties that some parents have in getting in to meetings, for example, shiftwork commitments or childminding problems, with only one opportunity to go in to see the teacher, it is not surprising that some never made it. A few parents among those who are able to meet their children after school have taken the initiative in checking their children's progress, a few ask every week, but such parents are sometimes seen by the teachers as 'pushy' or 'fussing' rather than as 'involved' and 'interested'. Whichever way they are viewed, it is fortunate they are such a minority, or teachers would be overwhelmed with ad hoc requests for interim progress reports. One or two mentioned being 'fobbed off' by the teachers, with the reply: 'Oh, she's doing fine' or 'Yes, she's coming along'. This is an understandable response from a busy teacher who simply cannot afford the time at that moment to embark on a detailed discussion of one child's educational development, even though there may well be a need for dialogue with the parent, and indeed with the parents of the 30+ other children for whom she is responsible.

Such opportunities for dialogue between teachers and parents need to be built in to the normal school schedule, and not relegated to two brief evening encounters a year.

Conclusion

To summarise my findings from all sources, although there appears to be a significant gap in the knowledge parents have about the school world and their children's education and despite a general desire for more information, many parents do not know how to go about getting hold of it. Interviews with parents brought out many feelings of awkwardness with teachers. The teachers certainly feel similar reticence about opening the doors completely to parents, fearing a lack of control. Teachers already have a stressful and heavy work load and faced with the daunting prospect of having to deal with all the children's parents as well, tend to close rather than open doors.

At a time of demoralisation in the profession, there is a need for teachers to maintain their expertise, and this is fuelling the rift between home and school, and is not necessarily what is best for the educational development of the children. While this is quite understandable in the present climate of low morale, poor conditions and extra work, it is part of a vicious circle, which needs to be broken. The atmosphere of schools has changed remarkably little in my lifetime, and walking back in as a parent revives some of those old feelings of inequality. This atmosphere and the few opportunities to meet teachers on an informal basis, mean few parents ever become completely at ease in school. Schools seem to see communication with parents as something to be dealt with through written notes, keeping parents informed of school 'events'. They also seem to think that such notes and newsletters are sufficient whereas parents feel they are being kept at a distance, and deprived of many details. Most parents would like the opportunity for more oral reassurance and personal contact with the teacher, giving them direct information about what is happening in school and an opportunity to *share* information about the child's progress. By sending out so many notes and regular newsletters schools *think* they are communicating, but in fact they are not.

In the schools I researched there was little evidence of a 'partnership' between home and school, but a lot which points to insufficient or poor communication between the two parties. Teachers somehow lose their personality and become part of an institution which views parents as unconnected with the job at hand, that of educating children. Clearly no-one is at fault, although both sides like to blame the other. It would be better if parents and teachers realised they are in fact on the same side, and started working towards improving communications and the education of our children.

Note
This project was carried out as part of an MA in Language Studies at Lancaster University.

Section 3:

Constituting Identities

Just as for spoken language, our uses of literacy and ability to control the written word go to make up our sense of ourselves — what kind of person we are, what social group we belong to and what it seems possible for us to achieve. A key theme in these articles is the importance of a sense of control over what and how we communicate so that we can express our own identity. The relationships around each person — child or adult — help define and negotiate what literacy means to us.

SHIRLEY CORNES

9: Gender-Engendered Literacy Needs

The above title was chosen deliberately to highlight an aspect of literacy work which deserves more attention than it usually receives in the mainstream literature. The term gender-engendered immediately poses the question: can it be argued that there is some distinction between the literacy needs of women and those of men? I believe that it can.

This conviction is rooted in two fundamental beliefs. First that whereas sex is biologically determined, gender is socially constructed within each society. As Stacey & Price (1981) put it, 'The "feminine characteristics" are not biologically determined or universally present among womankind, they are closely associated with particular social roles that women have played' (1981: 182). From this stance it is possible to explore how the separating out of 'female' and 'male' roles can give rise to different kinds, or different levels, of literacy needs both in fulfilling a gender role and in overcoming the stereotypes attached to that role.

My second belief is that literacy has to do with *all* modes of communication; this means that listening and talking, reading and writing are all forms of literacy, with listening and talking acting as the basis from which our various interdependent 'skills' of reading and writing can develop.

See Chap. 2

Furthermore, I would argue that it is through the development of a dialogue which involves all four modes of communication that people are best able to understand how our own society's gender roles have evolved and – through that understanding – to build a bridge of effective communication between them. In other words, awareness can form the basis of a more adult-to-adult dialogue of equality between and within the sexes.

Although there is a growing number of men who, through necessity or choice, take on what are considered to be the traditional 'female' responsibilities of keeping house and rearing children, these men constitute a fairly small minority. Acting as bread-winner is still seen as even the New Man's more natural role.

The present reality which projects that before the end of the century some 75% of the paid workforce will be female has yet to change radically the view put forward by Jean-Jacques Rousseau:

> The whole education of women ought to be relative to men. To please them, to be useful to them, to make themselves loved and honoured by them, to educate them when young, to care for them when grown, to counsel them, to console them and to make life sweet and agreeable to them – these are the duties of women at all times and what should be taught them from their infancy.

In 1792, Mary Wollstonecraft responded to this view:

> I have, probably, had an opportunity of observing more girls in their infancy than J.J. Rousseau. I can recollect my own feelings, and I have looked steadily around me . . . I will venture to affirm, that a girl, whose spirits have not been dampened by inactivity, or innocence tainted by false shame, will always be a romp (Wollstonecraft, 1972: 129).

Despite their opposing stands on this eighteenth century depiction of women as innately weak and therefore incapable of undertaking rational control of their own affairs, the message from each of these writers is that girls need to learn the contemporary rules governing 'feminine behaviour' since they would not necessarily conform unless taught to do so. There is no guarantee that by the year 2,000 such strongly rooted gender stereotyping will have changed very much.

Maybe we no longer hear so often the term 'pin money' attached to women's earnings, but attitudes usually lag some way behind social realities. This can be seen in every case where, regardless of whether she and/or her male partner undertakes full or part-time paid employment, a woman continues to accept the major burden of domestic and child-rearing chores as a *natural* division of unpaid employment.

See Chap. 18

As a consequence, women run a real danger of becoming relatively isolated from what is called the 'real world', the 'public world' – that is, the world outside their own front doors, where News is made so that whatever media coverage penetrates their homes serves to reinforce the comparative under-valuation of domestic events. Radio and television may be very informative, but cannot provide two-way adult dialogue. Children may be very entertaining, but cannot provide adult discussion.

Some women spend whole days without engaging in any form of adult conversation which is not about children or housework, or some other aspect of life considered 'feminine'; indeed, some (particularly single parents and older women) think it a good day when they have the opportunity even to speak with another adult. Many women, whatever their previous achievements in education or employment, come to doubt their ability to take in new ideas or to cope effectively outside the walls of home, and they come to doubt their own social human value.

See
Chap. 14

The 'Just a' Syndrome

Rightly or wrongly, 'private' domestic commitments are often accepted as a barrier to the establishment, let alone the pursuit, of personal ambitions in the 'public' world. This reinforces the process by which women learn that it is considered feminine to be supportively self-effacing.

Most of us recognise what I have come to call the 'Just a' Syndrome: 'I'm just a housewife', 'I'm just a wife and mother', I'm just an office cleaner', 'I'm just a secretary'; these are statements so commonplace that we don't really hear them. When we do not perceive the self-effacement behind the words 'just a', we reflect our own social conditioning every bit as clearly as do the women who use the term to describe themselves. This is not some radical 'feminist' argument about inequalities; it is a statement of the real effects of gender stereotyping.

The ability to read and to write was long ago described by Jeffery & Maginn as 'the narrowest possible view of literacy' (1979: 8). My point is that one of the aims of literacy practitioners should be to develop in their students not merely the 'mechanical' skills of reading and writing, but also those communication skills which help them to identify themselves within their own society, in ways which encourage a realistic exploration of their own social value and potential.

The word 'realistic' introduces a further strand to the basic argument. People who are isolated from the opportunity to assess and develop their abilities in areas which are accorded 'public' recognition, for instance through increased income or promotion, may well create an unrealistic picture of what they would be able to accomplish once given that opportunity. Those whose primary responsibilities are societally linked with the domestic sphere engage in work which is publicly invisible and privately conspicuous only by default. Personal empowerment incorporates knowledge of personal limitations.

A model which offers a broader approach to the recognition of literacy needs and which neatly illustrates the foregoing, is provided by Guthrie (1983) when he discusses an Equilibrium of Literacy. Guthrie points out that frustration arises not only where a person's environment demands greater ability than she/he can call upon, but equally so where a person's literacy level is higher than her/his environment demands. In either situation an individual is liable to feel alienated and unchallenged.

Women and Literacy Needs

Every adult who enrols for literacy tuition is seeking to change the effect of their present abilities on the balance of their lives. The tutor who uses a student-centred approach cannot automatically assume that the desired change is concentrated only upon self-improvement within an existing role. Taking the decision to become an Adult Basic Education student is a statement of frustration. It is for the tutor to enable the student to express the underlying basis of their dissatisfaction in order more effectively to set learning goals, and most ABE tutors would agree that enhancing a student's self-confidence is a major factor in achieving such goals.

What is being suggested here is that in a society which tends to ask 'What do you do? rather than 'Who are you?', women are less likely to feel confident in their responses. Because of their primary gender role as carers and supporters, women are more likely than men to experience the frustration described by Guthrie as relating to a lack of equilibrium between personal abilities and environment. More specifically, women are more likely than men to feel frustrated by the under-usage of their abilities.

However precisely a woman can follow a recipe, the meal itself is a transitory outcome; washing the dishes afterwards does not excite comment unless badly done or unless the question of who undertakes this chore is a matter for negotiation. Similarly, being able to read the instructions for a washing powder is obviously of basic importance, but so too is the ability to read 'behind' advertisements which imply that women have some innate superiority when it comes to understanding laundry chores.

This is not meant to imply that women do not feel a real sense of achievement in a domestic job well done, but it does raise questions concerning our interpretation of the word 'literacy'. A frequently attendant word is 'functional', and maybe we need to give deeper thought to whether we understand this to mean functional to the maintenance of a gender-role or to the fulfilment of informed adult citizenship.

One current debate raises the possibility of a basic difference in the way each of the sexes receives the language of the other, by suggesting that whereas a woman will use words to describe and share the detail of her life and her attendant feelings, a man will receive this an an invitation to problem-solve. If this is so, it would certainly help to explain why men often accuse women of 'nagging', while women frequently complain that what are intended as overtures in conversation are heard as demands for action. In this case, literacy and communication certainly could not be seen as gender-impartial.

Dale Spender (1985) goes even further by arguing that the very language available for self-identification has become male, so that a women is grammatically forced into using 'he' even when she is thinking of herself as representative of the human race. Elaine Morgan (1972) is cited by Spender (1985: 152) to exemplify this by pointing up the shock many readers experience when faced with the statement 'When the first ancestor of the human race descended from the trees, she had not yet developed the mighty brain that was to distinguish her so sharply from other species' (1972: 2-3).

See Chap. 14

One way of meeting the literacy needs of women is to address them within an all-female group and the following section looks at some of the arguments for making such provision.

Why a *Women's* Group?

On more than one occasion it has been put to me that a Women's Group is necessarily sexist. Whereas it is easy to understand the logic behind this argument, I will nevertheless stick to my guns concerning the need for groups which cater solely for female students.

First of all, the gender conditioning discussed above, which leads women to be relatively self-effacing, has a direct effect on the degree to which women may honestly express their feelings and opinions when they are in 'mixed company'. Women often voice their thoughts in ways which they think will be, or will be seen to be, most supportive of their menfolk. Leaving aside such sexually-orientated matters as flirting, or dressing and making up for mixed company, my experience (both as a woman and as a tutor) has been that in an all-female gathering, women are more forthcoming about individual aspirations. In the absence of men, they are also more frank about the hurdles standing between themselves and the fulfilment of such ambitions.

Women talk about the tendency of men to display dominance by 'taking over' meetings and discussion. Research points out the ways in which this dominant behaviour is often cultivated from early schooling. Sharpe (1976) for instance, explores how girls *learn* to be girls so that social factors of rearing override biological structures. She highlights social suppositions when she writes '. . . opposing the alleged passivity of women, men are supposed to be physically strong, aggressive, assertive and to take the initiative'. One of the operative terms here is that of assertiveness which runs counter to the old adage that girls should be 'sugar and spice, and all things nice'. Girls who display dominance are labelled 'tom-boys', a term which neatly places their actions as basically masculine and yet juvenile in feminine terms – something to be grown out of. Taking the initiative in mixed company, therefore, is not socially prescribed feminine activity.

Boys are generally expected to be more boisterous and vociferous than girls despite any natural inclinations of the latter. Studies carried out by Spender (1978) support the argument that in mixed classrooms girls do not have the opportunity to talk on equal terms with boys even where their teachers attempt to encourage equality. This is borne out by the findings of Millman (1984) that it was the boys who questioned, voiced protest and challenged teachers, while the girls tended to get on with the work set even if they too thought it was boring or irrelevant.

It would be simplistic to blame teachers for this situation since, as Sharpe points out, every teacher is a former pupil who has been through the process of learning gender-roles; teachers therefore reflect 'consciously and unconsciously their own attitudes . . . ultimately expect less from girls than from boys' and their expectations 'are picked up by pupils with devastating effects,' (1976: 151). One ongoing debate concerns the greater efficacy of single-sex schools for eradicating sexist bias, however unintentional, but as Sharpe recognises, in an all-girl school 'girls learn to perform well in their school work, but are left inadequately equipped to deal with the mixed social world outside' (1976: 153).

Although there is now a greater awareness of the effects of sexism in schools, most women who enrol for adult education have been through a less enlightened system. For them, there can be an additional dilemma: should they raise their children in a non-sexist fashion, or should they raise them to fit more easily into a predominantly sexist society?

From Theory to Practice

The following case study describes one ABE Women's Group which attempts to address some of the foregoing issues. For reasons of confidentiality, the use of names is avoided. The aim is to give the reader a flavour of the problem and some possible ways of tackling it.

Return to study: Communication skills for women

This group, for which I have been the paid tutor since its inception in September 1987, is the first provision of its kind to be funded by the Dorset County Council's AE Department. Offered free of charge to students and with the facility of a free creche, it demonstrates recognition of current demographic trends. The numbers of school-leavers had dropped and employers look to women to make good the shortfall by returning to the workforce, even at a time of growing male unemployment. This is not the place to explore the basis for that need in terms of women's tendency to accept low pay and low status jobs, but readers will draw their own conclusions regarding the way that particular factor links in with issues discussed above.

See Chap. 14

Like all such groups, the membership is a shifting one. There is usually a core of three or four women, while others join and leave according to their personal circumstances; the core itself changes over time for similar reasons. The group has attracted women of all ages, status, experience, abilities and aspirations.

Initially the creche was run by pairs of students on a local Nursery Nursing course, but a change of venue and time called for a different provision after the first two years. For two terms thereafter, the creche was run very successfully by one of the group's original students (with the assistance of a woman who had trained as a literacy tutor). When she joined early in 1988, this student was conspicuous by her tendency to maintain a physical distance from the rest of us because, as she then put it, she had nothing much to contribute and saw the group as a way of learning by listening. During the past two years, however, she has felt motivated to apply for a place on a Pre-School Playgroup Course, has become a registered child minder, is involved in running a creche for the local sports centre, has taken up part-time paid employment and is considering enrolment on an AE course to study the psychology of child development.

The number of children in the creche at each session obviously varies with overall attendance, but there have been anything up to seven pre-school children for whom creative activities have been provided. This of itself is a very important aspect of working with women since, even if no creche is available, any group activities have a strong 'knock-on' effect for students' children. This is so in terms of attitudes towards education in general and towards women and education in particular. A report compiled by the women attending in April 1989 illustrates the part played by the creche in the functioning of the group.

Our Report on the Creche for our Women's Group
On 7 April 1989 we spent some time evaluating our Creche and how we feel about having this facility. This is a list of our comments on that day:

- this is the only place I can go and be without the children for a while without arranging for babysitters
- I'd be a total vegetable if I had to wait for them to grow up and go to school before I could do something like this
- I just couldn't come at all if there wasn't a creche
- in the mother and toddler group the children stay with you, on your lap, and you can't really concentrate
- in the mother and toddler group they only talk about the children and husbands – they don't do the kinds of work the Women's Group does
- the kids get bored there; in the creche there's lots for them to do.
- they learn things in the creche – how to get along with other kids and grown-ups – learn about sharing things – learn to be away from Mum for a little while – learn about people's names
- they know we're nearby and they can see us if they want to
- it's because we've got separate rooms and can each get on with our own things
- my kiddy's always asking when we're going to see the ladies in the school
- when I was looking for something to do, some course, I was riveted by 'Creche', and then to get it free as well
- if you sort out a child-minder they can't get hold of you in emergencies
- it affects us all, even if we haven't got children to bring – it would be a very different group because a lot of women wouldn't come.
- the creche really made my choice for me
- is our Report going to be used to help get creches into the colleges? They ought to have them, we need them
- I'd come now even if I didn't have the kids – stretches my mind, makes me think

As stated, the group has attracted a wide range of women. There was, for instance, the psychology graduate who felt inadequate in her ability to communicate orally with other adults; she was highly nervous about joining because 'My grades won't be able to speak for me'. A newly-retired office worker whose literacy skills had been used mainly for transmitting the words of her boss, said '. . . can't express just myself on paper and how I feel, it comes out stilted and boring'. Or there was the battered mother of abused children, who felt the legal world was unsympathetic to her case because 'I can't talk posh like them'. One very articulate woman wept openly at the prospect of having to write 'in public' (i.e. within the group) because her self-esteem had been eroded; when eventually she did feel sufficiently unthreatened to commit herself to paper, her work was admired for its fluency and vocabulary.

One of the first questions any literacy tutor will ask is why a student enrolled with that particular group. Rather than offer more examples, let's look instead at how women themselves have responded to the question:

Why Are You Here? Why a Women's Group?
- to get back some self-confidence
- it's a possible stepping-stone to something else
- need adult company – maybe friendships?
- want to practise getting out of the house to meet other people . . don't know if I'm lazy or shy!
- need stimulation . . . I'm rotting away at home
- to stop vegetating – it's a chance to *listen* to other adults
- wanted to meet women of all ages; just because I'm a pensioner I meet only older women now . . . want to hear younger viewpoints
- can I do it? whatever this group does – want to find out
- to enjoy myself . . . love learning but don't know where to start on my own
- my husband thinks the house and the kids should be enough, but it isn't
- they don't understand . . . you end up thinking you can't do anything intelligent for yourself
- the men I know take over conversations . . . don't think my opinion matters because I'm a woman
- single Mums get seen as 'available', but not to talk to!
- can't do it on your own . . . need other women for bouncing ideas
- don't get creches usually in ordinary education classes, mixed classes
- miss having time for yourself, time to think
- you get out of the habit of digging deeper, stretching yourself
- think I can't even listen properly any more, let alone study

---

This was the outcome of a brainstorm exercise in January 1989. The comments came thick and fast from the eight women present. We ran out of time before we ran out of thoughts – each comment sparked off memories and anecdotes, so that it was difficult to hold the women to the concept of 'brainstorming' which, for several, was completely new and 'an education in itself, Shirl'.

Although ABE is subject to the same number-crunching pressures as other adult education classes, loss of membership is extremely satisfying when this occurs because individual women have gained sufficient self-confidence and motivation to make some change in their lives – to get a job, to go to college, to accept promotion, or to pursue an interest which they had thought 'beyond' them.

One cause for concern, however, is in regard to those women who recognise that learning means change but are afraid of changing. Precisely what it is that they are afraid of changing depends on the individual, but a pattern of sorts can be seen over time. These are often the women who begin sentences with 'My husband wouldn't let me', or 'My husband doesn't like me to'. They may well be correct in what they are saying, since one partner can feel very threatened when the other undertakes new ventures and new roles, meets new people and new ideas, and does this 'solo'.

Such women may also be saying that they find their own newly recognised needs and aspirations constitute a personal threat. What if, having acquired skills and assimilated new knowledge and ideas, they still feel isolated, unsuccessful or inadequate? What if they still cannot get the kind of job they want, pass an entrance examination or deal more satisfyingly with their personal relationships? What peg can they then use on which to hang their reasons for not 'measuring up' in their own terms?

In other words, a non-supportive, unsympathetic partner can be a rather useful barrier to personal change; an excuse rather than a reason for not putting oneself to the test, even if it does mean remaining behind that barrier and apparently discontented. These women are in a special dilemma since not only are they trying to balance their own conflicting needs with those of the people closest to them, for whom they have accepted a primary caring role, but they are also using the latter to avoid identifying how these personal needs are conflicting with each other.

Often I am told by women that the mere thought of taking time out for themselves is a revolutionary one – 'Read a book, Shirl? Where would I find the time?'. One or two women have actually left the group until they feel able to get to grips with the basis of this dilemma, but at least they have gone away aware that there is a problem to be faced and aware of the existence of a group which will support their efforts to resolve it.

Strategies

Creation of space and time in which to articulate and reflect upon reasons for attending a women-only group, paves the way for students to identify the issues which most closely concern them as *individuals* rather than as 'Just a's! Invariably these have been linked to the following: children's education; further education and training for women; getting a 'real' job with decent pay and status; personal relationships; health and welfare; law and order; the latest social, political or economic crises.

This is not necessarily the order of priority, but these are the areas about which the women have expressed greatest concern. When we remember that the traditional female responsibilities of today remain those stipulated by Rousseau above – i.e. the provision of nurture, emotional security within the 'private' sphere of home, family budgeting, nursing skills, initial education of offspring, care for dependants, maintenance of family relationships and friendships, and so on, it is obvious how each concern fits within the scope of an overall gender role. As one woman put it – 'Blimey, Shirl, what's left?'.

If we take one issue – 'getting a real job with decent pay and status' – we can see how this possibly provides a basic link to all the others. It highlights the position of women whose socialisation pivots around the importance accorded to an earning capacity versus the socially essential, yet financially unrewarded, role of providing a supportive environment for the 'earner'. If we, women and men alike, are brought up to believe that the real breadwinners are men and that women's contribution to earning is somehow different and therefore lacking in equal credibility, how can either sex begin to break through this barrier between them? The following offers some suggestions.

How I and others see my 'Self'

This is a potent exercise which I have used with various groups; it provides students with a method for constructing a kind of pictorial map of themselves as individuals and of their personal goals. I am indebted to a colleague, Tony Horowitz, for showing me its powerful effectiveness.

The students are supplied with a wide range of magazines, newspapers, etc. and asked:
(a) To select, literally to tear out and then to mount on paper, as collages, those images and symbols which they feel most appropriate to fit under three separate headings: How I see myself now; How others see me; How I would like to be seen.

(b) To write explanations and linking phrases on their own collage.

One outcome of this is the uncovering of feelings which are often kept buried, particularly when their verbal articulation is likely to create private or public discord. This has applied for both women and men in the groups where it has been used.

The key lies not just in the initial selection of images, but also in the process of having to decide into which of the three categories each piece of paper should be placed. It is very quickly recognised that these categories necessarily overlap. How we evaluate ourselves is strongly influenced by how we believe others perceive us, and vice versa; how we wish to be seen is tied in with our current self-image. The result is usually a jumble of shapes and colours which has great significance to its creator. The desire to explain this lack of distinct separation can motivate students to think, talk and write about themselves in a way they might never otherwise attempt.

The exercise has proved a very useful tool in helping women to look more closely at their hopes and fears concerning personal change and development. At the same time, it encourages women to communicate their feelings about the effect such change might have on their relationships with others. Obviously, it also provides valuable insights for planning further sessions.

Presenting oneself in a positive light : The CV

Another, if more pragmatic method of addressing such aspects is that of compiling individual curriculum vitae (CV). I will not describe the actual process, but merely make the point that the aim of a CV is to give information about oneself in a way which highlights personal attributes, experience and interests in a positive manner.

Many women have never tackled this exercise before because they have seen it as only vocationally relevant. Instead they find it a voyage of self-discovery which also practises such literacy skills as accessing memory, checking facts/figures, drafting, prioritising and producing information chronologically. The diagram below illustrates these factors; it shows statements over a period of time and is not meant to be a factual representation of the outcome of one single session with any one group of women.

Gender-engendered Literacy Needs

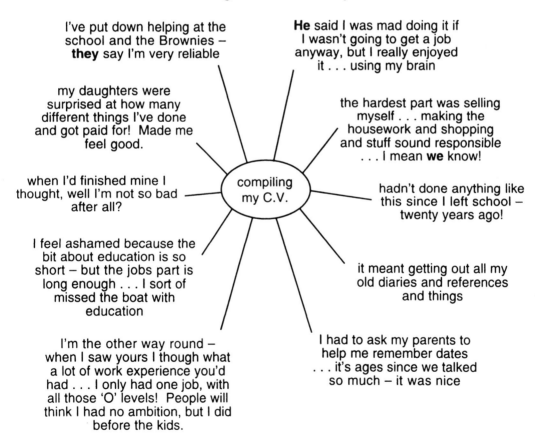

Literacy and Self-Identity

See
Chap. 13

The above two examples of working strategies serve also to highlight the fact that, in a literate society, literacy is very much a part of each person's self-identity.

Experience gained in working with a women's group leads me to believe that there are indeed gender-engendered literacy needs. Women have to accept that the 'private' sphere of home and family is socially considered to be their particular primary responsibility and activity, regardless of their 'public' status. Even should they avoid this role, they must still face up to the fact that the public world 'out there' operates under male control and uses gender-orientated language to prove it. Under these conditions, women's basic literacy needs appear to be:

- building self-confidence and self-esteem
- learning to communicate as equals within adult conversation
- participating in activities which positively value their skills and experience by placing them in a wider social and historical context
- setting realistic goals based on self-knowledge
- learning to be assertive (rather than submissive or aggressive) in exacting time and space to meet those goals
- making decisions concerning their own futures as adult individuals.

It would be extremely interesting to explore the degree to which these are related to gender and/or to sex. Perhaps we need more research into the experience of those men who do engage in a reversal of traditional roles? It seems fairly safe to assume that they have to deal with some negative responses from the 'public' world which is their more customary place of operation.

Unless their circumstances are exceptional, they will have internalised the traditional gender roles and reflect this in their choice of language to explain their situation, possibly leaning heavily on terms of temporariness or necessity in order to reassure themselves and their listeners. Certainly on some occasions they will be put in a position of having to explain why they haven't got a 'real job', however fulfilling they may find their gender-anomalous unpaid employment.

That we have had to invent a specific label for 'The New Man' proves my point; change does occur even if sometimes slowly and painfully, but it does seem that the media link this new term more with being helpful than with taking on a full half-share of domestic work. You only have to listen to women using phrases like 'He's very good' and 'He helps out quite a lot' to realise how our choice of words is deeply connected with our self-image. If the development of literacy skills is to be an empowering process, we need to take a closer look at that image and the reasons for its existence or perpetuation.

The last word should be left to the women. First a student who wrote on her half-term group evaluation sheet against the question 'What, if anything, do you know now that you didn't know when you joined the group?'

> Women are not just skivvies. I'm not the only one who feels guilty about reading a book in secret.

and secondly the student who told us about her attempt to participate in a discussion with her husband and sons concerning the Gulf crisis:

> I told them we'd studied it in the group, looking at the history over there for the past hundred years . . . gave them some facts and dates. They said this was just a woman's view and ignored me . . . it's always been the same but I'll keep trying anyway.

References

Jeffrey, J. and Maginn, C. (1979) *Who Needs Literacy Provision?* Adult Literacy Guides. London: Macmillan.

Millman, V. (1984) Are girls getting a raw deal? *Where.* ACE, Feb.

Morgan, Elaine (1972) *The Descent of Women.* London: Souvenir Press; New York: Stein & Day.

Sharpe, Sue (1976) *Just Like a Girl: How Girls Learn to be Women.* Harmondsworth: Penguin Books.

Spender, Dale (1978) Don't Talk, Listen! *Times Educational Supplement.* November 3rd.

Spender, Dale (1985) (2nd edn) *Man Made Language.* London: Routledge & Kegan Paul.

Stacey, Margaret and Price, Marian (1981) *Women, Power and Politics.* London: Tavistock Publications.

Weiner, Gaby (ed.) (1985) *Just a Bunch of Girls.* Gender and Education Series, Open University Press.

Wollstonecraft, Mary (1972) *A Vindication of the Rights of Women* (ed. M. Krammick) Harmondsworth: Penguin Books.

Further Reading

Allan, Graham (1985) *Family Life.* Oxford: Basil Blackwell.

Deem, Rosemary (1979) *Women and Schooling.* London: Routledge & Kegan Paul.

French, Marilyn (1986) *Beyond Power: On Women, Men and Morals.* London: Jonathan Cape.

Gavron, Hannah (1966) *The Captive Wife.* Harmondsworth: Penguin Books.

Guthrie, J. (1983) Equilibrium of literacy. *Journal of Reading* 26, 668-70.

Hochschild, Arlie and Machung, Anne (1990) *The Second Shift: Working Parents and the Revolution at Home.* London: Judy Piatkus (Publishers).

Malos, Ellen (1980) *The Politics of Housework.* London: Allison and Busby.

Nightingale, Camilla (1982) Boys will be boys but what will girls be? In Martin Hoyles (ed.) *The Politics of Literacy*. London: Writers and Readers Publishing Coop. Soc. Ltd.

Oakley, Anne (1972) *Housewife*. Harmondsworth: Penguin Books.

Radcliffe Richards, Janet (1980) *The Sceptical Feminist*. Harmondsworth: Penguin Books.

Rowbotham, Sheila (1979) *Woman's Consciousness, Man's World*. Harmondsworth: Penguin Books.

Acknowledgement

I am indebted to Dorset's AE Dept. and to the group itself for their permission to use the Women's Group as the case study for this chapter.

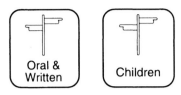

NIGEL HALL & ANNE ROBINSON

10: Power and Control in Young Children's Writing

Childhood could be described as a state of tension between being controlled and asserting independence. On the face of it children have little going for them when it comes to being independent. They are small, they are inexperienced, they have no economic freedom, they are dependent upon adults for food, clothing, warmth and protection. On almost any dimension one cares to consider children lack power and control over their lives. However, despite operating from a position of apparent weakness children manage in all kinds of ways to express their individuality, to take control of many aspects of their lives, and assert power over events and other people. Consider the following incident:

> On a hot summer's day two year old Suzy-Anne is sitting on the carpet in wellington boots which she is wearing despite the heat. On being told she has the boots on the wrong feet she pulls off a boot. In doing so she pulls off her sock as well. Mother stands patiently by holding a drink Suzy-Anne has requested. Ignoring everything else Suzy-Anne tried to put her sock back on. But, unlike the boot, the sock is difficult to control; it flops about and gets tangled in her toes. Offers of help are ignored and despite her obvious frustration she shouts, 'No, no, me put it on!' She continues to try and fail for almost five minutes until eventually the sock slips on, heel uppermost, and she replaces her boot on the wrong foot.

Despite offers of help Suzy-Anne holds onto power and attempts to see the process through. She does so with great perseverance and clearly achieves, to her own satisfaction, success. From the adults' perspective she has failed to get her sock on the right way round and has managed to replace the boot on the wrong foot, but they did not intervene; they judged the event, like Suzy-Anne, as a success. They recognised her achievement in getting her foot into the sock and were not worried about the bits that were not so perfect. Suzy-Anne was a learner, who through persistence, perseverance

121

and effort could now do something which before she had found impossible. She had exerted power and control over her own learning process. She had not been put off by the numerous times the sock failed to end up on the foot.

This event took place within a friendly, secure, and supportive environment where a parent, albeit probably intuitively, had matched their level of involvement to the level of the child's need to exert control in their learning, and had been able to recognise the validity of the achievement and respect it as successful. That Suzy-Anne behaved like a two-year-old was not seen as a disability or failure, but as progress from behaving like a one-year-old. Parents can be exceptionally sensitive to a young child's modest, but extremely significant, achievements. A few months after the above event two adults preparing dinner in the kitchen came running into another room in response to Suzy-Anne shouting 'I've done my letter, ALL BY MYSELF!' This was followed by exclamations of pleasure and 'What a clever girl' as they viewed the ill-formed and largely illegible squiggle which Suzy-Anne had used to represent the first letter of her name.

See
Chap. 12

The role of the adults in the two incidents outlined above was to be supportive, to accept Suzy-Anne's performance as representing achievement, but not to expect total perfection. They allowed her the freedom to explore, and resolve, something that, for Suzy-Anne, was difficult, and they acknowledged her desire to do something on her own, to be independent. By taking this stance the adults knew much more about what Suzy-Anne could achieve than if they had intervened early on and put the sock on her foot.

If the adult is renamed as a 'teacher' and the child is renamed as a 'pupil' can this 'independence' continue to be highly productive? In too many instances the answer has to be 'no'. The balance between having independence as a learner and being controlled as a learner is, in classrooms, usually upset to the disadvantage of the young child. For a start children do not elect to go to school; they are forced to go. Teachers are under much greater pressure than parents to demonstrate particular forms of success, and teachers are inevitably having to handle the competing individuality of between thirty and forty pupils. In addition, schools themselves tend to be products of a social system, that uses them to shape and develop young people in ways that are deemed 'appropriate' by that society. It is not surprising that in such circumstances children's power and control over their own learning is considerably reduced, and many manifestations of child power are defined institutionally as deviance; they upset the carefully regulated and organised patterns of classroom life. For many children such definitions are self-fulfilling prophecies as 'deviance' then becomes their main outlet for expressing control over their lives (Willis, 1977).

Institutional power intrudes into all aspects of schooling including curriculum and learning, and there are no aspects of curriculum which can stand outside such influence. The teaching of writing reflects, in many different ways, the power imbalance in classrooms. For most of this century children have been taught to be writers rather than authors. The very word 'author' indicates someone who has 'authority' over their text. Young children have too seldom been allowed to be authors of texts except at a very minimal level. From the start, success as a writer was defined as getting it 'right' and most early teaching of writing practices were skill-based, often totally decontextualised (like making endless patterns as a preparation for handwriting) and geared towards eliminating anything that was not perfect. There is one way to ensure perfection and that is to never do anything which involves any risk; in other words to always play safe. Thus teachers wrote things for children and the children copied them. At the point where children became better able to write a few words on their own it was not expression that was valued but accuracy in spelling and handwriting. The imposition of accuracy on beginning writers totally depowers them as authors. It devalues what they want to say and replaces what they want to say with writing which says only those things they know they can write correctly.

See
Chap. 5

We are not arguing that spelling, handwriting, and accuracy are unimportant; ultimately it is most helpful if they are part of the repertoire of authorial skills. However the demand for accuracy fails to reflect what Suzy-Anne's parents knew so well, that learners do not get everything right, that learners succeed when they see the object of the learning as purposeful, and that learners have a role to play in their own learning.

When a child's introduction to writing is copying, as in the following example, then nothing is being learned by the child about authorship, and the teacher is learning virtually nothing about the child.

All the teacher can say about this piece of writing is whether it has been written neatly. There is nothing more to be learned about the child as a writer. Although it looks like a 'perfect' piece of writing, it is in fact a 'perfect' piece of nothing. By imposing upon a child a process of simply copying, the child's ability to assert power and control over its own learning is reduced to controlling the craft of copying shapes.

It is not always easy for teachers to give up their role as controllers. If one stops controlling for absolute accuracy, then it has to be anticipated that there will be more errors, that children will not always write perfectly, and may not always write what teachers think children should write. Teachers have been led to think of themselves as people with status, who must keep control, and who must not get too personal with children. They also develop techniques of always asking the questions and controlling dialogue within classrooms. Just as they learn to act as teachers so children learn to act as pupils. It is difficult for teachers to change and it is difficult for pupils to change.

See
Chap. 16

Can it be otherwise? What would happen if teachers relinquished some of their power and allowed children to display more control in their writing? One way in which this has been explored is through the use of interactive writing. Interactive writing is essentially a written dialogue between two or more people which extends across a period of time and involves a number of exchanges (Hall & Robinson, 1993). Because it is an exchange between people the correspondents do not mark or criticise each other's writing but concentrate on exchanging meanings. It is our experience that when this happens in dialogues between children and teachers, power shifts so that both writers are able to express themselves in ways that they feel are appropriate. Each participant has the freedom to initiate topics, maintain topics or close topics. Hall & Duffy (1987) explored the tension of this change. The teacher began to use dialogue journals with her class of five-year-olds. Dialogue journals are simply a book in which the letters of both correspondents are both written. The book passes backwards and forwards between the participants allowing each writer to view all the letters that have been written (for further details see Hall & Duffy, 1987; and Staton, Shuy, Peyton & Reed, 1988). At first the teacher's letters consisted only of questions and the child's replies consisted only of answers. In other words a typical teacher – pupil exchange in a classroom. As a consequence the exchanges were fairly impersonal, contained little of the child's natural voice, and lacked any sense of dynamism. The teacher controlled the dialogue as her questions dictated the nature of the child's response. The teacher was unhappy with this and eventually it was decided that the teacher should simply stop asking questions and offer some information. It is not easy for a teacher to stop asking question but this one tried it. She simply wrote

Dear   Aileen

I have   a   friend

called   Judy

Love   from

Mrs Duffy

The child's response changed straight away. For the first time since the exchange had began she became a questioner.

Dear   Mrs   Duffy   wot
dose   she   luk   like
dose   she   luk   nis

Love   from

Aileen

From then on the exchange became much more like those in a person-person relationship. The child had learned that she had rights in this exchange; she could question as well as respond. Her own voice could be heard. The benefits to that child and the others in the class were significant. Hall & Duffy (1987) commented:

See
Chap. 13

> Aileen had discovered her voice in writing as a result of communicating to a real audience, someone who was not standing over her shoulder as she wrote, and someone whom she knew would be interested in what she wrote and would treat her words with respect. (p. 528)

However it was also the teacher that changed. By loosening her need to feel in control the dialogue became richer, she learned more about what the children could really write, and she began to appreciate that it was not necessary to exert tight control over what children wrote. The teacher learned to become a correspondent.

This was extended when the teacher worked a year later with another group of young children. The next example comes from a child, Georgina, aged five years and four months. In this journal the teacher wrote a sentence and then the child wrote one and so on. This type of interactive writing was carried out by the teacher when working with a group of children. The following entries are from one day.

T   What a nuisance? My car would not start this morning.

G   My daddy had to take it to the garage.

T   Why

G   Because the tyre wouldn't go.

T   My tyre was flat too!

G   Did you take it to the garage

T   I couldn't drive it there!

G   You could have rung up the man who gets the cars.

T   I'll do that next time. I am worried about my dog.

G   It could have got stolen last night.

T   No! She was sick!

G   Where was she sick.

T   She was sick on the carpet.

G   Did you have to wash it.

T   Yes.

G   Where did you put your dog after you had washed the carpet.

T   I took her to the vet.

G   What did the doctor say about her.

T   He gave her some medicine.

G   Was it nice medicine.

T   I don't think she liked it much.

G   I am worried now.

There are a number of points worth making about this dialogue of which the first must be that it was more like conversation than it was like any other genre. The topic derived from the everyday experience of both correspondents. The exchange contained twenty-two turns of about equal length. (In fact Georgina's sentences were a little longer than the teacher's; hers were, on average, 6.9 words long and the teacher's were 5.5.) As conversation however it was much more like everyday conversation between two adults than it was like a classroom conversation between a child and a teacher.

In the above written conversation Georgina had equal participatory rights, and could even be considered as the controller of the dialogue. It is true that the teacher initiated both the topics of this exchange but even a very simple look at the exchange shows that the rest of the dialogue was directed by the questions from Georgina. The teacher asked only one question; Georgina asked six. The topic was the teacher's but the direction was Georgina's.

Another side of this control was evident in Georgina's freedom to write what ever she wanted. She was not prevented from writing her part of the exchange by having to find a word book, queue up to get the teacher's attention, and then copy it out. She did not have to avoid using a word because she was unsure how to spell it. She was not worried that if she had a go at a spelling, the teacher would criticise her. These conversation journals were for exchanging meanings, for being authors, for having things to say. The conversation journals were not the only writing that the children did. Indeed, it was a relatively small part of their writing and the other aspects offered opportunities to explore language in more formal ways. The children understood perfectly well that the journals were for conversation, not instruction.

An important feature of the above dialogue was its length. Georgina wrote 76 words during the conversation. Too often children of this age are reduced to copying out short sentences (as in the example on page 123). Such children often copy no more than six or seven words a day, and never actually write any words for themselves. (It is also worth noting that those children cannot use writing in any other curriculum area because they cannot write on their own: Georgina could independently write reports, stories, recounts and observations. Thus Georgina's teacher could set work involving text production and know that Georgina could be getting on with it without needing constant support.) How can children learn to write if they don't write? When the exchanges of the children in this class were examined it was not unusual for them to range between twenty and eighty words. Thus even discounting all the other writing the children were doing, within these conversation journals the children were getting substantial experience of writing. They were not only getting experience of writing. The teacher's contributions were about the same overall length as the children's so each child had to do quite a lot of reading. Some times they needed help in reading sentences but it was all extra experience of acting as a reader. This is an aspect of interactive writing that is often not fully appreciated. It represents a real fusion of reading and writing.

The final point relates to what Georgina was doing with the words she wrote. Instead of a typical diet of copying teacher-influenced short recount or declarative sentences (the sort which go 'Last night I . . .' or 'This is me and . . .'), she was ranging across a variety of functions. She questioned and was prepared to hypothesise 'It could have got stolen last night'; she was prepared to argue 'You could have rung up the man who gets the cars', and she was prepared to respond affectively 'I am worried now'. In one day's dialogue Georgina had a rich, powerful and demanding writing experience.

It was an experience in which Georgina was able to exert control and have power. Like the parent of Suzy-Anne in the example earlier the teacher was not obsessed with Georgina getting everything absolutely right. She was prepared to accept that Georgina was a learner and that what was 'right' in the above extract was not the spelling or the handwriting but the use of written language to communicate feelings and actions. As a consequence instead of copying a few words, as did the child in the first example, Georgina was authoring over seventy words, and would author a substantial number of words every time she engaged in this kind of written conversation because she was not afraid to be an author of her own texts; Georgina was not a reluctant writer. It would seem that there is a much greater chance of spelling and handwriting improving if a child authors seventy words several times a week than when a child copies under ten words several times a week. There is also a much greater chance that Georgina's teacher has a more accurate image of exactly what Georgina does know and can do than does the teacher of the child who copied the first example. By relinquishing certain aspects of her control (but not her involvement and engagement) the teacher had created opportunities for Georgina to exert some control over her own learning process. It is quite clear from the above extract that Georgina relished the opportunities that this gave her.

See
Chap. 11

Chap. 13

One of the major factors in reducing children's power over their own writing is that for most, if not all, the time in school their only audience is the teacher. As we have already shown there are ways in which teachers can increase their sensitivity to the voice within the child's text. However a teacher's control can be relinquished even further by standing aside from the child's writing and allowing them to write directly, and without interference, for other audiences. This was the case in a letter writing project started with a class of 5 to 6 year olds (Robinson, Crawford & Hall, 1990).

Here the teacher's role was clear; she acted as a provider of resources, time and opportunity to write, and, by finding responsive adults, as a facilitator. Each child received a letter from one of the adults with an invitation to write back. These letters were presented to each child when the adults visited the classroom.

27 February, 1987

Dear

I have enjoyed being in your class. I hope you would like to write to me. I promise to write back to you.

Love,

I have enjoyed being in your class. I hope you would like to write to me. I promise to write back to you.

While Georgina and Aileen were both competent writers for their age, Matthew, at the beginning of the letter exchange, was one of the less able writers in the class. It took him some considerable effort to merely make the letter shapes and producing even a short text took a long time. But like Suzy-Anne in the previous example, finding things difficult did not stop him from persevering. Even the fact that he had been absent from school on the day the adults visited did not stop him wanting to write.

DearNige I wnoopeSchool Wen youca m olaindI Was ta homewen youcume mt frie hdmlantePhtuLme about tuwShAksLove

11·3·87

I was not at school when you came and I was at home when you came. My friend Martin told me about your two snakes.

This letter clearly demonstrates some of the difficulties Matthew was having. The letter format, the handwriting, spelling, and punctuation do not measure up to any kind of conventional correctness. Yet Matthew's message is powerful. He wants to be part of the writing exchange. He is in control of his text and says what he wants to say. He recognises the need of his correspondent for some kind of explanation and he chooses his words with this in mind.

In a different setting Matthew's letter might have been taken by the teacher, marked, criticised and corrected before it was sent out of school. In this case the letter was sent to his correspondent as it was. Matthew's right to control his own message was recognised and acknowledged both by the teacher and by his correspondent. For a five-year-old writing what may well be his first letter, a host of issues had to be settled. Questions like: 'Who is my correspondent?'; 'What is my relationship to him?'; 'What are the written manifestations of the relationship to look like?' and 'What will he want to know about?' need either implicitly or explicitly to be answered before a response can be orchestrated. Matthew had a free hand to compose the text he thought was appropriate for the context in which he was writing. We feel his choices were good ones.

His correspondent's reply was itself an acknowledgement of Matthew's integrity as a writer. The reply that came was a response to his meanings not a set of corrections. The link between the writers was established by their own texts and they responded to each other as people not as pupil and teacher/adult. Matthew's correspondent addressed the issues raised in Matthew's letter, in particular the fact that Matthew had not, like the other children, met him. What more motivating response can there be than to have your agenda taken seriously.

As the correspondence continued Matthew showed himself able to use a variety of strategies within his letters.

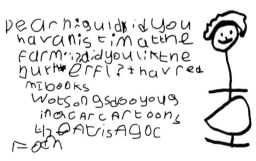

Did you have a nice time at the farm? Did you like the butterflies. I have read my books. What song do you sing in a car? A cartoon . . .

While this letter is short Matthew is able to maintain the social relationship by reference to his correspondent's previous letter, to provide information about himself and entertain his audience with a joke. In his next letter he showed further development in his writing ability when introducing the topic for the Whit Friday Festival. For the first time he extends the information about the topic, thus providing his correspondent with a more satisfying picture of the event.

20·6·87

I hope you are alright Nigel and I would like to go to california and I went to the Whit Friday Festival. There was stalls. The stalls sell sweets. I had a nice time.

By this time Matthew was well into his sixth year. In comparison with his classmates he was still not a 'good' writer. It would have been very easy for a less secure teacher to have decided that he needed to have his text written out so that he could copy, or worse still have decided that he was not ready for 'real' writing experiences and to have restricted him to an unceasing diet of copying. However, Matthew was allowed to be the author of his own texts and over the following year made slow but steady progress. It is important to appreciate that some children may never demonstrate spectacular improvements even given very supportive contexts for writing. The major change for Matthew was in his ability to maintain a theme in his letters. This is shown in the following letter written about fourteen months after the start of the correspondence.

I have been to Southsea, the capital of Portsmouth. This boat called Gotland came in and we saw the Queen Elizabeth and it was good. In Hong Kong is there trams. I hope you have a nice time.

It was written in response to a letter in which his correspondent told him about a trip to Australia. Matthew uses the theme of travel, reflecting on his own holiday and maintaining the ongoing relationship by asking a question about his correspondent's trip.

For a real measure of Matthew's progress we have to turn to a letter sent two years after the start of the exchange.

St Chad Primary school
Rhodes Avenue
    Uppermill
    Oldham
  30 January 1989
Dear Nigel I went too
Birmingham on Sunday. I crust
oh my gokart. I have got
droose We have made some naps
Old Worse We drowd it frst and then
we wrayt id abot it wich I have
bene doing. We have de to the
muesem to have a look at the
Old fasnd Cars and fire e nyes
it was good it was Uppre mill
muesem my Pantern Was Ben Morton
martin my Best Frend werct with me
and the fire was the dest
I dm ok yes scool is boring
I dm ingoy my self. Woke
is aboring. I have a istrmt
I dm get in a huoo wd nt to
higer it is a buritoh

    from

I went to Birmingham on Sundy. I crashed my go-cart. I have got a bruise. We have made some maps, old ones. We drew it first and then we wrote about it, which I have been doing. We have been to the museum to have a look at the old fashioned cars and fire engines. It was good. It was Uppermill museum. My partner was Ben Morten. Martin, my best friend, walked with me and the fire engine was the best. I am OK. Yes school is boring. I am enjoying myself. Work is boring. I have an instrument. I am getting a new one tonight. It is a baritone.

The length speaks for itself. But, more importantly, we can now see Matthew organising a number of topics within his letter. As texts grow longer so writers have to face up to a greater burden of organisation and orchestration. In this letter there is introductory information and detailed comment which provides a wealth of material for his correspondent to reply to. Matthew is functioning as an efficient and interesting correspondent. Throughout his letters, despite many difficulties, he continued to generate topics and maintain themes. His correspondent was throughout offering the greatest praise possible – a response which treated Matthew's letters as valid and successful communication. Despite areas where Matthew was less successful it was the elements of success that were responded to. Like Suzy-Anne, with effective support that allowed him ownership of his writing, Matthew displayed persistence, perseverance and effort.

In all the cases cited in this chapter the children were being treated as people. They were learners and were inexperienced but at the same time they were allowed to function as authors. Their successes were acknow-ledged not so much by praise, as in the case of Suzy-Anne, but by responses which treated their efforts as serious, meaningful and valid communication.

Lindfors (1990) reported that when she asked groups of students to write about successful moments in their education which had stayed in their minds (what she termed 'memories that endure') the response shared a number of features. Those moments were times when students felt 'I was competent', 'I was treated as someone special', 'I was able to do my own thing', and 'my teacher became a human being'. All the 'moments' reported in this study certainly have the potential to become memories that endure. Aileen, Georgina and Matthew would be able to say of their experiences during this moment that they were responded to as being competent, that they were being treated as someone special – someone with a distinctive voice, that they were able to write what they wanted to write, and that their correspondent related to them as a human being rather than as a teacher or superior adult. The worlds of literacy experienced by them were rendered powerful because they were allowed to exercise power and control. In Harste's terms (1988) a voice had been heard, a conversation started, and a mechanism established whereby that conversation could be continued.

See
Chap. 5

See
Chap. 19

References

Hall, N. and Duffy, R. (1987) Every child has a story to tell. *Language Arts* 64 (5), 523-9.

Hall, N. and Robinson, A. (1993) *Keeping in Touch: Using Interactive Writing With Young Children*. London: Hodder and Stoughton.

Harste, J. (1988) What difference does your theory of literacy make? Paper presented at 'Language and Learning' conference, Brisbane, Australia.

Lindfors, J. (1990) Writing is language: Creative construction of personal meanings. Introduction to paper presented at 13th World Congress on Reading, Stockholm, Sweden.

Robinson, A., Crawford, L. and Hall, N. (1990) *Some Day you Will No All About Me: Young Children's Explorations in a World of Letters*. London: Harper Collins.

Staton, J., Shuy, R., Peyton, J. and Reed, L. (1988) *Dialogue Journal Communication: Classroom, Linguistic, Social and Cognitive Views*. New Jersey: Ablex Publishing Corporation.

Willis, P. (1977) *Learning to Labour*. Hants: Saxon House.

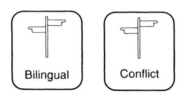

Bilingual   Conflict   Oral/Written

IRENE SCHWAB

11: Literacy, Language Variety and Identity

Introduction

The work described below took place at the Hackney Reading Centre over the last twelve years. During the course of teaching literacy and working on the publication of student writing, the issue of language arose constantly. We were enabled to step back from the day-to-day obligations of teaching and to spend some time examining and clarifying some of the language issues and to reflect on our practice because we were given time by the Inner London Education Authority's (ILEA) Afro-Caribbean Language and Literacy Project in Further and Adult Education. This project was set up in 1984, under the directorship of Roxy Harris, as part of ILEA's Language and Literacy Unit. Our original aim was to improve the handling of Caribbean language issues in further education colleges and adult literacy schemes, but we gradually moved from dealing just with Caribbean language to looking at language variety generally because of the need to make language issues relevant to all students in the multilingual, multicultural classroom.

See
Chap. 3

Chap. 7

Chap. 17

Context of the Work

During the course of this work I was the organiser of the Hackney Reading Centre, a literacy scheme in the borough of Hackney in East London. Hackney is an Inner London borough with a multiracial, multilingual population. As elsewhere in Inner London, students speak a wide variety of languages and/or types of English. The ILEA survey of schools in 1989 found 184 different languages spoken among ILEA school pupils (ILEA Research and Statistics Branch, 1989). One quarter of the school population was recorded as bilingual. Students attending literacy classes speak one of these 184 languages or a Creole language or a London variety of English or another regional variety. Some students, of course, will have a repertoire of several languages and varieties of English. Students whose first language is not English may be literate in their first language or they

See
Chap. 17

134

may not; they may feel their command of English is inadequate, but so also may students whose first language is English.

Standard English and Other Varieties

People coming forward for literacy help sometimes arrive with very specific learning goals, but they tend not to distinguish between different types of English. Most students are not aware of the term Standard English and think there is just 'good English', which they want to learn, and 'bad English' which they already know and use. There is a tendency to compare themselves and their language unfavourably with vague notions of 'correct', 'proper' or 'grammatical' written language, which they feel they have to produce to achieve success.

Equality of Language Varieties

Linguists talk about all varieties of a language as having equal validity; they say all dialects have equal status and Standard English is only one dialect among many. However, in the real world we know that this is not so. In England and in other countries we have examined, one variety has more power and status than all the others. For several centuries, spoken and written Standard English has been a measure of class, culture and social position. People using varieties of English other than the Standard have been taught to consider these variations as a sign of their inferiority – socially, economically and intellectually:

See
Chap. 19

> As a child I did not know what Cockney was. I thought I spoke English. It was not till much later in life that I realised the way you spoke could have class barriers. For instance, at an interview, the moment you open your mouth people seem to look at you as though to say, 'Oh yes, she is lower class', because people associate Cockneys with being lower class and unintelligent. (Student, Southwark College, London, quoted in ILEA Afro-Caribbean Language & Literacy Project in Further & Adult Education, 1990).

Creole

> When I arrived in England in the 1960s it was a cultural shock to me. I thought I spoke English when I arrived but I learnt I didn't. I was ridiculed and laughed at in school. Teachers said I was backward and uneducated because of my accent . . . I adapted myself to learn English and be accepted by my teachers and friends . . . Patois was my culture and yet I was made to turn away from my language; to feel ashamed when I heard fellow Jamaicans speaking Patois, and to think of them as uneducated people and me as more knowledgeable

because I spoke English. (Student, North London College, quoted in ILEA Afro-Caribbean Language & Literacy Project in Further & Adult Education, 1990).

See
Chap. 7

A cogent example of this is Creole. A large number of students in Inner London are Black, either born in the Caribbean or with parents from the Caribbean where people speak Creole languages. These are languages where the vocabulary is mainly drawn from English, French or another European language, but whose grammar and pronunciation patterns stem from African languages.

Caribbean Creole languages were formed as a result of the violent and unequal contacts between African and European people during the Atlantic Slave Trade, and the establishment of the slave plantation societies in the Caribbean. In order to justify slavery, Black people were regarded as 'inferior', and the languages they created were held in contempt by the white rulers. This explains why, historically, Creole languages have been treated with scorn and regarded as 'broken' or 'bad' versions of European languages.

Many students have retained the idea that the Creole languages they speak are not separate languages in their own right, but inferior versions of languages like English or French. This idea has been reinforced by the education systems both in the Caribbean and in Britain. Schooling has not usually provided the opportunity to analyse the structure and use of Creole grammar and the ways in which it is different from Standard English. As a result, in attempting to write Standard English, Afro-Caribbean students have often tended to use a mixture of Standard English and Creole features.

Language Variety and Literacy Teaching

In working with people, teaching literacy, decisions have to be made about which variety of language to use (I am not, in this case, talking about mother tongue literacy, but about English). The dilemma is what to teach. The Language Experience Approach used frequently and successfully in literacy teaching is based on the use of the students' own syntax, style and language patterns. The wealth of student writing published over the last 10-15 years bears witness to the success of this method in enabling students to find their voice. They are able to write and to read what they have written because the language is their own.

See
Chap. 13

See
Chap. 4

However, there are many different uses for literacy and those that are not just about self-expression, but about getting jobs, following further or higher education courses, dealing with bureaucracies are as, or more, important and often more pressing for students. The pleasure and pride at realising that one's own variety of English is a valid means of expression has to be offset against the knowledge that the same variety of English has low status and will not help one to get on in the world. George, a Black volunteer tutor at the Hackney Reading Centre, put the problem very succinctly and accurately:

> They don't have to come to you to learn to speak, they want to learn to write things. I'm not saying you shouldn't teach them how to write in dialect, but at the same time, the reason most of them want to, is not because they want just to write to friends, but some of them want not to feel left out of this society, and so putting them into a dialect mould isn't really helping them. OK, it's helping them to be able to express themselves among their own kind . . . (quoted in Schwab & Stone, 1986).

One answer to this problem seems simple. Teach both. Start with the variety most familiar to the student and when confidence has been built up and the basic skills have been learned, teach Standard English.

However, there can be problems with both aspects of this approach. Firstly, there are difficulties for white teachers who are not teaching Standard English, but are helping students to write in their own form of language because, in general, they do not know enough about Creole forms to know what is a Creole form and what is a mistake in any language. The tendency then is either to 'correct' the work into Standard English taking the control of the language form away from the student, or not to 'correct' anything, in which case the student feels that they are being short-changed and the teacher is not taking their work seriously.

A second problem with this approach is the transition from ideolect (each person's individual and personal variety of language) to Standard English. At what point should the learning of Standard English begin? Who decides – tutor or student, and how? In addition, even when it is agreed the transition point has been arrived at, how do we teach Standard English effectively? We may think we are teaching, but is the student learning? There is a long history of London schools and colleges failing to provide for the needs of their Black students which is why the Afro-Caribbean project was set up. Even with the most progressive, student-centred teaching methods, it is hard to change a lifetime's views and experiences of language. Indeed, often both students and teachers are more interested in the content than in the form of the writing that is being done.

The Role of Discussion

Clearly it is important to discuss the language variety with students so

See
Chap. 2, 9

that they are in a position to make their own decisions with full knowledge of the issues involved. Our work has been to look at ways of opening up the discussion in the classroom. Talking about language can be fraught because of the close link between language and identity. Many people feel threatened by such discussions, particularly when they are between a white teacher working with a group of mainly Black students. Feelings of resentment and anger are easily generated when students perceive that white teachers are telling them about their own language. We are all working within a context of a history of colonialism and its effects on the relations between Blacks and whites. In addition, in any mixed group of students, there is a desire not to be picked on/singled out with Creole taken as the only language that is examined.

Friday afternoon at the Reading Centre

Some examples of the issues that arise have been described fully in the report, 'Language, Writing and Publishing'. In this paper I am going to examine the experience of attempting to clarify and discuss the issues with one student, Isaac Gordon. The account is drawn from that provided in Schwab & Stone (1986).

Case Study

Isaac Gordon was a literacy student at the Hackney Reading Centre. He came to England from Jamaica 31 years ago and is now in his 50s. When he first started literacy classes 16 years ago, he had very few reading and writing skills, although he was highly articulate and had considerable skill at talking in his own variety of language, which was a mixture of Jamaican Creole and a London variety of English.

In 1979 he finished a book, *'Going Where the Work Is'*, which was published by Centerprise (Gordon, 1979). The book is an autobiographical account of his life in Jamaica, the USA and England. As Isaac could not yet write independently, the whole book was written by dictation. Isaac's speech patterns were written down by his tutor although obviously the process was mediated by how accurately she could hear and write down what was being said. As her ear became more attuned, she felt that her skill in representing his speech increased, but there was still a limitation on what he could say to a white tutor, how he could say it, and what could appear on paper.

The language issues continued to be discussed in class, but Isaac always agreed (or was persuaded?) that it was not appropriate to change yet. His tutor says her general policy at that time was to edge his writing towards Standard English but to keep it as close as possible to what he had said or written originally. His writing shows that he is beginning to understand and use Standard English, but still retains many Creole features in his writing. For example in one sentence he wrote: 'My brothers them never work, especially the lawful one them'. This demonstrates that Isaac has learned that most Standard English plurals are made by adding 's'. He has not, however, managed to unlearn the Jamaican use of the word 'them' to indicate a plural. The sentence thus uses both methods of forming plurals in juxtaposition.

Isaac's group continued to discuss the forms of English they used for writing. However, despite taking a vocal part in these discussions, Isaac still had a lack of knowledge/understanding about concepts of language variety, as illustrated by his description of another student in the class whose accent could be described as Cockney. 'I know she born in England, but she don't speak proper English. She speak like she born in the West Indies.' There he appears to be making a negative judgement based on his perception of the status of her language.

In 1983 Isaac wrote a second book, covering some of the same material as his first but expanding on it and including information about his first visit back to Jamaica, 21 years after he had left it (Gordon, 1985).

He was encouraged to write the book by a woman he met at work and he wrote it on his own during the summer holidays. He arrived back for classes in September with a manuscript written in pencil on the back of about 50 foolscap leaflets. The writing was covered with 'corrections'. As there were no classes at the time he had asked someone he knew to look through it.

> I asked her to look at it for me, and she take it, she check it more so into 'proper' English, and my teacher didn't really please about how she put it into 'proper English', and I agree with my teacher too in that way, for I remember most of the other book everybody like how I speak . . .

His teacher responded:

> What I 'didn't really please about' was that the corrections had been made without any discussion with Isaac. If he had decided that he wanted to learn Standard English, he could only do this if he were actively involved in making the necessary alterations to his writing and with some understanding of why these alterations were required.

Isaac Gordon

In a taped conversation about their work on the book, the tutor remarked: 'The issue of whether we used Standard English or Jamaican English was going on all the time.'

Isaac responded: 'All the time, but I would prefer the English' (i.e. the Standard English). The conflict here for Isaac was between achieving success through writing a book in his own variety of language, and the recognition that in other aspects of life his language is not considered 'correct' or 'educated'.

The report describes in detail the problems of trying to work on Isaac's writing. Isaac and his tutor eventually agreed to put the dialogue in Creole and the narrative in Standard English. Even this caused problems both because of the many interwoven influences on his language and because of her lack of knowledge about Creole forms. It raises the question of how difficult it is to discuss things openly and fully when we all lack complete information and knowledge.

Conclusion

Our work with Isaac and other students led us to conclude that discussing the issues with students is vital but often extremely difficult. It is difficult to shift prejudices and entrenched attitudes about language, which are held by all of us – tutors and students. Our attitudes are based on experience and on received information. People have a lifetime's experience of language and we can use this experience to change attitudes if there is enough information available.

We need to be aware of the following factors:

- There is a need to understand the history and development of the English language, how the language has changed through time and how some varieties have gained a higher status than others.
- We need to understand the social and political factors that helped to determine the development of Standard English.
- We also need to learn more about the history and development of Caribbean Creole languages.

In recognition that we work in multicultural, multilingual classrooms, we must look for common ground between the languages and experiences of all our students and draw on their own considerable experience and knowledge of language. There is a need to provide as much information as possible about language in general and, in particular, the relationship between language and power. This we have tried to do when producing materials for helping students to discuss these issues, e.g. in *Language and Power*. We believe that the more we all understand about language, the

See
Chap. 19

easier it will be to learn to manipulate it; the more awareness we have about our own world of literacy, the easier it will be to have some control over that and, when necessary, to be able to move from one world of literacy to another.

Isaac recognised this, when he described how a new world of literacy had opened up for him:

See
Chap. 22

> I now just regret it hiding from school when I was a young man. It was a hell of a mistake because of the suffering from no education and no expert. It like a disease to me especially when I first came to Britain with no education to lead me and guide me through the world we are living in now. I feel like I was locked up in a wardrobe. Now I am out of it. I feel like I am into the world now with light and star around me shining down on me.

References

Gordon, I. (1979) *Going Where the Work Is.* London: Centerprise.

Gordon, I. (1985) *It Can Happen.* London: Centerprise.

ILEA Afro-Caribbean Language and Literacy Project in Further and Adult Education (1990) *Language and Power.* London: Harcourt Brace Jovanovich.

ILEA Research and Statistics Branch (1989) *Language Census.* London: Inner London Education Authority.

Schwab, I. and Stone, J. (1986) *Language, Writing and Publishing.* London: Inner London Education Authority.

Children Gender Adults

SARAH PADMORE

12: Guiding Lights

> *Dick:* He was a character my grandad. Would he be my *guiding light?* ... I spent most of my time with him. If my aunty didn't read me a Rupert story and I told my grandad, she'd get a clip round the earhole. She'd be waiting to go out with her boyfriend – 'Get him that story read before you leave this house'.

Dick's phrase *guiding light* sums up something which we keep coming across in our research. When talking about their literacy lives, people quite often mention a particular individual, other than a parent or partner, who has played a significant role in their upbringing or adult life; someone who has encouraged their literacy development, and someone who is spoken of with affection, respect and trust.

We did not ask people who they admired or who had been a major influence on them but information about *guiding lights* seemed to appear by magic. And we have the feeling that had we asked this question directly they might have had some trouble answering; but more importantly it had not occurred to us to ask them. This is significant. If the interviews had been more formal, more structured, this information might not have come to light.

Project Methodology

The Literacy in the Community project, which started in 1988, is a collaborative research project based at Lancaster University. For the past three years we have been collecting and analysing data about local people's everyday uses of literacy; finding out how people use reading and writing in their daily lives; how they feel about different literacy practices and how they cope when they are having difficulties.

We began with pilot interviews of 20 adults who we contacted via the College of Adult Education. I was a tutor there at that time and knew some of them quite well. Everyone involved had left school at fifteen or sixteen. Eighteen of the twenty had attended basic education classes at the college.

The people, whose *guiding lights* are discussed in this article, were interviewed at this stage in our research.

Interviews were as informal as possible – not easy sitting in an empty classroom with a tape-recorder – but possibly helped by frequent technical hitches; pressing the wrong buttons on the machine; noisy drills in the corridor; or on one occasion the sudden Spiderman appearance of a grinning window cleaner. This was my first job as a researcher. People were keen to put me at my ease.

Sessions were semi-structured. We had compiled a questionnaire of 160 or more questions under a variety of themes or topics such as borrowing and owning (using the library, the market stall book-exchange, borrowing books, magazines, knitting patterns from friends and relatives; buying or being given books as presents or Sunday School prizes etc.). People were asked what reading and writing practices went on in the home; where, when and how often these took place; who was involved; were there family rules about appropriate and inappropriate times for reading and writing; did people read and write in public or did they need privacy; what materials were used and why (preferences for particular pens, pencils, paper; or types of reading matter); how they were acquired; how people set about writing (note-making, making rough drafts and re-writing, looking information up, or asking for advice or support); how they set about reading (personal ways of going through magazines and newspapers; how they dealt with difficult reading material); how they felt about particular reading and writing practices (were they seen as work or leisure; what was enjoyed, what was not); did they have strong feelings about anything they read (moral or critical objections to the subject matter or the way it was written; did anyone in the family censor reading).

We asked questions about the present and the past. People talked about their childhood homes and changes in their literacy practices and values over time. I usually had the questionnaire with me during interviews but I tried to hold the questions in my head. We felt it was important to go beyond the questionnaire, to encourage people to talk as freely as possible. The questionnaire simply acted as a check list of the areas which we had already thought about and wanted to cover. People were given space to come up with topics of their own which we might not have considered ourselves, and a degree of 'rambling' was positively encouraged. Sometimes people told me stories which I enjoyed but suspected had little relevance to the project. I was often wrong. Once people are focused on a subject they seem to stick to it; when studied, a 'ramble' can often prove to be useful data.

It was only on studying the transcribed tapes of these 20 interviews that we discovered the *guiding lights* theme. The importance people attached to a particular friendship or relationship was a subject people brought up of their own accord.

See Chap. 20

Adult Guiding Lights *(Neil and Sean; Liz and Barbara)*

Some people talked of support and guidance friends gave them in adult life. Neil and Liz talk in their own words about such friendships.

> *Neil:* He's really helpful. He's the same age as me and he's one of the most helpful people I've ever known . . . a great lad. It's her brother, (his partner's brother) and he was alright at school so he could have gone further but he left school at sixteen and went to work in a shop. He could have gone for further education but he just went and got a job. If I don't understand a word . . mainly spelling he'll help me with. I can't say a for instance – just say, like punctuation, commas and that . . and try to read out clearly to me. This was before I came to College he was helping me do things like that. It's him who got me here really. It took me three years to get here. He got me . . he forced me . . . 'Get yourself there, lad'. He's my friend, my mate. He goes round with me all the time, everyday near enough. And you know he's really helpful. I couldn't do without him in a way. He's reliable . . . if I'm stuck or owt I ask him.

Liz, who is now an avid reader, has had a history of writing difficulties. At one time she had a job which involved writing reports. Barbara was supportive. She was also importantly, a friend.

> *Liz:* My friend Barbara makes me (write to her) 'cos she knows and she accepts it so it's not too bad. But if somebody doesn't know . . . a lot of people don't know . . . I feel a bit concerned. It was terrible when I first started (her new job) but Barbara, the one who makes me write to her, she taught me how to go about it – how to word them. She said – it's basically the same words all the time just different actions. She lives in Birmingham 'cos that's where I lived at the time . . . well thirty six miles away, but we worked for the same company.

Neil is in his late twenties, Liz is in her late thirties. Although they had reading and writing difficulties neither had felt any great concern about this on a personal level, since leaving school. Nor had it apparently affected their job chances. Both had been employed for a number of years before new job opportunities brought new literacy demands.

Liz's story

After working for years in jobs with no formal writing demands, Liz found herself in a job where she was expected to write reports. For the sake of anonymity I cannot disclose her job title, but such a job would demand a good deal of self-confidence, the ability to act decisively and independently, and the willingness to be held accountable for action taken. Liz had no apparent worries about her personal skills on this score. She seemed frankly puzzled at my suggestion that the responsibility of such a job would scare me. Her worry was quite simply to do with the mechanics of wording and spelling when writing reports.

Liz turned to her friend Barbara because she was a friend and because, working for the same company, she would understand exactly what was involved. It is doubtful if Liz could have received such appropriate support from any outside body. Report writing is not standardised. Colleges may offer help with it, but with the best will in the world, they cannot hope to cover the exact demands of report writing in each and every avenue of work.

Barbara was the only company employee who really *knew* about Liz. Liz would not have approached anyone else at work for support. Barbara's help was not just specific to the expectations of that particular job, but specific to her understanding of Liz's needs, and her understanding of Liz as a person. A *guiding light* is not simply someone you respect and trust, but someone who really knows and respects you.

See
Chap. 4

When suddenly faced with new literacy demands at work, people may feel that their work identity, their fitness for the job is called into question. They may worry that the company they work for will find out, if they seek help, and lower their opinion of them; perhaps they will bump into someone from the workplace at evening classes and have to account for being there – explain themselves.

Liz did not consider external help as an option. She had been working for years; she had always coped in the past. And she had Barbara to turn to. It appears that at this point in her life, eight or nine years ago, she did not really see literacy as an issue for her.

Sometimes it may be particularly hard for people who are having some success in their working lives to seek help. Liz remarks that it can be hard admitting to yourself that there is something that needs sorting out. It was many years after this episode in Liz's life, long after she had left the company, and when she was living very much further away from her friend, Barbara, that Liz decided to sort out her English. She made the decision to go to college.

Although there appears no direct link between this *guiding light* relationship and her return to study it would seem likely that Barbara's ongoing friendship and support encouraged Liz to seek outside help. Barbara accepted her difficulties; Barbara had successfully supported her in her report writing; Barbara respected her as a person. It was possible that someone else would do the same.

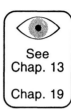

See
Chap. 13

Chap. 19

Families may also give this type of support (often they don't) but some people may value the support of partners or children less than that of a friend, perhaps feeling that families accept and support you because you are family, and so it does not really count. A woman's family roles – mother, housewife, lover – tend to interfere with or confuse her identity as an individual anyway. And to gain the confidence to deal with something that needs sorting out, such as working on literacy skills or in order to pursue other educational ambitions, perhaps you need to discover personal space and personal identity, away from the family; to feel respected and trusted as a person in your own right, in order to recognise your needs.

Liz, who avoids communicative writing in her daily life, corresponds with Barbara quite happily. Barbara is still the only person, outside of her immediate family, who really *knows*. When Liz writes to Barbara she does not have to write a letter in rough, get it checked by her husband or daughter, and then make a top copy, as she does with other writing tasks. Barbara is the only one who she writes to independently. To appreciate this trust it should be put in context. In recent years Liz has become far more self conscious about her literacy skills. She has taught herself to read fluently, but at the time of interview, was still having problems with writing. She had so little confidence in her spelling she hardly dared to write a shopping list. If she needed her daughter to shop for her she would write in a personal abbreviated code – that way if the list was dropped, and picked up, her spelling difficulties would not be exposed.

See
Chap. 14

Neil's story

New demands at work forced Neil to reassess his literacy skills. Working his way up at a local chain-store, Neil was sent on an area training course for promotion. He found himself surrounded by people, his age and younger, who had qualifications, and he was unnerved by this, and by his own difficulties with paperwork on the course.

See
Chap. 4

Neil was lucky. His best friend, Sean, supported and encouraged him. Neil respects Sean's abilities – 'He could have gone for further education'; Sean is someone like the people Neil has met on the training course, someone who would have no problem with the paperwork, someone he can trust to help him. But he is also someone who did not 'go on for further education'. Like Neil, Sean left school at sixteen and got a job in a shop; Sean and Neil have experiences in common. They understand one another. If Sean had gone on and got qualifications might the relationship have changed? Neil would not ask other people on the training course for help. He saw their qualifications as a barrier between him and them.

Drawing by
Milan Ivanic

Most of all, Neil respects Sean's helpfulness. In his brief speech he refers to Sean's help, or helpfulness, four times. 'He's the same age as me and one of the most helpful people I've ever known.' Neil is struck by the fact that someone his own age is so helpful; but also perhaps by their similarity. There is not mention in this extract of the ways in which he helps Sean but elsewhere it is implied. Sean has few friends; he is something of a loner. Neil is sociable and friendly. The relationship is almost certainly mutually supportive. Sean sees Neil nearly everyday. 'He's my friend, my mate . . . I couldn't do without him in a way'. Neil's *guiding light* is far more than a literacy broker or adviser. The speech speaks for itself.

See
Chap. 19

Like Liz, Neil eventually sought help at the local college. Sean was directly responsible for getting him to go. But as Neil says, 'It took three years'. Perhaps like Liz, Neil needed to reassurance of a long-term friendship and support to gain the confidence, or to accept that there really was something that needed sorting out.

Childhood Guiding Lights

Some people talked of a close friend in adult life; others described adult relatives, other than parents, who had played a major role in their upbringing and/or early literacy life. Quite often people appear to have taken a grandparent, aunt, uncle or elder sister as a role model and in some cases these people have been a source of lasting inspiration.

Here in their own words are some example of this.

> *Julie:* My maternal grandmother was very into reading and told me it would open up new worlds for me and that everywhere wasn't the same as here. And I remember my grandmother teaching me how to use the telephone. It'll come in handy', she said 'because there will be a lot more of these about when you get older'. She was quite bright I think. She was quite my mentor, I think, when I was that young, you know, five to eleven.

> *Dick:* He was quite a character my grandad . . . would he be my *guiding light?* He sort of kept me in order. Then with me being the eldest I used to have to look after the kids at home while my mum went to work. She used to do what they called the 'housewife's shift', 6.00 till 10 at . . (names local mill). I spent most of my time with him. If my aunty didn't read me a Rupert story and I told my grandad, she'd get a clip round the earhole. She'd be waiting to go out with her boyfriend – 'Get him that story read before you leave this house'. And his football coupons . . . and Sporting Life . . . pick horses out and that. It was, you know – great this, putting the little crosses on the coupon of the racing form.

> *Cath:* My aunty used to write . . . well, she used to write to Canada and America and all the relations over there. She used to write poetry. Yes, she used to write poetry and things like that. She was educated at the Grammar School – she was very clever, very well read . . . she was a marvellous person. She was very broad-minded. She never married. There was never such a thing as black and white . . . she always understood people. She was a beautiful person really. I used to . . ah, she was me best friend really, me favourite aunty. She had a lot to do with bringing me up. When I was fourteen she was the first person to ever take me out to a cafe.

Dick's story

Dick's grandad may or may not have consciously encouraged Dick's literacy development. What is apparent is that literacy was embedded in his everyday life; in allowing Dick to put the little crosses on the racing form coupon he was wittingly or unwittingly acting as literacy broker. This was a shared literacy event between adult and child, and one which was mutually enjoyed. Dick was being trusted to perform an adult task, with implications for his grandad's household's finances. Dick's writing had a definite purpose which he was almost certainly aware of – the little crosses he was making could lead to a wind-fall. He was learning the power of literacy and at the same time sharing dreams with his grandad.

Whether Dick's grandad saw making his daughter read Rupert to Dick as the need to exercise his authority over her or as important to Dick's literacy needs is irrelevant. Dick's grandad made sure that the story got read.

See
Chap. 5

Dick has discovered new worlds through his own reading and adult education. At the time of interview he was feeling under some pressure to go on to university, and was uncertain if it was what he wanted to do. The dramatic changes in his life over the last few years – marital break-up, injury at work, unemployment and, return after more than 20 years to education – have not been easy. He feels he has left a whole way of life behind: family, work mates, friends, life-style and beliefs. He does not regret it, but there is certainly a sense in which he feels trapped between two cultures. He has entered a world which his grandfather, who set him on the literacy path, knew nothing of; and yet I get the feeling that Dick's grandad still influences him, and is a source of strength.

Julie's story

Julie, Cath and Dick all spent a lot of time with their *guiding lights,* as children. For Julie it was something of an escape. She used to rush home after school on a Friday, grab a bag, and go to her grandmother's for the weekends. In her grandmother's kitchen she used to play with words on the newspaper table-cloth. Julie suggests that her grandmother enjoyed being shocked by scurrilous stories in the tabloid press; she remembers this with affection, although as an adult she has fierce views about such papers and the people who read them.

Literacy was both embedded in Julie's grandmother's daily life, and consciously valued. When Julie entered her grandmother's home she became part of a rich literacy world which seemed very different to her world at home. Her relationship with her mother was difficult, and her grandmother appears to have had more time and more inclination to share literacy practices with Julie, and to encourage her literacy development. Julie's grandmother's home was full of reading materials. There were books stacked on shelves, newspapers on the table where they ate. Julie was allowed to write on the paper, to play with the words. Her grandmother read to her and told her that reading would 'open up new worlds'. She read to herself in front of Julie and discussed what she read with her. Julie learned the power of literacy both by being told about it and through witnessing her grandmother's horror at stories in the newspaper. Perhaps this exposure to the tabloid press also represented an early lesson in critical reading. Finally, her grandmother acted as literacy broker in teaching Julie to use the telephone.

Cath's story

Cath looked up to her aunt, respected her grammar school education, her cleverness, her literacy practices. But a *guiding light* is not simply someone who is respected. Cath's aunt was also her best friend. She opened up new worlds for Cath, through discussion, reading and writing and also gave Cath new experiences. The example of being the first person to take her to a cafe is good one; she acted as cafe broker just as Julie's grandmother acted as telephone broker. There are a set of literacy skills involved in using a cafe: working out if it is self-service or table service, and if self-service how to use it; reading the menu and looking at the comparative prices; asking for and understanding bills; maybe leaving a tip, or finding the toilets. And these literacy skills are interwoven with social skills that also need learning – general cafe behaviour. These days when most people are used to cafes this may seem trivial; but Cath is talking about a time when her social world was very restricted. She was fourteen and it was an event.

Cath's aunt had a strong influence on her. She was broad-minded, single and independent; she wrote letters abroad, and poetry. Her world was very different to Cath's mother's world.

Mothers

None of the five whose transcribed extracts are shown above had mothers who could help them. Cath's mother had little education and was far too busy bringing up younger children and helping Cath's father to support the household, to encourage her literacy development. Her parents devoted more time to her younger brothers; by the time they arrived the family was more financially secure. Julie's mother was a harassed single-parent throughout most of Julie's childhood, and her only ambition was for her to marry. She actively prevented Julie from reading; Julie suggests she was scared of education – husbands didn't want educated women. But she also suggests that her mother was afraid that too much reading would give her ideas above her 'station' – 'peas above sticks' is the phrase she uses. This implies some real fear of losing Julie; of Julie leaving her family and community, her working-class roots behind. Ironically, Julie's mother wanted to prevent her daughter from discovering the 'new worlds' which

See
Chap. 8

her own mother, Julie's grandmother, was advocating with such success.

Liz's mother died when she was very young. Dick and Neil tell similar stories: their father left home and their mothers were overworked. It is not surprising that their literacy role models came from outside the home. Only two of the twenty people interviewed directly blamed their parents for a lack of interest in their education or for contributing to their own sense of school failure.

Education

Positive and negative school experiences obviously influence people's career and educational choices as adults, and their confidence in learning. None of the people interviewed had very happy memories of school. No-one expressed fond memories of a particular school teacher. Neil talks about an episode in his first year at secondary school 'destroying' his English and his confidence. A teacher read out something Neil had written to the class and made sarcastic comments about it. Neil feels this single incident affected his whole secondary school career. This is a common story. Had people developed *guiding light* relationships with teachers at school, might their lives have taken a different course?

See Chap. 10

Bad school experiences made people wary of returning to education. Neil might never have made the decision if Sean had not encouraged him. Dick arrived at the doors of the local college three times before he finally went through them. He was afraid it was going to be too much like school. And he did not have an image of himself as the sort of person who went to college; interestingly, his experience of college backed-up this pre-conception. But he stayed. He says that he was lucky in meeting someone like Julian (his tutor); perhaps implying that someone else might have put him off from staying. Dick's relationship with his tutor was important to him; there is an element of *guiding light* in it. Dick passed through basic education and went on to Open College courses. Perhaps Julian provided something which his grandfather could not – an academic role model. Though Dick suggests that he never really changed to fit in; he has 'too many rough edges' to do that.

Several people mentioned, as Neil did, a friend or relative finally persuaded them once they had returned. This ongoing support from someone outside the immediate family may be important. We are aware of the kind of pressures many women, perhaps some men, face if they do return to education. Rockhill (1993), in her study of Hispanic women, talks of the point at which women's literacy or language help is suddenly seen as 'education' by their partners; and men who have encouraged their wives to develop functional skills, enabling them to deal with household management, become alarmed and withdraw their support. Education is a threat.

See
Chap. 14, 9

We have evidence of this in our data too. Some of the women who were interviewed talked of pressure at home since they had started adult education classes. One said that her husband resented the time she spent on homework, and the way she shut herself away from the family to do it. When she had started at the college, he had encouraged her. As her learning increased and her confidence in writing grew, he became less and less supportive.

Another woman in our data had switched from studying sociology to health and beauty at her husband's request. She had done very well in sociology but her husband suggested she studied something more appropriate to her needs.

Liz mentioned getting into arguments with her husband over essays. She originally joined a spelling class at college. But once she began telling him about group discussions on social issues, and showing him essays expressing her point of view, he began to challenge her. Sometimes they would spend a whole weekend arguing. This confused Liz and made her uncomfortable. She would end up uncertain what she believed. She and her husband are close. Before she started college they had not had disagreements of this sort. Some women might have dropped out at this point, but Liz was determined. I suspect she took to talking less about her writing at home.

We understand the importance of friendships within basic education classes, and how these affect people's confidence, course attendance and learning outcomes. Perhaps in our discovery of *guiding lights* we have come across an additional factor – the significance of supportive friendships outside of classes.

Julie, Cath and Dick were adults before they reassessed their education. These significant childhood relationships do not appear to have helped their school careers. But then there are many ways in which schools fail to meet the needs of children. Children may not be seen or heard; invisibility is a serious problem in large schools. And visibility can also be a hazard if it results in sarcastic exposure or disruptive labelling. We might guess from what we know about their backgrounds that there would have been very little communication between home and school and perhaps a conflict of interests. But what about their personal motivation? Perhaps they found school dull in comparison to the time they spent with their *guiding lights*. How could any teacher compete with Dick's grandad, Julie's grandmother, or Cath's aunt, and their special treatment? How could a school provide such richness of literacy experience, total individual attention and affection?

See
Chap. 8

Shaping identities

It is possible that the influence of an adult *guiding light* in early life only becomes apparent when a child reaches adulthood. There are some striking likenesses between people's *guiding lights,* as they describe them, and themselves: Julie's grandmother, sounds very much like her; Cath's aunt seems to have an awful lot in common with her; and Dick, who talked of his grandad as a real character, has himself in middle-age begun to challenge what he sees as expected norms of behaviour. Talking about Neil and Sean, and Liz and Barbara, I have already mentioned their closeness and their shared experiences. A *guiding light* seems to have many similarities with his or her follower. In fact the word 'follower' is quite wrong. There is mutual respect. Even in the adult/child relationships there seems to be some sense of equality, or of being treated of an individual rather than a child; perhaps this is partly due to the fact that they lived alone. Company was company.

See
Chap. 13

Julie and Cath both felt that their childhood relationships with women relatives had given them a sense of strength in adult life. Both are very interested in women's issues; both are avid readers and write poetry, and both were determined that their own children would be better educated than they were.

The five people whose transcribed extracts on the guiding lights themes are discussed here, all talk of relationships with people who are the same sex as themselves. This is not surprising; our role models and closest friends are commonly the same sex as we are. But in other data which we have collected, there are examples of *guiding lights* who are the opposite sex: one man, Mark, talks of an older sister who influenced his literacy development, and, like Julie's grandmother, made him aware of new worlds and possibilities. Mark, who struggled through the bottom division at a local secondary school, eventually followed his sister, who had flown through the Grammar School, on to Art College. We finally have one example of someone whose *guiding light* was both her best friend, and a sexual partner, but perhaps importantly not one she lived with.

See
Chap. 20

Neil's son has just started school. Neil is going to ensure that his son will have a better education than he had. Neil's difficulties prevent him from reading for pleasure and he finds writing too frustrating to enjoy it, but he is determined things will be different for his son. He is actively seeking help for himself, and advice on his son's education. He and his partner, who also has some difficulties, encourage their child's literacy development by reading to him and hearing him read, and by organising literacy activities for him after school. Neil's *guiding light* has made him aware of new possibilities.

Conclusion

Some *guiding lights* appear to have been adopted as role models in preference to parents, helping people to shape their adult identities; and making them aware of new worlds and possibilities beyond the confines of their home. Most have provided conscious literacy help and support, but sometimes literacy was simply embedded in their everyday affairs. Some *guiding lights* are relatives, but each relative has been one of close friendship.

The implication of childhood *guiding lights* may be that the literacy world of home is not necessarily as important to an individual's literacy outlook as the world of literacy in someone else's home. Parental attitudes may be less influential in shaping children's views of learning/education or ambition than those of another relative or friend who has more time to take an interest in them, and who makes some active literacy contribution to their lives – someone who makes a child feel special.

Schools cannot create their own *guiding lights*. They are not prescribed; they are self chosen. But might Julie, Cath and Dick have got on better at school if there had been some communication between their *guiding lights* and their teachers? It seems probably that Julie's grandmother, Cath's aunt and Dick's grandad would have had more inclination, certainly more time, to talk to teachers about them than their parents did. And it is possible that they might have talked in a more informed way, given their special relationships with the children. Should parents evening actively open out to include friends and relatives? Should children be asked who they would like to come in to school to talk about them and their learning? Perhaps children could also be encouraged to talk about special friendships outside school, everyday literacy activities and how they value them.

See
Chap. 8

Adult *guiding lights* who are friends may have more influence over someone's literacy development and outlook than a partner, or another member of the immediate family. Adult *guiding lights* may play a vital role, helping people to gain confidence and discover a sense of personal identity, or changing identity. And in encouraging and supporting people returning to education. It is possible that adult educators could draw on such friendships; talk to students about them, the nature of their support, and how they feel it has helped their learning. Maybe informal, and self chosen, helpers have something to teach tutors.

See
Chap. 19

We cannot say exactly how significant *guiding lights* are in terms of educational attitudes and outcomes, but our feeling is that such a relationship – whether it acts as some kind of literacy/caring bonding, as it would appear in Dick's case with his grandad, literacy inspiration/and friendship, in Julie and Cath's childhoods, or the literacy trust and helpfulness in Neil and Liz's adult friendships, may help to counteract negative experiences of learning and encourage people to return to education.

Reference
Rockhill, K. (1993) Gender, language and the politics of literacy. In B. Street (ed.) *Cross-Cultural Approaches to Literacy*. Cambridge: Cambridge University Press.

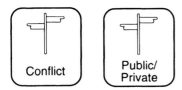

PAUL DAVIES, STELLA FITZPATRICK,
VICTOR GRENKO AND ROZ IVANIC

13: Literacy, Strength and Identity

Our sense of identity is very important to all of us. The value we give to ourselves and our talents helps us to make links with other people and to operate successfully in the world. All of us identify ourselves first and foremost as human beings with personal and everyday life strengths, but how we *show* these strengths is often limited by the world we live in. Other people's view of our personal strengths can be a source of power and freedom or can diminish us in the eyes of the world, and often in our own eyes too.

See
Chap. 12

In this chapter we will write about how literacy relates to our identity and our strengths. The ideas we develop began during discussions at the Worlds of Literacy Conference and this paper has grown from continuing interest and collaboration between four of us from the group, with ideas and comments from others. First we will write about how literacy can rob people of self-confidence in a world where some people read and write better than others. In this part we will give examples of how literacy robs people of their strengths when they are job hunting, and we will suggest some ways in which they can regain their strength. Then we will look at the positive side of literacy; how writing, particularly, can help us find ourselves, feel strong, and join our voices with others. Next we will write about how writing can sometimes portray us as different from the way we want to appear: literacy and conflict of identity. Then we will write about the writer's relationship with the reader: questions of identity and trust, with more examples from jobhunting. Finally we will speak out for alternatives to literacy: other ways of showing our strengths which we think ought to be treated as seriously as literacy.

Literacy as Robber

Imagine three different 'worlds of literacy'. By 'world' we mean mini-world, that is, society, community or group.

157

World 1

In a world without literacy, that is, where no one reads and writes, people are recognised and valued for all their other abilities, physical strength, intellectual strength as demonstrated by their spoken words and actions, their wisdom, their moral strength, their caring, and many other qualities.

World 2

· In a world where some people read and write better that others, like most industrialised countries in the 1990s, those same people suddenly take on a different identity. Instead of being those strong, valued people we just described, they become identified as 'not literate'. They are identified by what they cannot do rather than by what they can. What rubbish! They are still the same people.

In this sort of world, the one most of us live in now, we'd like to suggest a new metaphor for literacy: *Literacy as Robber*. The existence of literacy as the be-all and end-all in this sort of world, *robs* some people of their strength and identity. Later, we would like to take some examples of this from the experience of one of us as a careers adviser, working for twelve years with school pupils, and working also as a researcher, exploring the job application problems of long-term unemployed people who had problems with reading and writing.

Phil Baber

World 3

The third 'world of literacy' is like the second, where some people read and write more than others. The difference is that literacy doesn't have the power to rob people of their strength and identity. Literacy is useful for some things, but words, written words, are not the be-all and end-all. Some of the case studies in this book show the many different strengths people have without needing literacy. We think this is the world the co-authors of this book live in. It is the world we are all fighting for. At the same time, we acknowledge that the sheltered world of the conference which this piece of writing and this book springs from, can deceive as well as seek the truth, because of the presence of 'World 2' beyond its walls. It's easy to feel your strengths, and be noble about writing, your writing, within the world of the conference, but in the real world people judge you and your lack of technical skill harshly. For many people, what they might feel about their strengths apart from literacy is one thing, but in the real world they keep their head down and maintain a low profile. Here is one example:

How literacy can 'rob' personal strengths in the job market

In written job applications, you have to put forward your strengths to persuade the employer to give you the job. You are writing as evidence of your strength and identity. It may also be necessary to disguise your weaknesses. Writing about your strengths is extremely hard, because many people feel that this is 'boasting' and 'showing off'. Also, writing about your strengths is a hard thing to do if you have difficulties with reading and writing for not only might you have the technical difficulties of forming letters and getting the spelling right, but it is likely that your personal identity would have taken a battering. Your confidence would probably be low both as a writer and as a potential employee.

See
Chap. 4

Paul, one of this chapter's co-authors, works as a careers advisor. During 1989-90, he carried out a study of people who have been unemployed for a long time. This study has shown that people find some aspects of their lives easier to write about than others. It is relatively easy to write down a list of your school qualifications and achievements (if you have any). It is also quite straightforward to give details of previous jobs you have done if they follow a logical sequence, that is, traditional steps on a career ladder, for example bank clerk, supervisor, assistant bank manager, area bank manager. It is much harder to write about other talents, skills and achievements, such as being strong, being honest, being good at fixing things, being able to do a repetitive task well. One of the people in the study of long-term unemployed people said that the main thing he had to offer an employer was, 'Two strong lungs and two strong arms', but he would feel 'silly' writing this down on an application form. People who feel that the main things they have to offer an employer are physical rather than mental attributes often prefer to talk to employers in face-to-face meetings. A very large majority of the long-term unemployed people interviewed in the survey, had successfully obtained jobs in the past by turning up at the factory gate and building site and, 'If the employer like the *look* of you, you got the job. In those days there were no application forms'. Another man said that there was something unmasculine about applying for a labouring job, '. . . sitting down in a centrally heated room with a pen and paper. It's better to be out there in the wet and the cold walking from site to site, show 'em you can do the job'.

However, there is evidence to show that recruitment is becoming more formalised even for unskilled manual work. Although the people who took part in the study had done a wide variety of work, most generally found jobs at the semi-skilled and unskilled level, so they were surprised that they were now required to fill in application forms. All of this shows that the unequal weight given to literacy takes away from people's other strengths and skills.

Ways of regaining strength

If literacy robs you of your other strengths and your identity in 'World 2', what can you do about it? There are several ways of taking more control over the situation. Here are three examples of how to win back your strength when job hunting.

See Chap. 20

(1) It is better to write application forms in groups rather than individually. Your confidence will be higher if your friends reassure you that your experience and skills are the ones employers want. Jobclubs can sometimes help. For example, there is a literacy class held at a job centre in Bradford where people meet and write applications together with the help of tutors.

(2) There are other ways of writing apart from pen and paper. It can be useful to spend time writing a Curriculum Vitae (a list of your past education and experience) on a word processor, then when a good copy is produced, you can photocopy it and send this attached to the application form. In this way your mistakes disappear as soon as you press the delete button, and do not linger on the page as crossed out words to remind you of the difficulties you had.

See Chap. 9

(3) Personal strength leads to better written applications. 'Good' writing is as much to do with confidence in yourself as a person as with knowing spelling rules. That is why a lot of ABE work concentrates on this. Assertiveness training is useful here too, because it helps to give the strength to value your own opinions and ways of expressing yourself.

Literacy Gives People Strength

It isn't paradoxical, in the light of what we have already said, to point out that reading and writing can also develop and demonstrate people's strength and identity. The importance of reading and writing skills is undisputed. What we would argue for is an equality of status for the parallel talents that people use in order to cope adequately with life. In this section we will write about the positive role of literacy in helping people do what they want to do and be who they want to be.

Why *writing* is especially important

Writing and reading are different. When you are reading, you have to hold on to your identity hard and make sure you don't necessarily give in to the ideas you are reading just because they are written down. Written words don't have *that* much strength, though some people seem to think they do. Writing is the side of literacy which can give you the chance to express and share things which matter to you, with many more people than you can ever meet face-to-face. That's why lots of teachers (including Nigel Hall & Ann Robinson in Chapter 10, Jean Hudson in Chapter 16) and adults who return to learning, concentrate on writing. If you share what's important for you through writing, it makes it possible for new realisations of experience to be noticed. For example, if enough women write about what is true for them, then women's experience is differently perceived by other people and by women themselves. Writing allows this cumulative building of opinion. All of us need to join our voice with the rest, to show our strengths, to be the ones who influence as well as the ones who are influenced, and writing is one good way of doing this.

See Chap. 10, 16

See Chap. 18, 19

Some advantages of writing

Because writing can be slow and considered, the writer can work at developing his/her line of thought, drafting the writing as many times as is necessary, to get a satisfactory end-product. This can be a source of confidence and strength. Two of this chapter's co-authors have worked as writing teachers in literacy and academic courses for some years. In our experience, there are a number of arguments and affirmations to be made about the value of writing to people for whom writing, more usually, has felt an alien medium. Here are some of them.

- Writing is convenient because we don't have to be there to get our ideas to other people.
- It's got status, and we all want to share in that.
- It gives you extra communicative power; lots of people can respond to you through writing that gets made public.

- It's a way of reminding ourselves of what we were thinking at a particular time, a way of recapturing ideas and impressions, scenes and people.
- It's very satisfying to express ideas through writing. It's gratifying when other people give you feedback about what you've put and how you've put it. This makes writing worth working on, though hard.
- It's a way of collaborating with other people. One way of gathering strength through writing can be to use discussion to trawl what's going on below the surface, then to use writing to share with other people what you've discovered. A warm-up time is necessary for everyone who writes, either alone or with other people. This can be a source of bonding between people who share talk about common themes they feel are worth writing about.
- Writing is a way of communicating open to everyone, as long as we include getting writing down through tape recording or scribing for other people. Many wonderful books have been written by people dictating to 'scribes'. For example, *Never In A Loving Way* by Josie Byrnes or *Going Where The Work Is* by Isaac Gordon, give people the opportunity to learn from the experience and strengths of these writers. They were able to establish their identity and communicate to others in writing, with the help of tape recorders and secretaries.

See
Chap. 2, 9

See
Chap. 11

Why the medium you write in and the way you use language is important

The *medium* you write in can show your personal strength, just because it can be a personal statement. Whereas typewritten material is uniform and impersonal, using handwritten, perhaps brightly coloured text where practicable, is less expected and slightly riskier. For many of us, typing our writing enhances it and lends it the authority of print. But handwriting in coloured inks gives an opportunity to put a more personal stamp on the message. Choosing between typing and handwriting says something about your identity. Like the way you choose your words, it gives readers an impression of who you are. If you choose long words and write them in long sentences it gives a different impression from when you choose short words and write short sentences.

See
Chap. 20,
5, 22

The relationship between a person's thoughts and their way of expressing these in writing is very close to their sense of self. Deciding to put your personal stamp on your writing through keeping your own ways of expressing ideas can be a source of satisfaction and also shows personal strength. People who develop this strength are less dependent on other people's opinion of their writing. It still matters that other people understand and respond to the ideas in the writing, but the expression of the ideas belongs very strongly to the writer and matters a great deal to that person.

This belief in yourself as a user of language is a strength worth developing. Most of us rush to conform. This strength has more to do with your sense of self than with your technical ability to write. People who use a scribe can make this choice and have this strength.

Ways of showing yourself in your writing: Literacy and conflict of identity

Written language gives you more flexibility, and that's the reason why many people return to learning after they leave school. But new reading and writing abilities bring with them different identities. When people grow up only reading and writing a certain amount, their other strengths create their identity. When they start to read and write more, or different, sorts of things, this changes their identity. Examples of this are in Chapter 5, where Rachel Rimmershaw, Nichola Benson, Judith Harrison and Sarah Gurney write about how when you read and write at university, you can become, through choice or a sense of compulsion, a different person from who you are outside university.

If you decide to challenge this and deal with these increased and different writing and reading tasks in ways that use your personal strengths, it can be hard, but rewarding. In Chapter 20, Denise Roach and Angela Karach write of how they learned to deal with the academic requirements of being university students, in ways that used their personal strengths and sense of identity.

Showing strength and identity through writing can mean taking risky, different or unsafe routes to express your ideas. It means allowing people to judge you through your writing. One of the things aural technologies like the telephone, radio and television (though this is visual too) have done, is makes us more aware of the many accents and dialects in spoken versions of our language. To some extent, there's more appreciation of difference, less outlawing of people because their (spoken) language is different. Can it ever be the same for written versions? Not non-standard spelling necessarily, but recognition that as long as it 'means' it's allowable. Could a flavour of ethnic or regional difference be allowed in written language without being considered 'wrong'? Perhaps this would allow a different 'strength' to emerge. In 'World 2', writing has been 'standardised', so that is doesn't show your age or where you come from. For example, in Chapter 19, Joe Flanagan says that his identity depends very strongly on the fact that his family come from Ireland. This shows very clearly when he talks, but not when he writes. This is another case of *literacy as robber:* writing robs you of the identity you have through the way you speak.

It's tempting to hide behind language. Long words are assumed to mean intelligence, on a superficial level. Putting an everyday word in place of a long word seems like giving up a kind of power. Yet using everyday words means that we are understood by many more people. This helps us to see that using 'closed' ways of writing are not about sharing understanding, but are about holding on to ideas and keeping them only for certain people. Putting an everyday word in place of a long word, as a conscious act, can be a source of personal strength. So by giving up one kind of power you gain another, and you empower others. This is the principle which has guided the four of us in writing this chapter, as well as the other authors of this book. Our purpose has been to try to write about complicated ideas in a way that is plain and readable. As we said at the beginning, we want a world where literacy (in this case, our writing) does not rob others (in this case, our readers) of their own identity.

Questions of identity and trust

See
Chap. 5

One of the difficulties with establishing your identity in writing is that you don't know who you're dealing with. It's not like speaking, where you can see other people's reactions to you and adjust accordingly. You can't tell whether the reader is going to be on your side or not. In some situations you can trust people to acknowledge your identity and treat you with respect; in other situations you have to be on your guard. Let us return to our earlier jobhunting example. When writing about yourself for a job application, you have the problem that the person to whom you are writing is a stranger to you. All you know is that this person has the power to either reward you with a job or to reject your application completely. How will your application be received? Is there a particular form of writing which will impress the employer; will she/he prefer long words and complex sentence structures because these will be interpreted as a sign of intelligence? Should your style be straightforward and businesslike or should you try to convey your own personality in your writing? Should you use humour? How do you make your application stand out from all the others?

As well as style, there are difficulties with content. Should you be completely honest? Should you write that you resigned from your last job even though you were sacked? Will writing something like, 'I have not worked for the past four years because I was at home with my young children' be read as, 'this person is going to ask for time off at regular intervals to look after her children.'? The vast majority of job applicants will have some problems in this respect, but those who have reading and writing difficulties will have greater difficulties.

Alternatives to literacy: Other ways of knowing yourself, and letting others know you

It's important to know what your personal strengths are, and to be true to yourself. Although writing is a way of defining yourself, of saying who you are and what you know, it's not the only way. Talk, body-language, clothes, personality, painting, drawing, video, are means of expressing ourselves and what we know. Each way communicates something different about us and how we see the world. We're partly fulfilling a need we all have to interact with others, to give and receive information and to show who we are. Seen as part of these many ways of expression, writing can only ever say a little bit of who we are and what we know. It's always incomplete.

Another important way of communicating is through drawing. Pictures bring lots of messages, conscious and sub-conscious. They encourage a very personal interpretation. This 'picture literacy', while less valued than being able to read and write, is just as rich and powerful a skill to learn as verbal literacy. Listening to someone who can 'read' pictures and say what a particular picture holds for them can be a revelation. A cartoon is good to look at and easy to 'read'. Cartoons without words can be understood by everyone, whatever their language. They are a straightforward and popular way of communicating. (See Chapter 21 where Victor Grenko and Stella Fitzpatrick discuss this more.)

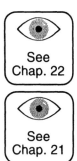

See Chap. 22

See Chap. 21

In books, pictures of the writer offer more than the written word alone. Whereas some writers feel that their words stand alone and to link the person with the writing is unnecessary or even wrong, in other kinds of books, like those published by Gatehouse or by a literacy scheme, a picture of the writer is a bond between reader and writer; a part of the promise that you could do this too; you, the reader, could also write a book. To summarise, instead of thinking of written language as 'the best way', we suggest that it is one among many ways of thinking, learning and communicating. The reason for learning written language is to increase your options, give you more flexibility. This is very different from saying that without literacy you can't think, learn or communicate adequately.

Conclusion

We have written about the relationship between literacy, strength and identity. We explained how literacy can be like a robber, sapping people's strengths and submerging their identity. We discussed how literacy, especially writing, can help people form their identity and share their strengths. We wrote about the conflict in identity literacy can bring, and about how we entrust our identity to the safekeeping of readers when we write. Finally we wrote about other ways of communicating which don't depend on literacy.

Our strengths create our identity. For some people, one of their strengths is literacy. For many others literacy is a negative force, sapping their other strengths. We all need to fight against that negative force:

- we need to value people's other strengths;
- we need to disagree when anyone treats literacy as if it is the be-all and end-all;
- we need to ensure that no-one gets their identity submerged in written language;
- we need to help each other use literacy, especially writing, as a positive force for getting to understand each other better.

Talking about literacy, strength and identity at the Worlds of Literacy Conference helped us to think about these issues. We hope this article has helped you think about them too.

Section 4:

Choice and Change

Learning literacy — or a new form of literacy — involves change: change of identity, of relationships with others, practical life changes. As part of this, the variety and power of different literacies often face people with choices. These changes and choices help shape people's lives and can also pose dilemmas and conflicts. Choice and change can be difficult and may have far-reaching effects.

Gender | Conflict | Inside/Outside | Adults | Public/Private

JENNY HORSMAN

14: The Problem of Illiteracy and the Promise of Literacy

People who are illiterate are described as 'chained in prison', 'disabled', 'caged and blinded', victims experiencing only 'death in life' (Callwood, 1990: 39). These media images screamed at us from the newspapers in Canada during 1990, International Literacy Year. Images that silence women judged to be illiterate, that portray people as helpless victims.

When I think back to the Nova Scotian[1] women I met in 1986, while researching women and literacy,[2] I know that these images do not reflect the role of literacy in their lives. The images do not allow the women I met to speak about their lives, about what *they* see as wrong and what *they* want to change. The women I interviewed were not victims, they were strong women surviving in the face of much violence.

Women's dependence – on men, on inadequately paid work and on social service assistance – is threaded through the lives of many women I interviewed. This dependence leads to violence: the violence of women's isolation in the household and sometimes actual physical violence; the violence of the drudgery of inadequately paid, hard, monotonous jobs; the violence of living on an inadequate welfare income and enduring the humiliation of receiving assistance. Some of the violence is spoken of and shared, but much is endured in the silence and isolation of the home.

See Chap. 18

The illusion that illiteracy creates women's problems obscures the violence of many women's lives. Our attention is focused, not on the way women's lives are organised, or *dis*-organised, but on women's failure to become literate. These women's lives are the context in which they experience the 'promise' of literacy, and dream of how different their lives will be when they improve their education level. Yet for these women there is little chance that this promise will be fulfilled, particularly through many of the training programmes women are offered, which serve instead to embed them more firmly in their current lives.

169

The Problem

The disorganisation of women's lives starts young. For many of the women I interviewed in Nova Scotia violence was a central feature of their experience at home and school. Frieda spoke of school and the violence she knew there:

> I couldn't take the criticism of the teacher, he just stood me up in class, I just couldn't do math at all. He used to call me retarded in front of the whole class of children and then they used to chase me around the school grounds when I went out for recess: 'Hey, look at the dummy. Look at the dummy'. And he put a dunce's cap on me every time he got a chance.

The construction of her as stupid was a silencing process until:

> One day he called me names and put me up at the front of the class on a chair with the cone cap that he made, and I felt stupid. So he said: 'Get up and go to the front of the class and sit on the chair please'. And I said 'You go to hell, please'. And I walked out the door.

But when she told me about her rejection of his authority she called herself 'stupid' for leaving school. She could not avoid the label of stupidity: if she stayed she was called stupid; if she left, that, too, was stupid:

> . . . when I quit school – well left school for reasons I just don't want to talk about – because it was *stupid* I guess to do that.

Girls are frequently shown that for them the valued education is preparation for a role of household work. The gendered division of labour in the household means that when help is needed in the home – especially when adult women are at work – it is often girls who are expected by their family to help out. Their school work is seen as less vital than their labour in the household. Barb explained:

> I was housekeeping, babysitting for Mum because she was working. The rest of them were in school. And then (my younger brother) came along. At the time Dad took me out of school and Mum had (my younger brother). I wasn't . . . (in school) for very long because Dad yanked me out . . . He said: 'She'd learn more at home than she'd learn there'.

Few of the women felt school was a place to think of careers:

> School never pushed . . . a career. They never pushed study hard, be a scientist or stuff like that . . . They just didn't seem to care, just as long as you go out of there. That's all they cared about.

For those working class girls, school was not a place that offered alternatives and options for the future. It was a time to get through, a place to leave.

The women who were living with men were often limited and controlled by the man's wishes. Jill had expected to be quite a traditional wife, but she had expected *some* life:

> Being married – I always believed myself to be married – you are there to cook and clean, look after the kids if you have them, look after the housework, but I always thought you'd get out too, you'd do things together. Like I don't believe a wife should go out, like a lot of them will go out to bars. I would never do something like that. But we didn't have *any* life at all.

Jill spoke of her husband's refusal to allow her space to continue her education:

> I never got through with it – just the studying – nobody would leave me alone long enough to study, between (my daughter) and (my husband). He didn't think that was such a hot idea either, I think he was afraid I would get a higher income than him.

Many of the women spoke of men stopping them from going to work, going to literacy class, or getting out of the house to go anywhere. Perhaps the description of 'death in life' is not a bad description of Jill's life at that time. I think she might have used it herself, as she said:

> If I had stayed, even now if I was to come back, I think I'd end up in a nut house because you can't just live with *no* social life, *no* communication. You just can't do it.

It is misleading to focus solely on literacy as limiting options. It makes the role of the man invisible.

Of course, the men were not solely responsible for the limitations set on the women's lives. For many women, children too, played a role. As Jane said: 'You're shut off from the world if you're just bringing up a child and working and nothing else'. It is not the children themselves though, so much as the assumption that women are solely responsible for their welfare that creates the limitations. Even if the women live with the children's father they are still seen to be *her* children and her responsibility:

> Even like at nights, if I can't be bothered with my own kids – which happens – he puts them into bed and says: 'Let your mother alone, let her study'. Which I find is good and for tutoring and stuff, he'll babysit.

In her account that he 'babysits', she is clear that it is *her duty* that he only *helps out* with.

Many of the women I talked to were bringing up children alone. As there are very few subsidised day care places available in the province, single mothers are in the impossible position of not being able to afford to work because childcare costs would eat up most of their income. The lack of services and the gendered labour market with few jobs paying adequate wages to women make it extremely difficult for single mothers to get off welfare.[3] With a minimum wage job, women could not pay the cost of transportation, babysitting and all the expenses of a family.[4] Many were left with no option but to endure the humiliation of welfare, but still feel as if there is something they should do to get off welfare. Many felt they were being told:

> You've put yourself in this position and you're not a very 'nice' person, a very 'good' person because you've *allowed* this to happen to you, you've *let* this happen to you, you've *made* this happen to you.

The women often talked about how awful they felt being on any form of assistance. As Alice said:

> I don't know, it must be the system, the ways it makes you feel. It's not a nice feeling, it's almost like the money is coming out of a worker that is sitting in front of you asking you all these questions, it's almost like it is coming out of his pocket or whatever.

Illiteracy is often considered to lead to isolation, especially for rural women. But women's isolation is created by many other aspects of social organisation. The power relations between men and women – men's control over access to a vehicle and over what women feel able to participate in – lead to women's isolated situation in the household, yet are usually seen as 'natural'. The gender organisation of society also makes it appear natural for families to live in a location suitable for the man's work and for women to stay at home as 'housewives'. When illiteracy is seen as the 'cause' of isolation, the illiterate woman is seen as responsible for her own isolation and attention is diverted away from sources of isolation embedded in the social organisation of women's lives. Many women suffer from their 'nerves' because of the isolation they experience and are desperate to find something that will take them out of the house:

> I've got to do something outside the house because, I don't know, I just get so tired of sitting here twenty-four hours a day, every day. I wouldn't really say I was depressed, but my nerves bother me, I get

real edgy real quick after so many days, and my head starts pound-
ing, I get migraines. I think it's just tension from being here all the
time.

With limited literacy skills, the only jobs available are hard heavy
manual labour. There is little 'choice' of jobs available in the Maritimes,
simply one minimum wage job or another. Women worked in factories,
laundries, or restaurants. There is little else available in the region, a
traditional area, for women who are unable to take on the clerical work
carried out by women with a higher education level, although even for those
with an education there are few jobs. Marion described the work at one
factory:

> You work seven days and get one day off, work seven days and get
> two days off, work seven days and get three days off, or whatever.
> And you work . . . 7.00 to 3.00, 3.00 to 11.00, 11.00 to 7.00. And it just
> got too much and I was bringing her up by myself at the time and
> living at Mum's . . . My nerves, my nerves were bad . . . I don't want
> to go back there. I find it too hard. I just get so tired.

Dorothy's experience shows the problems of doing shift work when caring
for children:

> There was a *very* lot of lifting, it really was . . . With the hours that you
> put in it was a long strenuous day and I had kids home to look after.
> I couldn't go home and go to bed and sleep, I couldn't do that because
> I had little kids to look after. So it really made it hard for me, you
> never got your sleep, that was the big thing, you never got your rest.

Rather than illiteracy chaining women to a 'prison', it is the disorganisation of some poor women's lives which creates many aspects of the
situation which traps them in the home, in routine, monotonous jobs, and
in dependence on men or welfare. No wonder women want to believe that
literacy will open the door to a different life. But, if we present their problem
as one of illiteracy we miss the disorganisation of the women's lives. This
disorganisation is often simply taken for granted as natural and will
continue to haunt many of the women, even if they obtain better literacy
levels.

The Promise

The promise of literacy is the promise of access to a different life. The
media tell us repeatedly that literacy is the 'key to a new life' and that, for
example, the wonder of letters has taken one woman from 'public assistance
to employment as building caretaker' (Crawford, 1990). Literacy offers the
promise of life free from worry about money, the possibility of surviving

from pay day to pay day, and a job with meaning. The popular image is that literacy offers access to an 'everyday life'. Susan described the life she hopes for:

> I'd like to have a career that I really want to do, not something you have to do because you need to live. And . . . further myself and some day be the president or be the owner of a company instead of always sitting down there being $4.50, $5.00 an hour. And I feel if you have a good job your life has a little more meaning to it, I really do, instead of this I don't know what I'm doing. My life has no meaning to it, other than getting up, going to school, looking after her, but if I had something to get up to in the morning, dress nice for, go out and meet the world, meet the . . . everyday kind of life – the things that go on in life, the things that go on in life that you need to handle. This way the least little thing gets you down because you don't go nowhere you don't do nothing. If I had a good job I could have a nice little home and do things that most parents do, take them to Florida, go to the Toronto zoo. Where can you go if you're here on mother's assistance?

She sees an 'everyday kind of life' as having a job with meaning and being able to afford to take her child to Florida. As she struggles with day to day survival, she dreams of the sort of life that the media implies is simply ordinary – the result of hard work through which anybody can become 'somebody'.

See
Chap. 13

Women felt that becoming 'somebody' and going 'somewhere' were the consequences of literacy. Betty contrasted how she felt when she was always at home and the sense of possibility generated by participating in the upgrading programme:

> As it was I wasn't going anywhere. I'm not going anywhere right now except for trying to study to get my Grade 12.[5] But now I can actually see a light at the end of the tunnel. There is something out there, all I've got to do is work.

Jill explained that being something was connected to having money: 'Well I am something, but I mean I'm not going to be poor. I want to be able to support us myself'.

Women said they were bored and had little to do and hoped that literacy and training programmes would provide something to fill the time. As Sandra said to her sister-in-law Frieda:

> . . . you must get bored. You don't go nowhere, do nothing. Her outing of the week is getting groceries. No wonder she's enjoying the school.

Taking on a literacy class offered the possibility of access to a broader world than that in the house. As Judy made clear: 'I'm even feeling better just learning, having something else in my mind besides the everyday'.

Women sought, through literacy, to achieve a different life for themselves, different possibilities for their children, a job or career which would provide meaning and offer freedom from continual worry about survival. As Alice said:

> I want to work . . . I want to work at something that I can enjoy getting up in the morning, where I think I'm accomplishing something, *where I can get paid a reasonable amount to live on.*

Questioning the promise

Although women pursued the promise of literacy, they also questioned whether it was really likely to be fulfilled. They knew, like Alice, that to ask for so much was 'asking for the moon and stars and everything else'. They contested the presentation of the reasons that literacy will make a difference. They doubted whether it really would make a person able to do a better job. As Betty said:

> People seem to like to have a person with a Grade 12 or college or university or whatever you want to call it. They seem to prefer that to somebody with a Grade 7, 8 or 9. . . . I don't know, they think you're smarter, they think you can wait on people faster and easier if you've got a (Grade 12). I don't think it (makes a difference) . . . I don't know, it seems to make them happy if they get a person with a higher education.

Women questioned whether literacy and the GED qualification (exams intended to be equivalent to a High School Diploma) really had the value that was claimed for it, at the same time as seeing it as the only way out from their current situation. As Alice said:

> The GED makes no difference to me, other than being able to say I have a Grade 12. But what good are they? I still haven't had anyone answer me that. They're as good as the paper they're typed on and you can say I have a Grade 12.

Many of the women knew that getting qualifications would not mean that they would get a job. Even with Grade 12, Alice did not get a job. She took one training after another, but in spite of all her qualifications, her problem is still presented to her by social workers as a lack of skills. Alice's real problem did not seem to be a lack of literacy skills or other qualifications, but the lack of jobs in the area. Although there is a common perception of an unproblematic connection between education and work, the social construction of the labour market sets many constraints on what work will be achieved with or without education. The dual labour market creates a category of exploitable workers and the gendering of the labour market 'ghettoises' women in underpaid areas, justifying low wages for women's work and categorising it as requiring little skill. However, skill levels are determined within a social context and are not an abstract measure. In addition, underdevelopment in the Maritimes provides a reserve army of labour for the industrial sector in central Canada. When the demand is high in Ontario or in western Canada, men leave the Maritimes to take up jobs. But in slack times they return, increasing the competition for jobs in the region. For women in the region, even with an education, the labour market is stacked against obtaining a job at an adequate wage.

Women swung between a belief that there were jobs out there and all they needed were qualifications, and fears that even with their GED there might be no light at the end of the tunnel – no job, no changed life.

> There's probably plenty (of jobs) out there, but you need a Grade 12 and qualifications and everything.

Several of the women said they were taking their upgrading classes so that they could get a job and then commented on the lack of jobs even for those with qualifications:

> When you go to get your education, there's a lot of people who still can't find work or get a job of any kind.

Women dreamed of careers, so different from 'just a job'; they hoped that literacy might open the path to this 'everyday life' as the media constantly told them, but they did not expect it. Finally they hoped only for the minimum – any job.

> It's more or less what grade you have nowadays. You hear it on the TV all the time: the better the grade the better the job and oh its stuck in my head – I get a better grade I get a better job – one job, it doesn't matter just as long as I get out to work, things would be a lot easier on (my husband).

Promises not fulfilled

Women hope that the promise of literacy can be fulfilled, although they know that it is unlikely. When women reach the literacy and training programme on offer in rural Nova Scotia many more of their hopes are dashed. Instead of helping them to escape from the web of dependence and the social service net within which many are entwined, the programme often embed the women more firmly in the social service definition of need.

To be eligible for many of the programmes, women had to be recommended by social service agencies which then evaluated their 'need' for them. It was not clear whose needs were being evaluated – social services 'need' to get a person off their 'rolls', or the woman's 'need' for a job. But, at the programme, women are told they must 'make a commitment' not just 'come here because you have to'. The women are in a double bind. They are referred to programmes and believe that their welfare is dependent on them going. One programme worker thought that when welfare workers sent the potential participants to her programme:

> It's their way of saying, 'Hey we can't give you welfare any more. Now, you have (to get some) skills and you have to look for work'.

The intertwining of programme and social service agency has consequences for the way in which women experience training programmes. Instead of escaping the social service system they become more firmly entangled in the client and worker relationship which characterises the social service system. One programme worker explained that her programme's close link to social services meant participants expected the educational programme workers to be like social workers:

See
Chap. 4

> They expect when they come in here . . . that we're going to set them across from the desk and that we're going to say: 'What have you done about this? What have you done about that? And are you going to do this and if you don't you are not going to get any more assistance'.

This relationship is structured into the interactions by the social service system and has implications beyond the individual success or failure of the client/worker encounter. Like the doctor-patient relationship, the client/worker relationship relies on diagnosis and prescription external to the learner.

Instead of being helped to free themselves from traditional expectations of femininity which can contribute to trapping women in the home, confirming the importance of an evaluation of their worth based on appearance, and limiting the jobs which it seems appropriate for women to do, training programmes frequently reinforce these values. Women are taught anger management and success is described in terms of appearance. Concern with appearance and attitude may seem appropriate to the programme workers, because such things can make a difference to whether the trainees have a chance of obtaining a job. However, this stress can reinforce traditional values and encourage women to accept gender roles and consequent limitations.

Training programmes also frequently locate women's problems of unemployment in their 'bad attitudes' rather than in the lack of employment in the area or in the gendered labour market. One job preparation programme combined upgrading skills and 'life skills'. The programme taught the skills of a 'good worker' such as punctuality, proper dress and attitudes through the rules and structure of the programme. The programme was organised to get the participants to acknowledge that they have 'barriers' to employment: they must learn 'appropriate' behaviour, appearance and communication.

See
Chap. 4

See
Chap. 9

Many of the programmes can be criticised for working towards creating 'good workers', rather than helping women to challenge the assumptions that 'the better the grade the better the job', and that 'they pay you good if you're good'. They do not often help women to question the assumption that they will be able to get office work if they take a training, even though the evidence of many women who have been unable to get work belie these beliefs, the women are left assuming that:

> All you have to learn is the secretarial skills like filing and shorthand and stuff like that. Then you can get into an office where you can make good money, $7 or $8 an hour rather than $4.

The promise of literacy for many of the women is that taking part in a programme will lead to qualifications which will enable them to get work and leave the house regularly. But, some women are not able to embark on training because the 'needs' of the basic literacy student are often identified as ones that cannot be met in upgrading and basic training programmes. Instead, they are offered tutoring in literacy by a volunteer,[6] often in their own home. The Basic Job Readiness Training Program excludes participants who do not reach a Grade 6 reading level on a test. One of the training programmes was considering excluding participants with less than a Grade 8, and another was considering testing potential participants and setting a minimum standard for entry to the programme. Frequently, students who need to work on basic literacy are accepted into a programme and then judged as having needs which cannot be met within the programme. Volunteers are brought into work with them using the Laubach Literacy materials (a structured set of phonics based materials). Literacy learners' needs are judged as too basic to be included within the institution. One of the instructors explained the problem and how she felt it would be perceived:

> For some of these, this place is their last hope and if we start saying that (they can't be in the program), they're going to say, 'Oh boy am

I in trouble because there's nowhere else to go'. Some of them really need that training, some of them really need a job, once they get a job even (as) a dishwasher then if they want to continue their academics they can go to upgrading class . . . or have a tutor or something, but the number one need when you're an adult is to get out there and earn yourself a living.

Women seek a changed life, often they look for meaning through the literacy programme, the challenge to think of something other than their daily life. But instead the programmes prepare women to fulfil their roles better. They offer women 'functional' skills for the life they lead: to write their shopping lists, cheques, letters to family. As one programme worker said:

> I think we have to go in and say literacy enriches this lifestyle, literacy will help you with better parenting, literacy will also show you how to make that welfare cheque or your husband's minimum wage go farther, through literacy we can show you how to build a garden and do it a fun way so that you can do it with herbs and seeds and cook with these things. In other words, we'll enrich the style of life that you like.

This position offers an alternative to the assumption that 'illiterate' people *should* change their lives, suggesting that they may not *want* to change their lives. Yet there is, in this formulation, the danger of concluding that without literacy, parenting is not adequate, money is wasted, or gardening cannot be done well. It can lead to women being offered a programme to do the 'everyday' better, when they are seeking to pursue dreams of a different life.

Finally, the minimum demand that many women have, is to get out of the house, to reduce their isolation, to share their experiences with other women. But many programmes offer only individual tutoring at home for their students. It may seem that this addresses the practical problems women often have attending classes. However, this 'solution' leaves the social organisation of women's lives not only unchanged but also unchallenged. Women remain isolated in the home and denied social contact and problematising discussion, unless opportunities to interact with other participants are structured into programmes. Women are denied even the minimal promise of literacy, to get out of the house and make some social contact.

See
Chap. 15

Even in the programmes where women do get to meet other learners in a small group the social time is often seen as irrelevant. Tutors frequently made a distinct separation between the social time, the chat, before the lesson started, and the *real* lesson. They spoke of trying 'not to get off track too much' and getting the students 'into their work' as quickly as possible. As one tutor said:

> I guess as I taught them I realised the only reason they had me here was so they could bake cookies and have tea and a social group. And one group, they never ever wrote their GEDs, they came about three times and they wouldn't write them. And we kept going out and going out and they just didn't write, so we dropped them off our case load because we came to the conclusion that they were there just basically (doing it) so that I'd come out and a couple of neighbours would come over and they'd have tea and cookies and they'd learn, but . . .

See
Chap. 9

This distinction between what is social and what is learning seems to differ from the intertwined sense of learning *as* social that the students appeared to want.

New Possibilities

Many literacy and training programmes do little to fulfil the promise of literacy. I would argue, along with many of the women I interviewed, that the promise cannot be fulfilled in the way that the media suggest. Instead, programmes *can* support women in their analysis and critique of the promise of literacy at the same time as helping them to improve their reading and writing skills. Programmes can help women in exploring and understanding the disorganisation of their lives. Programmes can help to reveal the myths embedded in the characterisation of the problem of illiteracy and the promise of literacy, as well as helping them to pursue their goals of literacy.

Programmes which listen to women's own accounts of their needs and support them in thinking critically about their own lives can help to free them from dependence and violence. When programmes are set up to encourage women to take greater control over their own learning and over the programme as a whole, the learning of literacy becomes, in itself, a tool for reflection and change.

Where programmes create space for the discussion of issues and for questioning the meaning of literacy, this can lead to exploring the unproblematic connection between education and 'getting ahead'. In this way the nature of the challenge of literacy can be broadened and the possibilities of social change strengthened.

Notes

1. The county where I carried out the study had a population of approximately 44,000 in 1981 (Department of Development, 1987). The population of the county is largely of British origin. Although early settlers of the area were Acadians, they were driven out of the area in 1755. There are three small communities of Nova Scotian black people in the County town and there is a small Micmac Indian community on the outskirts of the town. Both the black and native communities remain very separate from the white communities in the county.

   I interviewed 23 women with limited literacy, 22 were white women. One woman interviewed was mixed race, Native and Black. I have not identified this woman's race in my description of her, as that would deny her the promised confidentiality. The failure to explore the experience of Native and Black women in this study, was a joint result of the limits of my efforts and the process used to locate interviewees – referrals from programme workers of women in educational programmes. The separation of the Black and Micmac from the white community meant that few Black or Native students were involved in the education programmes I located, so I was only able to identify the one mixed race participant whom I interviewed. Although this was not my intention, it is clear that I have carried out a study of white women with limited literacy skills in the county.

2. A full account of the study appears in Horsman (1990).

3. Single mothers who need support must apply first for local assistance (municipal or county), then for family benefits from the province. A single mother receives $8,100 per year on provincial family benefits. On Municipal Allowance, a single mother would receive only approximately $5,220 per year (quoted in Williams (1988). However women are not eligible for provincial assistance until they have taken the father of their child to court.

4. Incomes in the area are generally low compared with Ontario. Many jobs, both for men and women, pay minimum wage which is four dollars and hour. For women much of the work available to them is part-time shift work. 47.6% of income tax returns in 1983 reported incomes of less that $10,000. The Statistics Canada poverty line was an income of $11,850 for a two person family in 1985.

5. Grade 12 is the top grade level in Canadian schools (outside Ontario). Grade 12 exam passes are needed for many jobs and to get entry into further or higher education.

6. I do not wish to argue against the use of volunteers *per se* as I believe they can be part of a programme where both volunteer and literacy student are learning in a more equal relationship. However they are often used simply as a method of saving money and cutting costs.

References

Callwood, J. (1990) Reading: The road to freedom. *Canadian Living* 39/41.

Crawford, T. (1990) I can read. *Toronto Star.* February 17.

Department of Development, Nova Scotia (1987) *Northeastern Region Statistical Profile.* Halifax: Dept. of Development, Nova Scotia.

Horsman, J. (1990) *'Something in My Mind Besides the Everyday': Women and Literacy.* Toronto: Women's Press.

Williams, R. (1988) Malign neglect. *New Maritimes* 11-12.

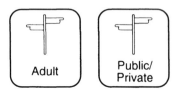

Adult   Public/
         Private

MARGARET HERRINGTON

15: Learning at Home: Distance Learning in Adult Basic Education

Introduction

Adults learn about literacy and numeracy in a variety of overlapping, and sometimes competing, literacy/numeracy worlds. At its most imaginative, adult basic education provision takes explicit account of these when students gather in particular settings to develop their basic skills. The issue of the relative access and quality merits of the various settings used is an ongoing one but is still under-researched. In this chapter I shall discuss how the Distance Learning Scheme within Leicestershire's Adult Basic Education Service has explored the curricular implications of learning basic skills in *home* settings. This has involved the use of the home both as a place for official sessions given by a paid tutor and as a main context in or from which students carry out a range of literacy and numeracy activities. I shall also attempt to clarify the relevance of this exploration for centre or college based ABE work.

Background

Although most current ABE provision is located in colleges and centres, it has not always been so. At the start of the Adult Literacy campaign in 1975, and up to the present day in some areas, adults who wished to develop their literacy skills were taught largely at home on an individual basis by volunteer tutors. Some aspects of this experience were well described but in general it remains an under-recorded part of ABE history. Any enabling qualities of the home context (for example, its accessibility) were heavily over-shadowed by its perceived disadvantages, namely, the isolation of students from each other and the difficulty in adequately monitoring and evaluating the provision with such large numbers to each organiser. The near wholesale shift to group[1] provision, fuelled by different access and quality criteria, also reflected a desire to banish both the hiding away of illiteracy and what some organisers perceived to be an over-reliance on volunteers. In addition, by basing groups in centres and colleges, literacy work could not be so easily marginalised and students would find more options for progression.

In turn, however, the full complexity of group provision was not properly described or evaluated and so in the access developments of the late 1980s (Open Learning Centres and Work-Based Learning), the so-called 'traditional group' began to be seen as static, old fashioned and unable to deliver, according to the new access and flexibility criteria. Despite this general dearth of in-depth evaluation, when Distance Learning was established in 1983 in Leicestershire (ALBSU Special Development Project 1983-85 and mainstream funding to the present day), the experience provoked a series of questions about the effects of particular settings on student/tutor roles and on student control over the time, place and pace of learning. In particular, it drew attention to the confining effects of those kinds of group provision which suggested to students that:

- the group or class was the sole or major place in which literacy and numeracy skills could be developed
- they would always learn best in the presence of other students
- tutors needed to be present for them to perform literacy and numeracy tasks.

The Leicestershire Distance Learning Models

Leicestershire's project was initiated in a rural area in which regular ABE groups met in community colleges, libraries and community centres and in which home tuition by volunteers was still offered when available and appropriate.

Its main objective was to establish a form of provision which would improve access to ABE by removing the practical problems of transport and by responding sensitively to the continuing confidentiality problem. There was some evidence locally that adults did still wish to hide their difficulties from their neighbours and indeed that they would not seek provision from local volunteers who may be known to them.

The first form of distance provision involved individual tuition at home by a paid tutor and on a regular four to six weeks basis, with distance tuition by post and telephone between sessions. The sessions themselves provided an opportunity to discuss and evaluate the work done and to negotiate an agreement about the subsequent four to six weeks. The distance work did not generally involve the selection of packages from shelves; an agreement

See
Chap. 6

See
Chap. 8

See
Chap. 4

could, for example, include tasks for the student such as undertaking a number of 'functional' activities (visiting a child's school teacher, the Job Centre, the Social Security Office), producing a first draft of a piece of writing, working on particular spellings; *and* tasks for the tutor, viz. preparing teaching material on a spelling topic, responding on tape to a piece of writing, collecting and sending off educational guidance information. A second form developed alongside this involving distance students meeting as a group once a month in students' houses. Individual work was negotiated and continued at distance and the group sessions were devoted to discussing, evaluating and planning the new work. Students therefore continued to use their homes for the bulk of their work but a general home setting was used for the official group sessions.

The Curriculum Effects

If 'curriculum' in this context is defined as a negotiated mix of content and process (what will be learned, when and how) aimed at enhancing student control over learning, *the experience of distance learning shifted the relative power of the negotiators and extended the choices available to both students and tutors.* These effects derived from the major elements in the model:

- learning in and from home settings
- devising individual programmes
- students working largely in the physical absence of tutors and other students
- the use of student-centred distance methods.

It is not possible to describe and analyse these in full here but it is important to record key observations about the significance of the home setting as a place of learning, and there seem to be three which are noteworthy:

(1) *The home is the student's territory.* In addition to the obvious convenience and accessibility of this setting, the student/tutor roles were altered. The tutor was a guest there; with permission, on the student's terms. As one student put it: 'If you had been snobby, I wouldn't have let you in'. For the tutor, exclusion would have involved a far clearer rejection that non-attendance at a class; it was a more exposed position. Students both felt more comfortable and also, in offering hospitality, were engaging in a more evenly balanced relationship.

(2) Most of the work done at home is carried out in the *absence of the tutor or other students,* and *at a time and pace of the students' own choosing.* This does not imply that students were operating in ideal conditions with no constraints; simply that they could and did choose very different time and pace combinations.

A recent student settled down to her writing every evening until a major piece was finished. Having hated history at school she decided to explore and write about the 17th century. This lady in her sixties had suffered a major stroke, had lost her ability to read and write, and had been wrongly informed by her GP that very little could be done: in fact, she recovered most of her literacy skills over a two year period in which she produced many sustained pieces of work. 'I get a longer time at it, plenty of time in my own leisure'. Other students have shown that they prefer to work in bursts and may then have some fallow periods. Several students have indicated that they get up at night to write. It is difficult to summarise the extent of the variations and, of course, insofar as other forms of provision emphasise the importance of writing outside group situations, then similar effects can be achieved. However, this kind of distance learning by definition involves these choices.

See Chap. 5

The effect of working without the tutor's presence needs more explanation. Once decisions had been made and materials devised as appropriate students reported: 'I like working alone . . . it feels my work . . . I've done it . . . nobody else' and 'If you'd been there, I'd have asked for help. In fact, I solved it myself'.

Students knew, however, that they had access to their tutor by telephone. They also knew that when the regular session arrived, they would have the opportunity to discuss both the process and outcomes with a familiar and interested 'partner'. Tutor presence at the regular sessions was geared to encouraging students to build up their self direction further; to the sharing and supporting of their curriculum decisions; and to evaluating outcomes jointly.

Students also noted the advantages of not having other students present when they were carrying out literacy and numeracy work (less noise, fewer interruptions, less chance of being watched by other students, freer to try methods which may be embarrassing in the presence of others). Those who used the group model drew the distinction between completing reading, writing or numeracy tasks when alone but then *discussing* and *evaluating* with others.

See Chap. 9

(3) *The home is a world of literacy in its own right* and often acts as a clearing house for a whole range of external demands. At the monthly personal sessions everyday literacy tasks could be considered in situ: manuals for various pieces of equipment could be examined as needed; private letters about financial or legal matters could be discussed; difficult phone calls requiring information or advice could be made on the spot; students with children having literacy difficulties at school could discuss possible courses of action and the tutor could meet the children concerned if appropriate; and relatives or friends who were also inter-

See Chap. 3

ested in seeking provision but who were too shy would sometimes sit in to see if they liked what was on offer. Overall, curriculum content seemed to be more real, more related to individual requirements and to involve more options than is often possible in centre-based work. This should not be taken to mean an undue concentration on functional tasks; the sheer range and quality of discussion in *private* settings was a notable feature of this work.

See
Chap. 12

In addition to this extended curriculum, tutors also gained from the opportunity to meet the students' 'significant others'. The tutor could see at first hand the constructive or destructive effects on the students of the family members around them. The question of how to build on or to counter these effects was an ongoing one. It was particularly difficult to witness the irritation with the 'brokering arrangements' when they involved unacceptable burdens for some partners: 'I don't want to do everything. He's got to learn', and distress for the students. Tutors could see when significant others were personally transmitting societal prejudice about 'illiteracy and lack of intelligence' to students. Sometimes it was possible for the tutor to discuss and work through these issues; even when it was not, these matters influenced curriculum process and priorities.

See
Chap. 14

In the case of the distance group model mentioned above, some of the advantages of the home were retained; students felt comfortable and able to take ownership of the curriculum in the group setting. When a new tutor arrived at one of the distance groups with a piece of work for them to do, they told her to put it away saying 'We'll show you how we prefer to work'. However, some part of the privacy was traded for the advantages of interaction with other students. In offering students a choice between the two, they decided whether or not they wanted to trade off in this way.

Though enabling in very significant ways, the home setting also carried some disadvantages. First, it was impossible to sustain work in that setting if the students' 'significant others' opposed it. Distance students in that position would arrange to meet tutors in neutral places and would use informal mailing arrangements. Second, in a very small minority of cases, students could not work in home setting when they had no physical space within the home to call their own, and no control over what members of the family might do with their papers. Third, and this was a question rather than a proven disadvantage, did successful and adult-centred home based work make progression through the rest of the education system more difficult? The actual progression of many distance learning students would suggest the opposite but for those who did not move into other courses the access and quality gap between distance learning and the available progression routes (few in rural areas) was marked. This of course is an argument for improving the quality of those routes rather than for jettisoning home-based work.

Conclusion

In terms of the early opposition to home-based tuition, this work suggests too hasty a rejection of it based on a narrow view of how it could be developed. The experience of these models of learning emphasise:

(1) The accessibility and potential quality of home-based work.
(2) The vital importance of remembering how little power many adults who have not succeeded at school feel they have in relation to colleges and centres used for educational purposes.
(3) The necessity for centres and colleges to build outreach/access programmes which harness official home-based work rather than ignoring it. (This is particularly important for Open Learning Centres which should not be restricted by the view that all literacy and numeracy work must be visible at the centre. They can be the bases from which distance work is organised.)
(4) The necessity for ABE workers in other educational settings to harness the potential of the home setting as the 'unofficial' base. If they organise ABE sessions which concentrate solely on task completion and if they regard home as the potential 'black hole' for homework, then they will not activate this resource. However, if the session also becomes the place in which work done elsewhere is discussed and evaluated, learning at home can be well harnessed. The question is not always one of home or centre-based work but of what kind of work is appropriate or best achieved in each place for any particular student.

See
Chap. 3

Notes

(1) Adult Basic Education Groups vary widely; they include groups of student/ tutor pairs who share a room but who otherwise work largely in isolation from each other, as well as groups which operate with joint themes and which often preclude any work based on individual interests. Many involve some mix of individual and group activity.

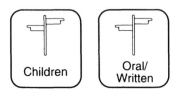

JEAN HUDSON

16: Catherine's Story: A Young Child Learns to Write

This is a story set in a particular world of literacy: a young child's development in writing during her first two years at school. In it, she progresses from purposeful early expression, which does not easily communicate to confident composition and control of standard English orthography. This very limited picture of her early progress in writing could be replicated in any infant classroom in Britain today. Teachers are becoming increasingly aware of the complexity of the writing process, and of the need to support more than spelling and handwriting when encouraging development. The implementation of the National Curriculum in English (1990) at Key Stage I has also increased many teachers' competence in devising appropriate activities for the development of both composition and secretarial skills in writing.

Catherine started school in September, 1988. She was four years and one month old. She is the older of two children, and like many young children entering schools today had enjoyed a wide experience with books and stories in her preschool years. She had also demonstrated an interest in letters and words and had attempted to copy them for herself.

See Chap. 10

She entered a classroom in a small rural school where children were encouraged to write independently from the very beginning, where many real purposes for writing were embedded in the ongoing classroom activities, and where children received very positive responses to their early attempts to convey meaning through making marks on paper. Catherine was therefore encouraged to see herself as a writer from the very beginning of her school career. Typical classroom purposes for writing included writing rotas, labelling displays and illustrations, recording observations from ongoing science experiments, writing stories and descriptions to share with other children, recording home and school activities and making posters and writing letters in connection with planned school events.

The teaching/learning strategies in the classroom included many wide and varied experiences with written language and promoted a lot of oral discussion about writing. The teacher also arranged a writing corner in the classroom which contained a wide variety of different things to write about, to write with and to write on. She was also concerned to provide practice in letter formation, and to develop children's awareness of word structure. Catherine was part of many shared writing activities with other children and with the teacher who often acted as scribe for the children's oral compositions. This scribing activity provided many opportunities for Catherine to share her ideas with others, to see speech translated into written symbols and to observe and discuss how written language works (top to bottom, left to right, spaces between words, etc.). The teacher also used this group activity to provide meaningful and relevant experiences connected with the formation of letters, the structure and conventional spelling of many common words, and the use of punctuation. Many of the scribed compositions were illustrated by the children and made into books of various sizes and formats to be added to the classroom reading collection. In addition, the teacher shared a wide variety of books with the children throughout the school day and she also shared her own writing. In fact, one of Catherine's favourite stories was the teacher's written memories of her own grandparents.

In the early stages, children were also encouraged to 'copy' their own recorded oral language, but this activity was only a small part of the much broader beginning writing curriculum provided for all the children. Before the end of her first term at school Catherine could perform this copying task without difficulty as illustrated in Sample 1.

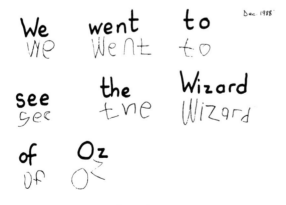

Sample 1

Her ability to compose written language independently had also progressed, and during a class project on 'Helpers' in January 1989, she wrote at length about helping with the shopping.

Here, she has clearly differentiated writing from drawing, realised that written language conveys meaning and mastered many letter shapes although there is still some confusion between lower case and capital letters. She also demonstrates a developing awareness of sound/symbol relationships.

Sample 2

Two examples of her independent writing one month later (Samples 3 & 4) illustrate increasing phonological awareness and an understanding of how speech is represented by written symbols. In Gentry's attempts (1982) to define stages in spelling development she has definitely reached the phonetic/communicative level. Her writing is quite readable and most of her invented spellings represent the entire sound structure of the word being spelled. She has made use of the available classroom resources for words such as grandad and holiday. Her ASDA story indicates some uncertainty regarding the left to right sequence in writing, although it may be that the size of her picture (drawn first) in relation to the size of the page was the main cause of her confused sequence. The two examples also demonstrate the recursive, non-linear nature of early writing development.

Sample 3   Sample 4

Samples 5 and 6 were composed in March, 1989 when Catherine was four years and eight months old. She had been attending school for 7 months. Sample 5, done in connection with class work on Noah's Ark, indicates increasing control over sound/symbol relationships (luvly) and recognition of consistency in spelling (bowt). It is interesting that she has noticed the apostrophe in Noah's and attempted to reproduce it in her own writing. There is also evidence that her visual memory for words that she has experienced in books and in the environment is beginning to be utilised as she remembers the silent e in her spelling of 'insade'.

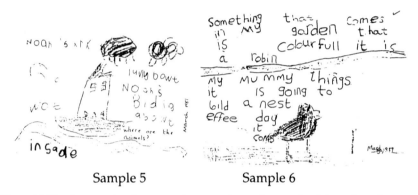

Sample 5   Sample 6

The riddle format in the opening section of sample 6 is related to a published text that she has experienced. Again, she has used the word resources that are available in the classroom, and her independent spelling increasingly approximates the conventional form. Catherine's spontaneous adoption of models from her reading experiences illustrates well the important link between reading and writing development at all stages of literacy.

Her 'news' in May, 1989 (Sample 7) is short, but word perfect and she also uses the apostrophe!

Sample 7

A final piece of independent writing at the end of her reception year (Sample 8) provides convincing evidence of the writing progress that has been made during her first year at school. She is keen to communicate her newly acquired ability to ride her bike (without stabilisers!) and recognises that writing is one appropriate medium for doing so.

She is writing in a most purposeful context and she has conveyed a considerable amount of information in this lengthier piece of writing. Indeed, she has even internalised the teacher's model in responding to the children's writing. After one year in school, Catherine is working well toward achieving all of the statements of attainment at Level 2 in the National Curriculum for Writing, Spelling and Handwriting (1990).

Sample 8

See
Chap. 5

Her non-chronological writing (Sample 9) at the beginning of her second year in school includes considerable detail and evidence of the use of writing for learning. The overuse of 'and' in joining ideas together is typical of early writers. It may be time for some explicit teaching about sentence demarcations, but the teacher's scribing and her experience with written language in books is also providing plenty of models for her learning of the conventions of punctuation. She has certainly noticed the question mark in written texts, even though she has not yet mastered its precise use.

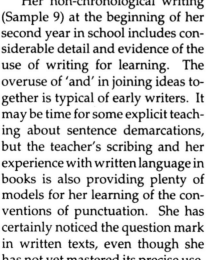

Sample 9

Her expertise in imaginative writing is shown in Sample 10, which demonstrates an increasing awareness and use of book language, and story content in her writing. There is also evidence that she is beginning to understand the structure of stories, and include a beginning, a middle and an end.

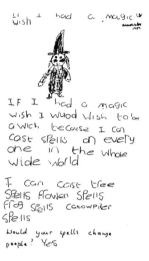

I wish I had a magic

IF I had a magic wish I wuod Wish to be a Wich because I can cast spells on every one in the Whole wide World

I can cast tree spells flower spells frog spells catterpiler spells

would your spells change people? Yes

Sample 10

Sample 11 (in March 1990) is another writing genre written in relation to a book about Norah, The Robot which the class have enjoyed. In it, Catherine demonstrates that she is a confident writer, and has an increasing awareness of the audience for her writing. She has mastered the conventional spelling of many monosyllabic and polysyllabic words.

Finally, she writes poems too, (Sample 12) and all readers can respond to her ideas about the hot summer sun.

Dear Nora   March '90
I hope you are having a nice time at the rubish Tip and I enjoyed reading your letters we have a wether chart up now and we are recording the wether we have got a thmoiter and it tells us how hot or how cold it is this is. Nora the end of my letter now
love from Catherine
xxxx xx ♡

Sample 11

At the end of her second year at school, Catherine is an avid writer, and a very confident one. She writes at length and has achieved Level 2 in the Writing attainment target of the National Curriculum. She is working toward Level 3 in Spelling, but ascenders and descenders in Handwriting (Level 2) have not been differentiated. The increasing use of lined paper in the classroom should help her to master this difference.

Catherine at age 6 enjoys writing, has a growing understanding of what being a writer means, and can identify many reasons

> The Sun   May '90
>
> The Sun wakes us up
> in the morning day at
> downing.
> The Sun is with us.
> Sweaty bodies in the Sun.
> Burning brintly.
> Cross tired Sleepy chidren.
> Hot lazy days.

Sample 12

for writing. Some purposes that she suggests are that people need to write to learn, to know what people said in olden days, to give a message, and to help other people learn to write! She also stresses that writers have to listen, watch, concentrate and think and that she can write poems, songs, jokes, stories, cards, letters and about her Barbie doll. When asked what happens to her writing, she is adamant that *it gets read*.

Catherine's future development in her world of literacy is dependent on her own choices, but it is also dependent on the school's plans for change and development. Many meaningful and relevant contexts for writing should be provided for her as well as continued positive response and encouragement from a wide variety of audiences. She also needs to experience many different purposes for writing with specific attention being drawn to the language and structure of different types of texts. Above all, she needs to continue to enjoy her writing activities, and to be surrounded by adults and peers who also enjoy writing and use it to fulfil wide and varied purposes in their daily lives.

Note:

From the samples included in this short case study, it is obvious that both Catherine and her teacher have contributed greatly to its writing, and I should like to thank them both. I look forward to following Catherine's writing development throughout her primary school.

References
Gentry, J.R. (1982) An analysis of development spelling in Gnys, at WRK. *The Reading Teacher* 36(2), 192-200.

National Curriculum Council (1990) *English in the National Curriculum* (No. 2). London Department of Education & Science.

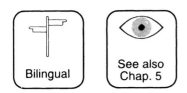

| Bilingual | See also Chap. 5 | Conflict | Oral & Written |

MUKUL SAXENA

17: Literacies Among the Panjabis in Southall

This chapter is based on an ethnographic study of the literacy situation that exists among Panjabis[1], particularly Panjabi Hindus, in Southall, an area of the Borough of Ealing, in the western part of Greater London. The total population of Southall is about 120,000. The South Asian population of Southall is approximately 69,000. Of the total South Asian population, about 77% are Panjabi Sikhs, 20% are Panjabi Hindus, and the rest are a mix of various other South Asian minorities, including Panjabi, Gujarati and Urdu speaking Muslims, and Gujarati and Tamil speaking Hindus. Since Sikh and Hindu Panjabis are in the numerical majority, one is more likely to encounter the use of spoken and written Panjabi, Hindi and Urdu in Southall than that of Gujarati, Bengali or Tamil.

The literacy practices in the Panjabi community in Southall, West London, have changed enormously since the first group of Panjabi men came to Britain in 1950s. The third generation Panjabis are now living and growing up in a much more varied and complex situation of multilingual literacies than the first and second generation Panjabis ever did.

See Chap. 3

In the first part of this chapter I present a case study of a Panjabi Hindu family. It shows how individual members of this family are exposed to and make use of different literacies in Southall. It also draws attention to the values they assign to these literacies. In the second part, I provide an historical account of the literacy situation in the regions of origin of Panjabis. It will be helpful in understanding their current literacy practices in Southall. In the third and final part, I look at the political, economic, social and religious processes that have shaped the multiliteracy situation in Southall since the Panjabis migrated to Britain.

Multiliteracy Practices in Southall: A Case Study of a Panjabi Hindu Family

This section provides an account of some of the literacy practices of individual members of a Panjabi Hindu family in Southall. It will provide examples of how they make use of different literacies in their daily lives and, hopefully, throw some light on the literacy repertoire and literacy practices of the Panjabi Hindu community and the larger Panjabi community in Southall. We shall see, in this section, how individuals in this community are exposed to different print media; how they make literacy choices for different purposes; and how they value different literacies in their repertoire.

This family consists of a 4-year-old boy, his parents and grandparents. I chose this family because its members are fairly representative of the Panjabi Hindu community in Southall. They are brought up and have lived in different cultural and linguistic environments in India, East Africa and Britain. They are of different age groups and sex; they have had their education in different political, religious and cultural climates; and they have different attitudes towards different languages and orthographies.

SCRIPT CHOICES AND RELIGIOUS IDENTITIES

> Panjabi is normally written in Gurmukhi script and associated with Sikhs.

ਨਸਲੀ ਭੇਦਭਾਵ ਦੇ ਵਿਰੁੱਧ ਸਾਲ
ਦੀ ਪਾਲਿਸੀ ਦਾ ਵਿਸਥਾਰ

> Hindi is normally written in Devanagari script and associated with Hindus.

नस्ली भेदभाव के विरुद्ध वर्ष
की नीति के बारे में बयान

> Urdu is normally written in Perso-Arabic script and associated with Muslims.

نسلی مناظرت کے خلاف سال ۔ پالیسی کا بیان

All three languages can be written in all three scripts. Everyday spoken Hindi and Urdu are very similar, especially in their grammatical structures. However, in certain contexts, users of these languages try to bring in the words of Sanskrit or Perso-Arabic origin in their speech and writing to show their allegiance to Hindus or Muslims.

This is one of the families in Southall with whom I have spent most time. Over the course of five years, I stayed with them on many occasions and observed their literacy practices. Initially, my visits to and stays with this family were a matter of hospitality extended to a student from their country of origin having the same linguistic background. However, over the period, the acquaintance gradually grew into a close relationship. As I was accepted and treated as a member of the family, I could participate in their day-to-day activities. This relationship also provided me with the freedom of questioning and discussing their actions and views, even though they were fully aware of my study and its purpose.

The literacy events presented below all took place but did not necessarily happen in one single day. In order to give the account more cohesion they are presented as if they occurred in a single day.

Grandfather (educated in the Panjab in pre-liberated India; migrated to East Africa before coming to England)
He takes bus no. 74 signposted in English 'Greenford' to go to the Community Club for the elderly people. There he reads a local newspaper in Urdu[2] about the South Asians in Britain, Southall's local news, and political news from India and Pakistan. He picks up a national newspaper in English, skims through it to get general news about British and international affairs.

He then walks down a few blocks to a publishing house which publishes a fortnightly newspaper to promote Panjabi nationalism in terms of its secular political ideology and Panjabi culture. He exchanges greetings with the editor in Panjabi and shows him a poem he has written in Panjabi/Gurmukhi in praise of Panjab rivers. The editor considers it for publication.

On the way home, he goes to a book store which specialises in print media (newspaper, magazine, children's and literary books, novels, etc.) from India, Pakistan and Britain in various South Asian scripts. He buys a Hindi film magazine from India for his daughter-in-law. He also notices advertising posters in English in the street.

At home, when his grandson comes back from school, he reads him a nursery book written in English.

Grandmother (brought up in East Africa with little formal education: learnt Hindi at home)
She waits for a bus, at the bus stop, to go to a Hindu temple. She does not read English. One of the buses that go to the temple is No. 36. When buses other than No. 36 come, she checks with the drivers (bus drivers in

Southall are mostly Panjabi) if the buses go in the direction of the temple. None does. No. 36 arrives with Hayes sign written in English. Though she does not read English, she recognises the shape of the word, because she sees it often. She also recognises the driver and the adverts on the bus. She boards the bus without feeling a need to check it with the driver. She compensates her lack of knowledge of written English by relying on her memory of certain objects, events, people, etc., and assistance from other people.

On entering the temple, she reads a notice in Hindi about the weekend's events at the temple. Inside the main hall, after offering prayers to each of the Hindi gods, she asks the priest about the date of a particular festival. The priest then checks a yearly magazine from the Panjab, written in Perso-Arabic script, about the Hindu religious calendar[3]. Later, with other women and some elderly men, she listens to a Hindu religious book read out in Hindi by the priest. Then she goes upstairs where there is a Hindu cultural centre and a library. She reads a Hindi newspaper from India there, and borrows a religious book in Hindi.

On the way home, she notices shop names displayed in bilingual signs in Panjabi-English, Hindi-English or Urdu-English. She goes into a *sari* (an Indian women's dress) shop. The shop has a English-Hindi bilingual sign outside. The shop owner is the president of the Hindi temple[4].

Father (Born in East Africa, but brought up and educated in England from an early age).

In the morning, he reads an English newspaper for national and international news before leaving for work. At work, he supervises about 250 workers of South Asian origin in a factory. As and when required, he also mediates, as an interpreter, between the workers and the factory bosses. He also has the responsibility of making available bilingual materials published by social service agencies on safety, workers' legal rights, medical benefits etc. in the factory.

After work, in the evening, he goes to a Hindu temple where he is a member of the temple executive committee. With other committee members, he prepares a draft letter in English about the annual general meeting to be sent out to the registered members of the temple. It was agreed that when the temple has enough funds, the committee will send English-Hindi bilingual letters and notices to its members, as one of the roles of the temple is to promote Hindi. At the moment, the temple has only an English typewriter. The committee members also prepare some hand-written notices in Hindi for the temple notice board regarding the agenda of the annual general meeting.

On the way home, he notices some new Sikh nationalistic and communal slogans on street walls written in Panjabi. He discusses these slogans with his family when he comes home. At home, his mother reads to him from a weekly Hindi newspaper published locally about some local news an some news from the Panjab. This newspaper also has a few articles on Indian Hindi films written in English which he reads himself.

Mother (born, brought up and educated in the Panjab during and after reorganisation period of the Panjab in India before coming to England for marriage)

In the morning, she takes her son to a nearby nursery. She brings back a note in English from the teacher about some activity which the child and the parents have contributed to. She shows it to her husband in the evening. He reads it and explains it to her in Panjabi.

After finishing the household chores, she gets a little time to read a few pages from a Hindi novel. Later, with her mother-in-law, she writes a letter to a relative in Delhi. They discuss and write the contents of the letter in Panjabi-Hindi mixed code using Devanagari script. She also writes a letter in Panjabi-Gurmukhi to a friend in the Panjab.

In the evening, before putting her son to sleep, she tells him a story in Panjabi.

Son (born in Southall)

In the morning as he enters the school, he sees bilingual signs. He can distinguish between Gurmukhi, Devanagari and Roman scripts. In the classroom, he is exposed only to the Roman script for teaching and learning purposes.

At home in the afternoon, his grandmother sends him with a small shopping list in Hindi/Devanagari to a corner shop next door. The shopkeeper records the goods sold to the boy in Hindi/Devanagari in his ledger[5].

During the day, the boy observes his parents and grandparents using different literacies for different purposes.

Dinner time

One of the topics discussed during and after dinner is why the child should learn Hindi or Panjabi. The grandfather wants his grandson to learn Panjabi in the Gurmukhi script when he goes to school, but not in the Sikh temple. He thinks this way his grandson can learn Panjabi and retain Panjabi culture. He favours Panjabi because it is also the official language of the Panjab state. However, grandmother, mother and father think that the child should learn Hindi/Devanagari. Grandmother and father take more of a religious stance whereas mother takes the nationalistic/secular stance. Grandmother and father think that it is important to learn Hindi to retain Hindu culture and religion; whereas mother thinks that the child should learn Hindi because it is the national language of India. A further argument put forward in favour of Hindi related to the interpersonal communicative functions of literacy: grandmother, mother and father argue in favour of Hindi by saying that with the knowledge of the Hindi script the child will be able to correspond with the relatives both in Delhi and the Panjab, whereas the knowledge of the written Panjab would restrict him only to the Panjab. Grandfather is outvoted, and it is decided that the child would go to the Hindi voluntary classes held in the Hindu temple initially and later would also opt for Hindi in school.

In the above section, I have talked about what individual members of this family do with different literacies in different situations, and how they value these literacies. In the following two sections, I will address the questions: why do these people make different literacy choices in their everyday lives the way they do, and how are these choices shaped in different social conditions in which they are living or have lived? These questions will help us understand that the multiple literacy choices Panjabi individuals of Southall make in their everyday literacy practices reflect their differing ideological way of thinking. Nevertheless, rather than restraining their actions, these choices provide them with multiple identities and freedom to operate in different worlds of literacies to achieve different goals. These questions will also reveal the fact that a decade or so ago one would not have encountered this kind of multiplicity of literacies in Southall as reflected by their literacy practices.

Literacies in Places of Origin of Southall Panjabis: An Historical Account of Cultural Practices in Different Social Conditions

This section outlines the historical literacy background of the Panjabis who live in Southall. The historical literacy situation presented in this section is reconstructed through in-depth interviews with Panjabi community leaders, elders and other individuals in Southall, and on the basis of various studies of Panjabis in the Panjab and Delhi.

Panjabi Hindus in Southall have migrated from India and East Africa. Those from India are either from Delhi or different rural and urban parts of the Panjab.

Literacies in the Panjab

There are three main phases in which people have been mobilised around language and literacy in the Panjab: from the turn of the century to the Independence of India in 1947; from the Independence to the reorgani-sation of the Panjab state boundaries in 1966; and from 1966 to the present time. During first phase, there was a movement to replace Urdu/Perso-Arabic in schools, courts and official institutions with the vernacular mother tongues, Panjabi and Hindi. At the same time, there was competition between those who wished to promote Panjabi/Gurmukhi or Hindi/Devanagari. In the post-independence period, during the second and third phase, the language/literacy cleavage has been exclusively between Hindi and Panjabi (cf. Gopal, 1968; Das Gupta, 1970; Brass, 1974; Jones, 1976).

There are Panjabi Hindus in Britain who were brought up and had their education around and before the independence period. At that time, the political and religious situation was such that among Panjabi Hindus a positive feeling towards Hindi-Devanagari-Hinduism and negative feeling towards Panjabi-Gurmukhi-Sikhism were running very high. Panjabi-Gurmukhi did not have any support in education, administration and mass media. At that time, the languages used as media of education in schools were Urdu/Perso-Arabic and English/Roman. Hindi and Urdu, written in either the Perso-Arabic or Devanagari scripts, were the language of literate exchange. Panjabi/Gurmukhi was only promoted by schools and volun-tary classes run by the Sikh religious and political institutions. Hindi was widely supported and learnt by Hindus and by many Panjab-speaking Hindus through religious and political institutions. Access to Panjabi-Gurmukhi and Hindi-Devanagari depended on religious affiliation, and the knowledge or Urdu/Perso-Arabic and English/Roman depended on whether somebody had had formal education.

Those Panjabi Hindus in Britain brought up in the post-independence period (1947) were socialised into a different socio-literacy environment. At that time, the Muslim population had become established on the Pakistan side of the Panjab and Urdu was no longer the language of administration and education. In the Indian Panjab, the main political and religious rivalry was between Panjabi and Hindi. As the education curricular options provided Panjabi and Hindi, educational choices by Panjabi Hindus and Sikhs reflected the wider religio-political environment prevalent at that time. Panjabi Hindus with strong Hindu tendencies learnt Hindi in Devanagari script.

Another group of Panjabi Hindus I encountered in the Southall context were those brought up in post-reorganisation (1966) period in the Panjab. At that time, Panjabi had become the Panjab state official language and

Panjabi in Gurmukhi script was the first and main language of education in schools. Hindi and English as subjects of study were introduced in the fourth and sixth years of schooling, respectively. Even those Panjabi Hindus who had very strong Hindu tendencies had to face this practical problem: if they did not encourage their children to be proficient in the Gurmukhi script, then their children would not stand good chances of competing with the Panjabi Sikh children. Therefore, the motivation for the children brought up during this third phase to learn Panjabi/Gurmukhi was of a different kind from the ones who were brought up before the reorganisation period. Hindi in Devanagari script in this situation acquired only a second place in terms of the comparative importance of the language in the lives of these children. This relative importance of Hindi and Panjabi was also evident in the mass media. For instance, as soon as the government started encouraging the Gurmukhi script in the school system there was a concomitant decrease in the publication of books in Hindi and an increase in the Panjabi books. The use of Panjabi also increased in radio broadcasting. The sociolinguistic situation in the post 1966 period shows clearly people's, especially Panjabi Hindus', sensitivity towards the change in the official importance assigned to Panjabi/Gurmukhi, as opposed to the religious importance of the language/script.

To sum up, in response to the domination of Muslim religion and their Urdu language and Perso-Arabic script in the Panjab, there was a growth of Hindu and Sikh religious revival movements and the literature associated with them at the turn of this century. In consequence, Sikhs came to attach increasing significance to the writing of Panjabi in the Gurmukhi script as the language of the Sikhs and of the Sikh religion just as Hindus developed an attachment to Hindi in the Devanagari script. Close symbolic linkages, therefore, were made between Panjabi, Hindi and Urdu with Gurmukhi, Devanagari and Perso-Arabic scripts for religious reasons.

However, all the three scripts can be and have been used to write the three languages, Panjabi being the main language for informal discourse. There was incompatibility between the competence in Devanagari/Perso-Arabic scripts and Hindi/Urdu languages if these languages were not learnt formally. As there was more emphasis on learning the scripts to appreciate the religious scriptures written in these languages, many people had passive knowledge of formal Hindi/Urdu. Many of them spoke in Panjabi in their day-to-day lives, but wrote it in Gurmukhi, Devanagari and/or Perso-Arabic scripts. A Hindu might write a letter to a relative in other parts of the Panjab or in the Delhi in Panjabi language but in Devanagari script. This choice of script could simply be a matter of mutual convenience for the writer and reader or a matter of symbolising Hindu solidarity. In the same way, the choice of Gurmukhi script might be made as much for practical as ideological reasons. Although people in the Panjab have learnt and used different languages and scripts in different political, religious and educational environments over the period of three different phases, the symbolic linkage between language and literacy has been maintained for religious identity since the turn of the century.

See
Chap. 11
Chap. 13

Literacies in Delhi and East Africa

Patterns of literacy of Panjabis who came from Delhi and East Africa are not as complex as those who migrated from the Panjab. Delhi saw the influx of Panjabi refugees after the partition of India who came from communal war—stricken Panjab. After independence Hindi/Devanagari became the official language and the language of education in Delhi. Sikhs and even those Panjabi Hindus who had strong loyalty towards Panjabi had little choice but to learn Hindi/Devanagari, and to operate in that literacy environment. The majority of Panjabi Hindus, on the other hand, identified themselves with Hindi – Hindu tradition and, thus, found the language and literacy situation of Delhi in their favour as compared with the Panjabi Hindus in the Panjab who had to fight for it. Pandit's (1978) and Mukherjee's (1980) studies show that the sociolinguistic situation among the Panjabi Hindus in Delhi was generally such that they chose to relegate Panjabi to the status of spoken language in the home, and use Hindi for social and written interaction, either as their religious identity or for practical needs. In contrast, Sikhs maintained the Panjabi language in Gurmukhi script as a symbol of their religious identity.

Panjabi Hindus and Sikhs in East Africa had similar attitudes towards Hindi and Panjabi literacies as did many of their counterparts in Delhi and the Panjab.

Minority Literacies in the British Context, 1950s-1980s: Differing Cultural Responses to Changing Social Conditions

The functions of literacies in the literacy repertoire of Panjabis have been changed, elaborated and redistributed, since they arrived in Britain. This section looks at the changing social conditions in Britain since the arrival of Panjabis and their differing cultural responses to these conditions in the context of proliferating functions of home/minority literacies (viz. Panjabi, Hindi, Urdu). The information presented in this section is gathered through my interviews with various people in the Panjabi community (such as businessmen, community leaders, teachers, intellectuals, factory workers, housewives and students); through detailed observations in Southall over

POLITICAL, RELIGIOUS, SOCIAL SUPPORT TO & USE OF MULTILITERACIES
IN THE LIVES OF PANJABI HINDUS: CHANGE & MIGRATION

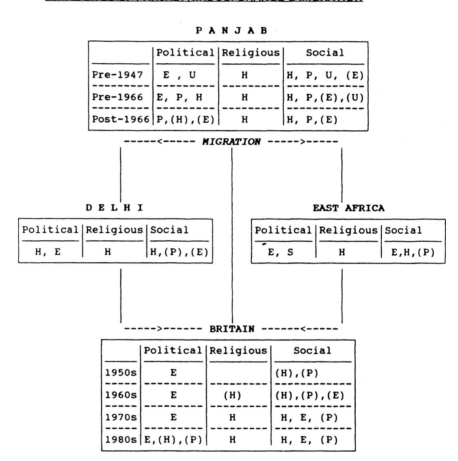

P A N J A B

	Political	Religious	Social
Pre-1947	E , U	H	H, P, U, (E)
Pre-1966	E, P, H	H	H, P,(E),(U)
Post-1966	P,(H),(E)	H	H, P,(E)

-----<----- MIGRATION ----->-----

D E L H I

Political	Religious	Social
H, E	H	H,(P),(E)

EAST AFRICA

Political	Religious	Social
E, S	H	E,H,(P)

----->------ BRITAIN ------<-----

	Political	Religious	Social
1950s	E		(H),(P)
1960s	E	(H)	(H),(P),(E)
1970s	E	H	H, E, (P)
1980s	E,(H),(P)	H	H, E, (P)

Note: In the diagram, literacies represented inside the brackets have or had
relatively less support and/or use. Literacy symbols: P (Panjabi), H (Hindi),
U (Urdu), E (English), S (Swahili)

the period of five years; and through various multidisciplinary studies of Panjabi communities in Britain.

Literacies in the 1950s

The first South Asian Panjabi-speaking men arrived in Southall in the boom years of the 1950s as a response to Britain's enormous need for an unskilled labour force (Harox & McRedie, 1979; Southall, 1981). Since then the composition of Southall South Asian population has changed enormously. Till around 1960, the Southall Asian population consisted of mainly Panjabi Sikh and Hindu men from India. The main literacy activity at that time was writing letters in Panjabi and Hindi to their families and friends in India. If one was illiterate, one could seek help through a friendship network. Since their aim at that time was to earn as much money as possible and then go back to India, these men usually worked on shifts, and lived in cheap accommodation shared by many others. They in fact preferred to rent houses with shared kitchens, bathrooms and toilets in order to save money to send home (cf. Jung, 1985). Men working on different shifts even shared beds to save the money. Sometimes, in such situations, the only way of communication between these men sharing beds or houses was to leave notes in Panjabi or Hindi. There were very few who knew English and those who did acted as interpreters and translators between the managements and the workers.

Literacies in the 1960s

The 1962 Commonwealth Immigration Act changed the demography of Southall and with it its literacy situation. The widespread belief that the impending legislation would be that of a complete ban on immigration increased the flow of immigrants from South Asia into Britain. By this time, these men were well enough established in Southall and were able to bring their wives and children to join the. Once here, these parents looked for ways in which they could advance the educational prospects of their children. As children started going to schools, literacy in English assumed importance. On the one hand, to survive and to be successful in the British system of schooling, children needed to learn English. On the other hand, once a contact was established between the schools and linguistic minority community, letters in English began to arrive from schools. They would be about, for instance, children's progress or events taking place in the school, etc. In order to communicate with the schools' staff or authorities, parents needed literacy in English too. In most cases they got help from someone who knew English in the community/friendship network. It was then for the first time, spoken and written English, the language of host community outside home began to make inroads into homes in the form of school correspondence and children's books.

The material ties in Britain were established when Panjabi men bought houses for their families and sent their children to schools. Socio-economic obligations in Britain, thus, began to assume greater importance. Other ways in which English literature made inroads into the homes were various types of house bills, mortgage and insurance papers, etc. For reasons such as better living standards, independence, prestige in the community, elimination of rent payments, or even income from lodgers, Panjabis were becoming owner-occupiers of the properties in Southall. This, inevitably, brought financial pressures on the families and many women had to find some kind of work. However, poor English, cultural barriers and responsibility for rearing children made these women an obvious source of cheap labour for the homeworking industry (cf. Wilson, 1978). For those men and women who were well motivated to climb the socio-economic ladder by securing better jobs and avoiding poor working conditions and shift work in factories, it became imperative for them to learn English. This brought about the need for adult literacy classes in the area. English was no longer just a language of the host society that one could get by using the friendship network, it was becoming a reality of their daily lives for the full participation in the wider community. They began to take interest in the social, cultural, economic and political aspects of the host country with which their future was becoming associated. This need was mainly fulfilled by radio, television and English newspapers since there was not much contact with the host community at social level. The absence of contact between the two communities was mostly because of lack of interest among the host society to let the 'immigrant' minority community participate in their social lives. The basis for this discrimination was racism.

A the settlement grew in size, the social networks of these people began to be confined to immigrants from specific areas, castes or groups of villagers. With the development of social networks, social obligations in Britain became more important than the links with families in India. As a result, written communication in Panjabi and Hindi became less frequent between India and Britain and more frequent within Britain.

Literacies in the 1970s
The period around 1970s brought further changes in the demographic situation and literacy environment in Southall. There were three reasons for these changes: (1) decline in the British economy; (2) increasing cultural and linguistic gap between migrant parents and their children; and (3) arrival of South Asians from East Africa as political refugees

South Asians, like other groups of workers, were involved in the industrial conflicts during the recession in the late 1960s and in 1970s. With the realisation that they would not be returning to India, and with the blockage of social mobility due to their low earnings or high unemployment conditions during the recession, they found themselves fixed in working class jobs (Westergard & Resler, 1975). Their greater participation in industrial disputes along with their white counterparts brought about a working class consciousness among them (cf. Rimmer, 1972). They became more involved in Trade Union activities at work and took greater interest in politics at community level. This brought in greater reliance on literacy activity among these people to achieve their political goals. English literacy became necessary to maintain and to develop contacts with the national Trade Unions, and to understand and to participate in their activities. Posters in Panjabi and Hindi were also used to inform the local minorities about the Trade Union movement and to encourage greater local participation. The local newspapers in Panjabi and Hindi also played a role in achieving this political goal. The second generation Panjabis, having gone through the British school system, found a new role in contributing towards written communication in English as they had a good command of English.

As the recession deepened, the level of unemployment increased along with discrimination and racism (cf. Rimmer, 1972; Taylor, 1976; Smith, 1977). Some politicians used the 'immigrants' as a scapegoat to create the myth that they were in the way of the native labour force in finding jobs. As the racism against these minorities increased in the wider society, the potential employers also discriminated against them. Demonstrations against racial violence in 1970s by British-educated South Asian youths in Southall (Southall SWP, 1979) proved that, unlike their parents, they were much more prepared to take direct action in defence of the interests and identity. As the British political and economic environment became instrumental in transforming the Panjabis' immigrant identity into a new British working class identity, it also created a social environment in Britain which made Panjabi youth think about their own cultural identity. The Panjabi and Hindi languages and associated literacies became significant resources for the construction of their distinct cultural identity.

The same period also saw the development of voluntary language classes in Panjabi and Hindi, with emphases on literacy. Also, a greater demand for these languages to be taught in the schools was made by the parents, as the linguistic and cultural gap between first and second generations began to surface.

In the beginning when the Panjabi families came to this country, the assimilatory forces into the 'host' society were compelling. The political trend of the host country was to assimilate the newly arrived immigrants into the host society through the education system as quickly as possible. A great emphasis was put on learning English. The Panjabi parents themselves saw English as a passport to success in British society and education system, but at the cost of home languages. Some people in the education system were convinced and led parents to believe that if children spoke and learnt their home languages, it would hinder their progress in learning English and thus, access to the school curriculum[6]. Gradually English became the main language of communication for children at school and home alike. This led to a communication gap between parents and their children. This was felt more by mothers who were not fluent in English. This further led to a conflict with their cultural beliefs, such as marriage and religion. Having been brought up in a western cultural system, the second-generation children saw the arranged marriage system and their parents' religious beliefs as backward (cf. Dhir, 1975). The parents found this situation very threatening to their cultural identity and, to repair the situation, the South Asian community made a concerted effort to open temples where children could learn and appreciate their religions, cultures and languages. The arrival of South Asian political refugees in Britain from East Africa around this time was of great assistance and morale boosting in building up this infrastructure. Unlike the Panjabis from India who came mainly from villages with little or no education, the new immigrants from East Africa were well educated and had had the experience of maintaining their languages and cultures through voluntary efforts there.

Literacies in the 1980s

The period of the 1980s brought in further changes in the literacy situation in Southall, mainly in the context of home literacies. For the first time since the arrival of these Panjabis, the religious division between the Sikhs and Hindus began to surface. Their sociolinguistic history provided them with the symbols, i.e. either Gurmukhi or Devanagari script, to emphasise this religious division. This process began to take shape with the politically motivated communal violence between Sikhs and Hindus in the Panjab state in India, which led to the assassination of India's prime minister in 1985. The assassination resulted in communal violence in the Hindi speaking states of India, the worst violence being felt in Delhi. Southall in Britain had by then become the main Sikh militant centre outside India which supported the cause of an independent Panjab as a separate Sikh nation. The self-proclaimed president of the perceived Sikh nation, the Khalistan, had his office in Southall. This office issued passports (to those Sikhs who belived in the cause) written in Gurmukhi, symbolising the Sikh nation. A Sikh temple there became the main centre for promoting the Sikh political cause and engaged in a renewed effort of teaching Panjabi in Gurmukhi script. Those Panjabi Hindus who used to visit the Sikh temple stopped doing so after the temple took this political stance. Some of them started sending their children to learn Hindi in the Hindu temple instead.

The Hindu temple had thus become a main centre for promoting Hindu culture and the Hindi language for those Hindus who dissociated themselves from Sikhs and the Gurmukhi script. These Hindus did not mind their children speaking Panjabi, but considered Devanagari, and not Gurmukhi, to be the fit written medium for a Hindu child to be able to appreciate the Hindu scriptures. However, there was a small proportion of these Panjabi Hindus who preferred their children to speak Hindi rather than Panjabi, and to learn Devanagari and not Gurmukhi script. Their preference for Hindi-Devanagari over Panjabi-Gurmukhi was not due to the fact that they were Hindus, but because of their positive attitude towards Hindi for different ideological and practical purposes. These Panjabi Hindus think that since Hindi is a national language and a language of wide communication in India, it is the right language for an Indian to learn in order to maintain an Indian cultural identity. In addition, the mastery of it also provides a better chance in keeping business contacts and links with their relatives in India.

Besides these three groups of Panjabis in Southall who are motivated by either the religious or nationalistic ideology, there is a fourth group of Panjabis. This group is comprised of both Hindus and Sikhs, and is motivated by a socialist political ideology. Unlike those who support the Khalistan cause, this group believes in an Indian national cause. They see the Panjab as a Sikh-Hindu state within the Indian political system. They also believe in the maintenance of the Panjabi language in the Gurmukhi script as an emblem of Panjabi culture rather than the Sikh religion. Similarly, they are very clear about treating Hindi-Devanagari as a national language of India, in contrast to those Panjabi Hindus who see it as an emblem of their religious identity. They disagree with the adoption of Hindi-Devanagari at the cost of Panjabi-Gurmukhi by the Panjabis. This group, therefore, has added a new symbolic value to Pajabi-Gurmukhi for one cultural identity to all Panjabis, Hindus and Sikhs. It is important to note here that the development of this secular identity among this grouping of Panjabis has come directly in response to the social conditions within the Panjabi community which divided the community on religious grounds.

Educational role of minority literacies

In the context of education, during 1980s, the Sikh-Hindu religious polarisation became prominent. In schools, most Panjabi Hindu children chose to learn Hindi and the Panjabi Sikh children chose Panjabi. By this time, Hindi and Panjabi were offered as part of school curriculum in the secondary schools in Southall. The print environment in the schools at all levels had begun to reflect the multicultural and multilingual nature of the local communities. During the period in which I carried out my fieldwork, multiliteracy posters in Panjabi, Hindi and English were seen on classroom and school corridor walls. They depicted curriculum contents (e.g. science and arts projects) and cultural aspects (e.g. food, religion, dresses, etc.) of the school and the community. Doors of head teachers' rooms, staff rooms, classrooms, school offices, toilets, etc. bore labels in multiliteracies. This multiliteracy environment in the schools that the third generation Panjabis are being exposed to was not experienced by the second generation.

Commercial role of minority literacies

Another development that became instrumental in boosting the home literacies was the boom in the British economy during the 1980s. During this period, the government's enterprise initiative schemes gave encouragement and support to new businesses. Many Panjabis in Southall, who were in low-paid jobs in the industry and other institutions, took advantage of these initiatives and set up their own businesses. Most of their business was in the area of trading consumer goods such as food and clothing, suitable to the way of life of the Panjabis in Southall and neighbouring areas. Since not many of these items are produced in Britain, the obvious market is India and other South Asian countries. The import of these goods has renewed the link of the Panjabis with their country of origin.

Those businesses that deal with large international exporters from India can communicate in written English, but those importing from small, local industry through friendship and familial network in India have to rely on Hindi and Panjabi literacies. This provided a new role for home literacies as facilitators of international business.

As the purchasing power of the local community increased, more people began to eat out, and the role of home literacies proliferated too. They find the Indian restaurants which offer multiliteracy menus more friendly and authentic and less intimidating. If one visits shops in Southall catering for daily consumer items – food, clothes, utensils, toiletries, jewellery, decoration, books, newspapers, magazines, stationery, etc. – one can see bilingual labels in Panjabi, Hindi and/or English on the items and the shelves. This literacy environment in the shops especially facilitates the shopping of housewives, and older men and women as they tend to have little or no command of written English. Also children are often sent with shopping lists in home literacies to corner shops. Many small family business make their everyday inventories of their stocks in home literacies. Children from such families learn home literacies informally while working alongside their parents in the shops.

Institutional role of minority literacies

It is only in the past decade that the social service provisions (DHSS, Police, Immigration etc.) have been made available in minority languages (through interpreters) and literacies (through translations) by the Local Authorities in Britain. This has come about in response to the continuing demand by the linguistic minority communities as citizens of their right to resources provided by the state. One can find in social service agencies (such as hospitals, community relation office, citizen advice bureaux) leaflets about health, safety, law, immigration, etc. written in Panjabi, Hindi, Urdu, Chinese, Polish, etc. besides English. Such information provided in home languages has helped many women, particularly housewives who, either due to poor command of English or due to other social and domestic reasons, cannot get independent professional help in areas of health, hygiene, child care, women's rights in marriage, etc. Similarly, for the general linguistic minority communities information regarding law, immigration, housing, etc. is now more accessible. This material, for those who do not want to rely on networks of friends and family, has meant that the personal problems need not become public knowledge. They are now, therefore, in a position to achieve personal freedom and independence.

As the minority languages like Panjabi and Hindi have gained official status, it has opened up the job opportunities for bilinguals who have good command of English and one (or more) of these languages, especially in the literacy skills. Although many of them have had school or college education in these languages in India, they need to pass professional examinations conducted by British language institutions, such as, the Institute of Linguists and the Royal Society of Arts to qualify as interpreters and translators. To obtain jobs as translators and interpreters, it is no longer enough to be able to speak, write or have had an education in these languages.

However, these recognised standards and the job prospects linked to them have given qualified Panjabis and the home literacies a professional status. For the first time, the younger generations of Panjabis born and/or brought up in Britain have seen the role of home literacies extended beyond their own community to an institutional level. This has motivated many of them to learn and to improve their knowledge of home languages and literacies to obtain the recognised qualifications. Jobs in 'community' interpreting and translation, especially part-time ones, have proved to be very popular among women who cannot get into full-time employment because of their domestic responsibilities. Also, these jobs have provided them with a respectable professional status as well as personal independence.

Summary and Conclusion

Historically and ideologically Britain has largely remained a monolingual, monocultural and monoliterate state; in this context, however, linguistic minorities exist as multilingual, multicultural and multiliterate subsystems both in terms of their ideologies and practices. The Panjabis in Southall are one such subgroup who, in turn, exist as constellations of differing languages and literacy practices and ideologies.

The different kinds of responses amongst different Panjabi subgroups to the changing social conditions in Britain are manifested in a variety of changing literacy practices and ideologies in the Panjabi community in Southall. External factors (such as inequality and racism in the wider society) and internal factors (e.g. different religious ideologies, and need for transmission of Panjabi cultures and maintaining cultural ties with the country of origin) have contributed to this manifestation. Until very recently, English literacy had a place in the material market, whereas the home literacies served the ideological purposes for these linguistic minorities. However, there has been a struggle to get Panjabi minority literacies a place alongside English literacy in institutional domains. Panjabis are now trying to create a multiliteracy market to serve their own needs and purposes. These multiple literacy resources are associated with multiple identities of Panjabi individuals, and are reflected in the choices that they make in their everyday literacy practices. As compared to the previous generations, the third generation Panjabi children now live in a very different world of literacies.

Hindi literacy, with or without its spoken form, has firmly been associated with the Hindu religion and is maintained by many Panjabi Hindus. Similarly, Panjabi language and Gurmukhi scripts are linked with Sikhs and the Sikh religion. On the other hand, Hindi literacy and Panjabi literacy are in competition on the issue of representation of Panjabi secular culture. Urdu literacy has only an informative function (e.g. newspapers) along with Hindi and Panjabi literacies, for those who had their education in Urdu before the partition of India. The constitution of these multiple religious and secular identities as exemplified by different literacy practices of Panjabis have come not only in response to the changing economic, political and social conditions of the wider British context, but also in response to the changing political, religious, economic and social conditions in India as well as within the Panjabi community in Southall itself.

The three distinct literacies and religious communities associated with the Panjabi language provide a particularly useful and important case for the discussion of different worlds of literacies. For instance, it exemplifies that being literate means one thing and being literate in a particular language/orthography is another. By being literate, a person can be identified with a literate world, whereas being literate in a particular language may imply identification with a particular cultural tradition or a particular ideology.[7] A study of a bi/multiliteracy situation like the one among Panjabis discussed in this paper highlights the salient issues of 'identity' and 'ideology'.

See Chap. 13

In multiliteracy situations, institutional support given to one particular literacy bestows power in the hands of the users of that literacy over the users of the other literacies. People who are literate in a lower status language but illiterate in the higher status language, may be subjected to similar negative experiences as would be an illiterate person from the higher status language background. Further, if the lower status language or literacy is associated with a particular ethnic background, people from that group may be subjected to discrimination or racism in the wider society. For example, in Britain, a Panjabi person literate in Panjabi, Hindi or Urdu, but illiterate in English, may find him or herself in this situation, and may be discriminated against in finding a job. But the same person may have a very different kind of social experience in his or her own community in Britain. Being literate in Panjabi, Hindi or Urdu, s/he may be identified with Sikh, Hindu or Muslim religion. But being illiterate in English s/he may be considered to be not westernised enough as English is often associated with westernisation, modernity and success in the wider Panjabi community. Therefore, in the British context, being literate in both English and Panjabi, Hindi or Urdu may mean taking on two complementary, rather than, competing identities, viz. western and Indian, either Sikh, Hindu or Muslim. Whereas being literate in Panjabi, Hindi or Urdu alone may imply taking on different identities, which may become competing and not complementary.

See Chap. 4

In contrast to a monoliteracy situation, a bi/multiliteracy situation readily identifies the categories such as 'diversity', 'choice', 'identity' and 'ideology' which are essential to the theoretical goal that sets out to look at a literacy situation in terms of variety of 'literacies' within an 'ideological model' (Street, 1984) or different 'worlds of literacy', as in this volume.

See Chap. 1

Notes

1. Mother-tongue Panjabi speakers belong to three different religious groups: Sikhs, Hindus and Muslims.
2. Generally, Urdu language is written in Perso-Arabic script, Panjabi language in Gurmukhi script, and Hindi language in Devanagari script.
3. One would expect a Hindu calendar to be written in Devanagari script, rather than in Perso-Arabic script. But the people of priest's generation, as himself, who were educated in the pre-partition period in India, still refer to magazines and other journals written in Perso-Arabic.
4. As I found out in interviews with shop owners, different linguistic signs represented their interest more in terms of their ideological stance and less of their commercial need.
5. Following the business tradition practised in India, some corner shopkeepers have separate accounts for the families living in the vicinity. These customers do not pay the shopkeepers for what they buy on a day-to-day basis, but settle their accounts weekly or monthly.
6. This view was held among some practitioners in education due to the narrow understanding of bilingualism in educational research (cf. Martin-Jones & Romaine, 1985; Romaine, 1989), and the low esteem in which the South Asian minorities and their languages were held.
7. For example, a person may become or aspire to become literate in Gurmukhi to be associated with the Sikh religious tradition and/or with the Panjab cultural tradition.

References

Brass, P.L. (1974) *Language Religion and Politics in North India.* London: CUP.
Das Gupta, J. (1970) *Language Conflict and Language Development.* London: University of California Press.
Dhir, R. (1975) Emotional and social conflict. In P. Parekh and B.. Parekh (eds), *Cultural Conflict and the Asian Family.* Report of the conference organised by the National Association of Indian Youth.
Gopal, R. (1968) *Linguistic Affairs of India.* Bombay: Asia Publishing House.
Harox, A. and McRedie (1979) *Our People.* London: Thames Television.
Jones, K.W. (1976) *Arya Dharm: Hindu Consciousness in 19th Century Punjab.* New Delhi: Manohar Publications.
Jung, G. (1985) The impact of Indian video films on an Indian community in London. Unpublished BA dissertation, University of Essex.
Martin-Jones, M. and Romaine, S. (1985) Semilingualism: A half-baked theory of communicative competence. *Applied Linguistics* 6 106-17.
Pandit, P.B. (1978) Language and identity: The Panjabi language in Delhi. *International Journal of Sociology of Language* 16. 93-108.
Rimmer, M. (1972) *Race and Racial Conflict.* London: Heinemann.
Romaine, S. (1989) *Bilingualism.* Oxford: Basil Blackwell.
Smith, D.J. (1977) *Racial Disadvantage in Britain.* London: Penguin.
Street, B. (1984) *Literacy in Theory and Practice.* New York: CUP.
Southall, S.W.P. (1979) Southall: The fight for our future. London: Socialist Worker.
Southall (1981) The birth of black community. Institute of Race Relations.
Taylor, J.H. (1976) *The Half-way Generation.* Slough: National Foundation for Educational Research.
Westergard, J. and Resler, H. (1975) *Class in Capitalist Society.* London: Penguin.
Wilson, A. (1978) *Finding a Voice.* London: Virago.

Gender | Conflict | Public/Private

MANDY MCMAHON, DENISE ROACH,
ANGELA KARACH AND FIE VAN DIJK

18: Women and Literacy for Change

This article was written collaboratively by Mandy McMahon, Denise Roach, Angela Karach and Fie Van Dijk. During the final stages of preparing the article Mandy died on 25th December 1990. We had only known her for a short time, but were overwhelmed by her wit an determination. Without her enthusiasm, hard work and collaboration this article would not exist. Mandy's courageous spirit lives on.

For several years, Fie Van Dijk has collected postcards showing images of literacy. The pictures that accompany this article are part of her collection.

Introduction
We all come from groups of women that work collaboratively in the 'public' domain, both officially and unofficially, visibly and invisibly.

We worked together at the conference. Our experience of working together has taught us that one way forward is a joint one.

Collaboration

See Chap. 20

- supports us in a world generally devised and controlled by men;

- helps us understand our similarities and differences;

- helps us understand what women's distinctive contribution to that world is and might be and

- gives us strength, confidence, power and creativity.

We, and other women, live in a world of Western images, which tell us things like

- women only write and read alone, to children, to ill people, write and read letters from their lover and sons;

- women wear provocative clothing or nothing at all when they write;

- women let novels fall listlessly from their hands, lost in dreams of romance;

- literacy is a leisure activity for women.

Meanwhile men get down to business at desks in libraries filled with books.

Images of men's literacy are objective and valued, women's subjective and devalued.

We, like other women who work in literacy, may share these assumptions and other beliefs, just as damaging, about literacy and women:

See
Chap. 14

- literacy learning gives you a better life;

- literacy learning links you and your life with other people and their lives;

- literacy learning makes your own life and its relationships better;

- literacy learning gives you access to knowledge and power;

- literacy learning may let you 'speak' in your own voice as a woman.

'Literacy' learning fits into a world of many literacies. Some of them are 'public', and some 'private' but the two are interlinked, with each affecting the other.

See
Chap. 1,
Chap, 9,
Chap. 17

Many women who learn think that their 'private' literacy abilities

- their good communication skills for talking and listening,

- the letters and Christmas cards they send,

- the literacy skills they pass on to their children,

- or lend to their neighbours on request,

are not the same skills that will help them succeed in the 'public' world.

They are wrong and right at the same time.

The skills are the same, but defined and valued differently.

Where you do it shows the value of what you do.

See
Chap. 14

Men have the power

- to separate and define the 'public' and 'private' and

- to confer value or non-value.

The skills are the same, but the 'public' domain does not look like the world of interrelating people in 'private' domains.

'Public' domain images and values talk about individuals, not groups:

- individuals moving up,

- earning money,

- creating new things,

- making their mark.

There are other words for this, words like

- competition,

- individualism,

- elitism,

- hierarchy,

- power and

- wealth,

- isolation.

Skills here are not shared nor transmitted freely and equally.
Expertise is stolen, not credited to its source.
Expertise is bought and sold:

- one person to another,

- one company to another,

- one 'professional' to another,

- one academic success feeding a number of future individual successes.

We think these images lie.
It may be that jointness,

> collaboration,

> teamwork and

> sensitivity to relationships

Mutter und Kind mit Bilderbuch
(Bildarchiv Preussischer Kulturbesitz)

*Women only write and
read alone to children,
to ill people, to their
lover or their sons . . .*

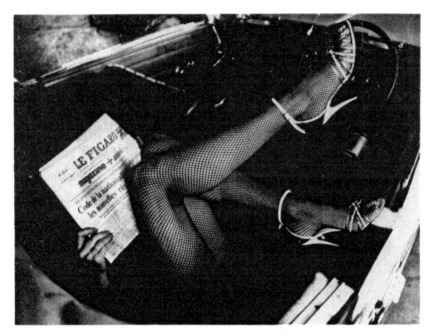

Reine d'un Jour (Photo: Cor Dekkinga)

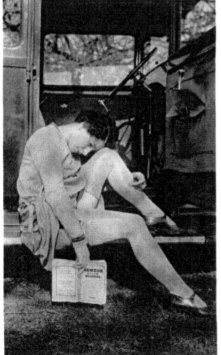

Französische Photokarte der zwanziger Jahre
Sammlung Robert Lebeck

*Women let words fall listlessly
from their hands, lost in
dreams of romance . . .*

*They wear provocative clothing
or nothing at all when they
read or write*

Cartoon: Len Munnik

*While images of women
and literacy emphasise
sexuality, images of men
and literacy emphasise
authority.*

Photo: Steef Zoetmulder

are as important in 'public' as in 'private', although that's not the way it looks.

Yet, ironically, without these commonly devalued and ignored practices and values, the 'public' worlds of literacy would not exist, nor continue to function.

★ ★ ★ ★ ★ ★ ★

Moving from 'Private' to 'Public'

So when women are afraid to move out into 'public', when they say they haven't got the skills and we as literacy workers say they lack confidence, they are wrong and right at the same time, and we are wrong and right at the same time.

Fear of change is a sensible fear.

Literacies position people in the world, and repositioning is painful, as is acknowledging powerlessness, choice and no choice at all.

Choices between literacies can be choices among identities and creating a new identity, like learning, hurts.

See Chap. 1, 17, 20

See Chap. 14, 15

See Chap. 14

Women manage transmission literacies in the 'private' and new literacies can put that at risk.

No matter how disorganised women feel – or are made to feel – their lives to be, there's a lot more disorganisation in learning and in moving to 'public' worlds of literacy.

Women in the 'private' domain know that the 'public' one is made to appear different.

Many women also know that they are devalued and excluded.

What they know of its values, its surenesses and its imageries tell them so, and we as literacy workers must learn from them.

It is not just a 'lack of confidence', but an awareness of things they do and do not know, feeling dislocated from the male-defined and male-valued 'public' world of literacy.

They see their 'incompetences' more clearly and realistically than we as literacy workers do.

★ ★ ★ ★ ★ ★ ★

Literacy Workers as Part of the Problem

As literacy workers, we understand that literacy skill is not the problem.

What we have not yet learned is a name for the abilities and skills that women coming in to literacy have said they need.

If we continue to devalue women's existing skills, and if these new skills are not available to women, then they use the old one, and still become, in their own eyes and the eyes of others

See
Chap. 9

'justa' typist,

'justa' secretary,

'justa' housewife.

See
Chap. 5, 20

'Public' literacies ignore, devalue and trivialise women's experience.

Instead, we help people learn the 'public' rules by methods like

See
Chap. 14

- assertiveness training,
- 'impartiality' in decision-making and other management skills,
- 'objective' ways of understanding social life,

and

- an attention to the male-defined values of the 'public' domain:

    abstraction

    individualism

    competitiveness

    elitism

A celebration of the varied distinctive literacies women are skilled at is something we do not include or acknowledge in the courses we offer to women who want to study.

* * * * * * *

See
Chap. 4, 20

The New Public Literacies and How They Get Invented

'Public' domain literacies exist to do 'public' work – men's literacies exist to do what men think should be done.

'Public' work is not always done well.

Getting it done better may be harder than changing its goals or its aims or its methods of evaluating itself.

We should change the way it is done. The method is the message: how you do it is what you do.

We need new public literacies. Our problem is how to find them again and reclaim them for ourselves and others.

?

The new public literacies will reconnect falsely separated 'public' and 'private' domains which reconnect and re-value our experiences and subjectivities with the things we learn from the experience and knowledge of others.

We need to re-evaluate the extent of our individual and collective forms of power and powerlessness.

The problem is where do we begin and how do we get a new, holistic, form of public literacies invented?

?

See
Chap. 20

The 'public' domain is created and maintained by men.

Women entering singly,
    without support
    are forced to learn alien rule and values
    and abide by them.

What happens to women's specifically female experience?

Women literacy workers live in this 'public' domain, and have learned male rules and values.

They have been taught that 'public' literacies are more important than 'private' literacy ones, even though they may still manage their own 'private' literacy worlds,

Women literacy workers are losing their competence to understand what the new rules might be - those rules invented by women creating their

own,

new,

holistic,

public structures.

They accept the split between the 'public' and 'private' and, worse, they value one over the other.

They forget that, every day, they talk with women who still understand the 'private' in its many guises.

They forget that, every day, they may get support and strength from other women, unlike men, who usually want something in return.

See Chap. 10, 15, 17, 3, 11

The new public literacies and jointly re-invented ways of being in public, may benefit others who move from their own social class or cultural pattern of literacies.

Men may benefit.

Others who have had to invent ways of understanding the world by themselves may contribute and link, making the new public literacies able to do public work better.

See Chap. 19, 20, 21, 22

Those entering existing 'public' domains – including those apprentices whose method of learning (academic literacy) is also the proof they have learned – will find their choices richer.

✳ ✳ ✳ ✳ ✳ ✳ ✳

The Way Forward

Understanding 'private' domains comes from listening to experts.

In their observations about learning, women coming into 'public' identify differences between the 'public' and 'private' domains.

In what they say, we may see the beginnings of the new public literacies.

Section 5:

Collaboration and Resistance: Challenging Words

The articles in this section are about creating new ways of working and communicating through written langue. They are all collaboratively written articles and in different ways, they all emphasise that literacy is also oral, that change involves moving from isolation, listening and talking together with other people.

19: Forging a Common Language, Sharing the Power

We are a group of people who are working on our reading, writing and confidence. We had the chance to go away with others like ourselves on a week's course. We learnt more in five days than in months of weekly classes. We have formed a group, working to give others in basic education the same chance we had, by running weekend and week courses and by setting up a centre for these courses.[1]

Learning the Value of Life
JOE FLANAGAN

Secure world

I suppose I was happy with my lot. I was prepared to live in it till God took me out of this world. I had my food on my table, my family had their health. Life in general was worth living. Work was all I knew. If I didn't have a family, I would have worked because I was secure there. I didn't think there was another world outside my work. I had responsible jobs and I handled them responsibly, otherwise I wouldn't have got a second chance. Them were the days when you could get a job, when people wanted a good worker, an honest worker. They didn't want to know if you could read or write. They never asked.

Redundancy

When I got made redundant, I was afraid. I was afraid to go down to the office, to all offices, because of the forms – you couldn't imagine the fear of walking into the world of forms. I couldn't get anyone to fill them in without telling them I couldn't do it myself. Just to tell a person you couldn't fill a form in was the worst experience of my life. You didn't know whether to throw up or shit your pants, you were that scared. After working from age 14 to 54, then when I was made redundant, I felt like nobody. I felt like all those years were wasted, no meaning to them.

See Chap. 4

Basic education

Into a new world – it was like being born again. When I went to education, I expect a hell of a lot more time than I got, I expected every day. To make the decision to go, and to go – you can't describe it – to get in that door. Then you have to tell them why you're there and you may have to repeat it three or four times. What did I get? When I stopped looking round to see if there was anybody there I knew, I think the hardest part was to accept the tutors who were younger than me. I was old enough to be their father. That in itself was degrading. I couldn't go back. I had to go forward.

I think I can honestly say I didn't start to read until I went into the magazine group. I learnt because the story in the magazine was in my language, easy words. Of course, I read if I wanted to. There was no pressure. There wasn't in the other classes, I just felt there was, just the fact there was somebody in charge. What I liked about the magazine group, somebody was reading a story out while I was picking the story I was going to read, an easy one. The chance was I probably knew every word in the story because they were simple words. The magazine group was for students, by students. It was a magazine for people like myself. They gave me the courage to try something for myself. So with the help of a friend/tutor, I wrote my life story, put it on tape. It was typed out for me. It was pages and pages of letters, words, numbers, call it what you like, and when I decided to made a story of it, I decided to make it a part of the story of my life. I haven't stopped since.

> "My idea of the college I want, I would like to see and make happen, would be where people work *together*. If a tutor, what I want to see, if a tutor can take six people into a room and give the people enough of confidence to work together without the tutor, then she's done a day's work. As far as I'm concerned she's done a day's work".

Pecket Well College

The system being the system, there were many times we had to take the system on. And there was never enough time for me, for my education. By then, I'd got the bug. I didn't expect three months holiday a year. So we talked about a residential college. We knew the kind of college we wanted to see. We knew it wouldn't open overnight. That was five or six years ago.

I've been educated in a lot of ways, with the group that wants this college open, like being interviewed by people who are going to give us the funds. I think I've found out there's more than one way of being educated besides being able to read and write. You learn the value of life. I have learned if ten people said no to us, and one person said yes, I soon forgot about the ten people who'd said no. I suppose I got thick skinned in the process.

I settled down when I heard more people who can't read or write. Nobody was telling me he couldn't read or write. He was telling me of himself. It takes the weight off everybody. I'm trying to kid you, you're trying to kid me. You learn through the years how to bluff. All the hard work is paying off. This year we are opening Pecket Well College. One of our aims is to make 'literacy/illiteracy' part of our history, not a continuation of our future.

Our office is the roots of the college: what goes on here, today, tomorrow. The first thing people want to know is 'who's in charge', but we have to make it clear, we all are. I'm responsible for what I'm doing. The help is there if I need it. We are not here as students or tutors. We are all here to work together and to learn from each other. Those labels have gone out the door.

> "You wouldn't believe that eight or nine people could do so much in five years, and most of them with reading and writing difficulties."

How I work at Pecket
When I write something, I need scrap paper. I might need a couple of words from someone to get me started – talking about what I'm going to write. When I wrote the article for Network, when I wrote about getting married, it was just the start of the story. What I wanted was the words to go in to have an impact. All my story was around those two or three dozen words. What it means not to be able to read to your children. It had an effect on me when I wrote it. I wanted it to have an effect on people when they read it. It had an effect on my daughter – she thought I was blaming her. It wasn't the effect I wanted. If a young lad read it and he would think, this is not going to happen to me, I am the greatest writer in the country because at least I've hit one person in their gut to get off their backside.

What I have gained
The most important thing I gained out of the whole lot is some good friends. I've met people I otherwise wouldn't have met. I got to know a lot more about myself. I learnt how to cope with disabled people. Before I suppose I didn't care or wasn't interested. That's a good lesson. I'm glad I learnt that one.

What I have lost
But in my writing, I have lost my own language and I think it's a very

See Chap. 11, 20, 5

expensive price to pay. I lost it because, to get my point over, I had to do it the system's way. When it comes to writing, I can no longer write as I speak. What I write is for a purpose. Like what I'm doing now, for this book. If I write any other way, they probably wouldn't put it in.

I've lost my own language in writing and speech. Now people understand me who couldn't before. Even my own family understand me better, and my youngest is 25, and sometimes Babs, my wife, would have to tell them what I said. Now I have very little problem. The loss to me outweighs the gain. The people I've met throughout the country in my work for Pecket, have changed me. I had to get my point over to them and I couldn't do that if they didn't understand me.

I'm satisfied with what I've done. I would have preferred to have done things my way, not the system's way. It's important to me when you read my writing that you know my nationality. This is the price I had to pay just for your system, and it's a very expensive price. It's a price I didn't want to pay. The system wouldn't or couldn't change. I did it without realising. If I'd realised, I would have thought there must be another way. It wasn't a sacrifice because sacrifice is something you know you are doing and are prepared to do it. Sometimes I get angry about it but I have to live with it.

Note
1. *Side by Side,* by Pecket Well College, 36 Gibbet Street, Halifax, West Yorkshire HX1 5BA.

Beyond the Values of Reading: Something to Offer
PETER GOODE

> Where reading and writing was the scourge, the most undermining thing, instead of being a negative thing, it became a positive thing. It is why you put yourself in the position of going to talk to 20, 30 tutors, as we did at the Morecambe 'Worlds of Literacy' event. We had something to offer. There comes a time when the disability is not the fear. The disability is an enhancement, because you've faced this disability, it gives you a focus of vision.

> "Thank you wall, for giving me such a high advantage view."[1]

Basic education
Coming into basic education with my tongue and my name encouraged me to express my opinions and ideas verbally, and have some of them taken as important, as of value. There's something self-gratifying, self fulfilling, of someone actually writing them down, someone you can trust who's got

compassion, someone who can listen.

That's the main thing I got from basic education. It wasn't what I came in for. I came in to open up a parcel of reading and writing. I opened it up and found the world of gifts.

From these new worlds, we as individuals had the opportunity to go to Nottingham University with 'Write First Time' on a week's writing course. It was like somebody opening the door of freedom. You're used to sitting in a room, being slaves to the 'I can't read, I can't write syndrome'. You're afraid of freedom or even of expressing the fear. I had the pain of feeling that this was my first and last chance. What helped me was finding my way of expressing myself through poetry as there were people there to write down my words. And what helped me was meeting another once-was-manacled person with obvious scars of lack of education who had the common bond of poetry. Nottingham University was my cradle of birth. We went as isolated individuals and come back as a united team.

The vision of Pecket

We'd all played away and successfully could carry on a united dream of the future. One week had changed my life. By having a dream, a rosette pinned on you by someone saying, 'What about us building a college to make what we'd had possible for all?'

Everybody had come back to Halifax Adult Basic Education Centre either quietly confident or dramatically confident. At one time it must have sounded like a changing room of proud fathers and mothers, all boasting about their new babies. You only get that feeling with victory, with success. Everybody is a winning team, united behind our written voice 'Not Written Off'. We was, soon after, under threat ourselves. The adult education authorities wanted to close the class. It no sooner seemed that we were putting in place the fruits of freedom with one hand than someone was going to take it away with the other hand, to silence us.

They took away the water, heat and anvil. So a new anvil, a new foundry came. We were used to working with raw steel, making our own shape, working our apprenticeship but not having the plan of design. At that time Basic Education said there's a roomful of people here. You've all got to go from point ABC to form filling to certificates and maybe the world of 'O' levels.

At Pecket Well College we come in at our own level and actually sketch our own plan. This is where people start filing down the key finely or reshaping it. Pecket encourages you to go further on. It introduces people to a world that's denied them.

Re-inventing the wheel

The Pecket Well College group has a strong awareness of the written language because most of us have problems with reading and writing. So we started with the need to make the written word accessible to all of us. We are re-inventing the wheel. From fetching a word-watcher, we are now all word-watchers. We ask for translations from the formal world into a familiar language. We have the freedom to ask questions. We insist on our right to understand, so that we can make our contribution. We want information that's normally denied us so that we can give the information that's required of us.

But, with this history of denial and insecurity, until you see the bottom of the pan, you still think there's something left in it. One of the things we are beginning to be aware of is, it's never left empty. It fulfils and leads you on. It has a subtler taste and that's when it becomes tastier. What we keep forgetting is, it's us that's adding to the pan instead of it being someone else.

This works because we have people that understand the official world of writing. It gives me confidence to trust that relevant information will be shared. Part of the motivation is to be able to share responsibility and take the burden off others shoulders. Then the growing time comes.

From wanting language that is accessible to us, we moved to wanting language that is accessible and welcoming to disabled people, Black people, single-parent families, older people, young people and others.

Introducing people to a world that is denied them

Pecket introduces people to a world that is denied them. None are excluded. From tea mashing to computers, the vastness of a real working office and all its complexities are open to us. All of us are trying to break down the hierarchy of tasks. This has meant, for example that someone could move from the security of making tea to the challenge of being a company secretary. We are actually involved in giving advice and training to professionals and students about basic education, meeting funders, councillors, accountants, solicitors, academics, writing articles, publicity and funding, planning courses, recruiting paid workers, running workshops.

We are introduced to new skills. I have never had the chance to read a book but now I am involved in making a book, both the content and the print. The day-to-day skills are more strengthening to me. A regular phone to use, not once in a lifetime, for fire, police, ambulance, it's new to me using it for information and chit-chat. Pecket gives me the experience of travel, even now with anxiety but not so overriding that it makes you numb.

Writing messages and notes are a new-found skill. I can now leave notes lying around as people are not judging me in a disabled role. We are becoming ablers, not disabled, in the world of reading and writing. It is because we are not isolated as one or two people with reading and writing difficulties. The group is important as a support group.

See
Chap. 9, 14

I feel I am accepted. In the letters I write my language is accepted and my strengths are called upon. I am offered guidance and advice on structure. With this, I can make my contribution.

> "Not able to read is like having a thousand tons hanging over you and sometime someone will come along and cut the cord. But within this conference today, for the first time in my life I don't feel that thousand tons hanging over my head".

> "I couldn't speak in official language 'cause it isn't my language, if you will. One of the most fruitful things that I found out, there's been some words bandied round in here that I only met 6 weeks ago, what was it? 'Methodology'. Keep being fruitful, don't deny me those words because I'll be coming back and saying, yes, I need to know, I want to know – that's my journey forward."

Notes
1. From 'The Wall' in 'Moon on the Window' by Peter Goode, published by Open Township, 1991.

On the following page is an example of Peter's contribution, his letter to Paul Getty. It is by no means a standard letter to funders. It is Peter's language. The imagery is Peter's strength. The first draft and final one are included to show something of the process of working together. Peter does not let worries about spelling prevent him from getting his ideas onto paper.

First Draft

Der PoL Gate

it wos Pting The Poms to gethR
for TRos Thed at helpt we to
Find mi on vos to tok with
i dim thit a Bat Pnt in Pnetning
for wi self at th afte
                    and
the Potre is sent to yon
I an Praud to sa that I was
         R
veRe shcsesfL to The yoksp
          u
as a was I aAd 1 in 4o eshas
to og fowd so fam stel Raring
Potp. and tnc ing fowd to
Fening awt mi on BooE
      ch
fo Poms
   vo
           gos sinseLc Peter

Peter and Gillian together deciphered his writing and Peter then added to
the draft by dictating the rest to Gillian. He copied out the completed letter
and sent it to the Paul Getty Junior Charitable Trust. This letter is part of the
project's continuing relationships with the Trust which has brought us
much support, advice and further grants. A previous letter and poems sent
by Peter had impressed the Trust enough to award us a grant of £10,000!

Final draft

Dear Paul Getti

It was putting the Poems
together for your trust that
helped me to find my own Voice
to talk with. It helped to
give me the confidence to put
in for an award to writers from
the Yorkshire Arts Association. I
am proud to say that I was
Successful. I hed one in Forty
chances to go forward! So. I
am still Writing Poetry and
looking Forward to fetching out
my own book of Poems.

The Pecket Well college will be
one of the anvils that will fore
the chain of success to those that
faltered with reading and writing and
therefore left their words unbnded.
If this is so. surely

Pecket Well cllege is the foundry that
We can smithey together on by fetching
oun own Passion as heat, our own tears
to temper the steel. My admiration for
all that try to succeed With the written

Word goes with my own recommendation
Forward to link the chains to unite not
in desparation but in a common Knowledge
of growth. And then I Can Surely sey

I am proud of being a basic
education student

yours sincerely
Peter Goode

The Pecket Partnership
GILLIAN FROST

Pecket Well members have persuaded me to emerge from my invisible role to add my contribution to this chapter.

I see Pecket Well College as a partnership of people who have been through the educational system, with people who have been failed by that system. We are bonded by a common purpose, to set up a residential college where the people with experience of tackling problems with reading and writing are fully involved in the planning, running and evaluation of the courses and the management of the centre.

Because we have worked together, from the conception of the idea, through the development of the project and now to its fruition, we have had to forge a new way of working. We have had to develop a new language, not the 'academic/professional' language, not 'street' language, but one we all can understand. It is not a world that any of us are completely at ease in nor a language any of us are fluent in. This way of working puts enormous pressures on all of us but it is exciting, challenging and stretching. It is the only way we have found of sharing power.

In the early days of the project, I was the only one of the day to day workers with a 'professional' background. The world expected me to be the voice and public face of Pecket. Sharing power has meant I have had to retreat in an attempt to resist this pressure and am now perhaps over-reluctant to make my contribution publicly.

To honestly describe the Pecket 'world of literacy', those of us with an academic training should acknowledge our role. In the preparation for this presentation and this chapter I have acted as translator, putting over to Peter and Joe what was being asked of us. I have asked questions, acted as instant editor in the process of writing down their words by guiding people away from expounding interesting ideas in areas that I did not see as relevant for this purpose. This has not been imposed. It is what Joe and Peter asked of me. Equally Peter and Joe have helped me with writing this piece by persuading me it was important and by pointing out both inaccessible language and neglected areas in my first draft.

My training with ideas allows me to focus and provide the 'structure' that Peter refers to. My commitment to sharing power, my own passion against oppression of all kinds is one of the ingredients that have helped to fashion the project.

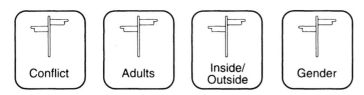

ANGELA KARACH AND DENISE ROACH

20: Collaborative Writing, Consciousness Raising and Practical Feminist Ethics

Context

'Collaborative Writing' was written in early 1990 as part of an Independent Studies research project we had designed in the third year of our BA (Hons) degree studies at Lancaster University in the UK. One year on, we still stand by our claims. As far as we are aware, in the English university system a critical undergraduate project such as ours – which involved our collaborative participation from the conceptual stages to the assessment stage with our 'assessors' – is non-existent. We hope we are wrong. However, we have never come across a similar piece of collaborative work, nor have been 'allowed' to undertake another such critical study of undergraduate women's learning experiences in our three years of study at university – in any of our varied disciplines. Our hope is that more undergraduate women will be encouraged to consciously position themselves within their higher education institutions and encouraged to write critical analyses of their own experiences, their strategies for survival and resistance and their proposals for change.

See Chap. 5

We wrote this paper out of the anger and concern we felt at the extent to which our and other women's forms and content of knowledge, and our experiences are excluded from what constitutes 'academic' knowledge. We wrote it also out of the anger and concern we felt at the extent to which we as women are dislocated and alienated both within the structures of the institutions of higher education, and the teaching practices. But as we more clearly see now through our lived experiences within the institution and our critical analyses, each – hierarchical definitions, structures, practices, dominance and subordination – follows the other.

Our other main source of motivation for writing this paper was that we also wanted to celebrate and share with others our own developed strategy of resistance – that of collaborative writing. Working together not only helped us to survive the institution with our identities and our previously held values more-or-less intact, but further, enabled us to create ways in which we could learn from each others' knowledge and skills, despite pressures on us to conform to the conventional ethos and teaching/learning practices of higher education. Working collaboratively or collectively has enabled us to become more critically conscious of and to challenge the individualistic, competitive, elitist ethos of 'higher' education. It has enabled us to challenge what constitutes 'academic' knowledge (unlike the partiality of subjective knowledge) which continues in general to be deceptive through the value placed upon it and its status and claims to be 'truthful' and 'whole' and 'impartial'. At the same time, it is clear that despite these claims, the majority of academic knowledge continues to exclude the experientially informed knowledge of women and other discriminated against and oppressed people.

See Chap. 13, 19, 22

Although our experiences expressed here are specifically with and about women collaborators, we acknowledge that this could be used as a positive method of working academically for male students also. However, this is not the focus of this paper. 'Collaborative Writing, Consciousness Raising and Practical Feminist Ethics' is the outcome of our three years of struggles as undergraduate women in higher education. Its practices were our strategy for survival and resistance, and our partial solution towards change.

Introduction

Studying at university as undergraduates, particularly as mature women, has often seemed like the worst times of our lives. We know ourselves, through conversations and our research of other mature women's experiences, that being on the 'receiving' end of the formal educational process often feels – and is – incredibly threatening to our identities, and to our experiential, subjective forms of knowledge. Being at university sometimes feels like existing within a huge sterile, impersonal machine, which grinds its way through time seemingly oblivious to the existence of the lost and confused tiny *you* within. Without doubt, we have gained new understandings and awareness of other people's views of the world, and have modified and expanded our own forms of knowledge. However, we feel we have achieved this largely through our own methods of learning rather than those conventionally prescribed.

Students find or create different strategies to help themselves through the higher educational system, and/or to help themselves gain the most from the education on offer. Through necessity at times, and sheer determination at others, we have found strategies to make gains and to survive the struggles through the institution. One of our most important strategies has been to work collaboratively on some of our written assignments together and with our other women friends. Through collaboration in our academic work, we have been able to incorporate new academic knowledge with our own forms while not losing total sight of our own multi-dimensional identities, in relation to our 'student' identity viz. academia, and to retain a sense of the value of our own varied forms of personal-subjective knowledge. We have learnt to recognise and to respect each other's differences, and have learnt much from each other's skills and knowledge. Our academic work has been enriched by our strategies of working together. Through these informal strategies of collaboration, we have created a network of women friends which has been an invaluable source of support and means of survival in what is often an alienating environment.

From our experiences in higher education, we can quite easily appreciate the importance and necessity of collaborative writing (CW) for all students. However, as women students, involved to varying degrees in Women's Studies, our particular concerns and interests are with the use of collaborative writing (CW) as a practical method of knowledge-making and gaining specifically for women students. A second point which follows on from the first, is to introduce the methods of CW as a feminist principle for women in educational institutions.

Both of us are mature women undergraduates in higher education. Denise is 29 and in the 3rd year of a 4-year degree scheme. Angela is 34 and in the final year of her 3-year degree scheme. We are both white and are from different working class and cultural backgrounds; but apart from these often over-generalised social 'categories', we find we have very different life experiences. The major thing we do have in common however, is that many of our past and present experiences in relation to men and male-controlled institutions, have been and are so similar that they have become a primary basis through which we have recognised our common identity as women.

Feminist Principles and Practical Feminist Ethics

There is no one set of feminist principles agreed upon and accepted by all women within the Women's Liberation Movement (WLM). The contemporary WLM, increasingly a truly international political movement, consists of women from almost all countries, races, classes, sexualities, creeds and other diverse experiences. Women within the WLM critique and fight for change in all areas of social life: political, economic, sexual, cultural and institutional. Spanning the spectrum from equality to liberation, women demand 'equality' with men to 'liberation' from men. Since the International WLM is diverse and complex, many different philosophies have arisen, each with their own distinct principles for working with women and/or together with men, for various prescriptions and visions of social change. However, underlying many earlier and to some extent present feminist working practices and demands, we find there is an ethos which is totally opposed to the ethos of liberal competitive individualism present in our western educational systems.

See
Chap. 13,
19, 22

This feminist ethos, underlying political practice, has its contemporary roots in consciousness raising (CR) activities – that is, activities through which women come together to speak of their own experiences, listen to those of other women, learn from all the women's experiences together and find strategies for change. Broadly, practical feminist ethics underlying women's activities in such groups, emphasised co-operation rather than competitiveness and conflict. Through *practice* rather than abstract theory, feminists have developed ethics which stress the importance of recognising and understanding women's differences as well as our similarities; ethics which involve articulating our experiences as individual women with other women; sharing of knowledge and skills rather than perpetuating elitism, hierarchy, objectification, and fragmentation of knowledge and of self. Co-operation in attempting to resolve our difficulties, problems and conflicts we have within ourselves and amongst ourselves. Community is emphasised rather than individualism in finding strategies for change, the building of collective consciousnesses and strength.

Women's politically defined CR groups developed originally and fundamentally out of women's oppression and exclusion from hierarchical, elitist male-structured and controlled institutions; and also as a fundamental attempt to (re)create bonds and understandings between women. These ethics and practices created and developed by women had not evolved directly from any explicit feminist theory of individual/group or social change. Rather, they sprang from social conditions which both enabled and necessitated these forms of activities, from where women were at politically, at that particular moment in time.

As mature undergraduate women, we find we continue to be discriminated against in higher education in Britain in the early 1990s. Perhaps naively, we did not expect the higher educational institutions to be hierarchical, male-centred and elitist. Nor had we expected to feel so alienated from the knowledge we hoped we would find and gain. We had not expected to find conventional disciplines continuing to largely ignore or trivialise the lives, works and achievements of women. Nor had we expected to be bombarded with the works of past and present male academic 'masters', who, we find, we are only allowed to criticise generally through the voices of other contemporary male 'masters'.

We had not expected academic knowledge to be so fragmented into specialisms, discourses and disciplines. Nor had we expected academic knowledge to be so divorced or separated from *real* everyday life experiences. We had not perceived that knowledge could be so distanced from ourselves and/or our real lived experiences and subjective knowledge. Nor that these forms of objectified knowledge would be so resistant to challenges and criticisms from women, and people other than academics. We had not expected ourselves to feel so fragmented and our identities and knowledge so threatened and undervalued.

Furthermore, we had not expected to feel so isolated and alienated both from most academic 'knowledge' and from most academics themselves. Perhaps most crucial of all, as undergraduate women we had not expected to be treated and viewed as sub-human, in what we have been led to believe to be a 'liberal educational institution'. We have in part gained knowledge, and increased our capacities to analyse in depth and criticise. We would like to have gained more and enjoyed more of our right to our time spent in education. But conventional teaching and learning practices we know have hindered and limited our opportunities to do so. Largely through our 'informal' and 'unofficial' collaborations on academic work and academic writing, through pre- and post-seminar readings with our extended women's network and through some of our Women's Studies courses, we have been enabled to learn and understand new forms of knowledge, and at times actually enjoy our education.

Our Experiences of Collaborative Writing

Below we will share our experiences of working together and some of our thoughts on what this method of working could do for other women.

Collaborative writing for us is a process through which students can learn, communicate and share skills and knowledge *with* students in similar, more equal positions to themselves, as opposed to learning in unequal, one-to-one relationships with reified others and academic texts. 'Unofficially', both of us have collaborated on some of our academic course work. We discussed topics and views, shared our knowledge, shared our skills – not only of reading, understanding and making sense of academic texts, but also our skills of writing academically. And even though the eventual piece of written work had, or was only allowed to have one name, we nevertheless were aware of and recognised the contribution the other had made – from an idea to a fullstop. Furthermore, one of our most important gains was the actual support we gave each other through the traumas of essay writing, and surviving overall in our hierarchical academic institution. Largely from the basis of working together in our first year at university, we have since developed and maintained a strong, lasting friendship and a wider network of women friends.

Working in collaboration, without positive encouragement and acknowledgement, as well as being fairly dissimilar women, has not always been an easy task, sometimes fraught with tensions, frustrations and disadvantages. However, the positive aspects of our experiences, we feel, clearly outweigh the disadvantages, since we have grown in ourselves and developed more realistic and critical attitudes to our relationship with academia, academic knowledge and methods of knowledge-making.

Talking together, writing apart

Denise: In my first year at university I often 'unofficially' collaboratively worked on academic assignments with Angela. Since I was fairly new to academic writing at the time, and often found the processes difficult to cope with, Angela would help me by pointing out some of the conventions (written and unwritten rules) of this particular form of writing. We would look at an essay question together, discuss what I knew about the topic and then she would show me how to structure my ideas and essay around the question, and how to make an academic argument. Our collaboration, then, was mainly in the thinking and discussing processes of academic writing, in the teaching and learning of skills, and in sharing emotional support. This initial basis enabled me to 'network' and collaborate with other women students, to find/give support and share our knowledge, skills and experiences.

In my second year, collaboration played a greater part in my academic work. The friendships I had made through this 'unofficial' method of working together extended into my/our social lives, which over time, have made our bondings and understandings of each other all the stronger and greater. Before coming here, my prior work experiences had mostly consisted of team work, and therefore I found it satisfying, comfortable and reassuring to be able to network with other women students at university – working together, sharing, understanding, accepting and giving support.

Talking together, writing together

Angela and Denise: The second example of our experiences of collaborative writing is this piece of work itself. Roz, our project facilitator, knew of our 'unofficial' collaborations. Through her initial suggestion we began to plan and eventually produce this piece of work together about our thoughts and experiences of collaborative writing.

The way in which we have written this and shared the 'division of labour' is as follows. Both of us discussed the content, form and argument we thought the piece should take over a period of several weeks. We jointly jotted down notes and tape-recorded one of our discussions to enable us to refer back to when we had begun the process of writing. While only one of us took on the task of physically writing up our ideas, knowledge and experiences, we both nevertheless feel we have produced this work more or less equally. Angela typed out the drafts which Denise read through, adding to, criticising and editing the text. Roz has also been part of this process of collaboration. As mentioned above, she had been initially part of the thinking process by suggesting we undertake this work by encouraging us, by reading through, commenting and editing our work in the draft stages.

While involved in these processes, both of us have been aware of, and have tried as best as possible in these circumstances, not to subsume each of our individual identities and thoughts into an undifferentiated 'we'. But this has been difficult, and for many reasons, not least time restraints and a lack of experience in actually *writing* together, I (Angela) don't think we have been very successful. Throughout this essay the reader will find it difficult in large parts to distinguish between myself and Denise, will be unable to see where we have disagreed and what compromises each of us has had to make in order for it to appear consistent and as though we both agree with everything said here. While each of us agrees with the overall contents and the arguments of this essay, minor things have not always been jointly agreed on, and compromises have been made. One crucial point I realised in this process of collaboration, is that each of us has power, and whether or not our individual power is asserted *over* the other, depends on the nature of the compromises made between us and the confidence that each of us may already have, express and/or gain during our work.

Besides the partial loss of our individual identities within the merging of the 'we', we have had to face and deal with other difficulties such as coming to terms with our own individual characteristic 'flaws', such as impatience, and guilt, of being frightened of 'holding back' the other and of not contributing 'as much' as the other, or 'too much', and of having too much individual control over this project. While both of us have in many ways found collaborating on this essay hard work and realise some of its limitations, *positively* it has forced us to recognise and come to terms with each other's differences and each other's and our own limitations now, more than at any other time of working 'unofficially' together during the past three years. Even more than before, we have been enabled to grow in ourselves, and to share more fully our skills and knowledge.

Consciousness-raising

Through 'unofficially' working together, we recognised the benefits of writing and working collaboratively for other women students. By working and discussing our experiences together, we began and continue to raise each other's awareness of the contradictions we have to deal with as mature women undergraduates at university. We have also been able to provide each other with strength and support, as well as have fun and learn new skills.

Informally we criticised the present ethos of higher education – the ethos of individualism, competitiveness and elitism. Through our experiences we found that this ethos and its consequent practices can, and often does, lead to isolation from other students within the university system; alienation from the staff and some of the knowledge we are supposed to 'receive' and from the knowledge we already have as mature women. Following on from this is the problem of experiencing confusion and loss of confidence in one's identity. Specifically as women, we find we are obliged through the nature and elitism of academic knowledge and teaching practices, to undervalue our own subjective knowledge, to lose sight of our own identities and consequently, to desperately seek approval from others in 'authority'. One of the most important aspects of collaboration for us however, is that we have been able to express, and to value our own and each other's experiences and knowledge, and to a greater extent than otherwise, hold on to our identities as multi-dimensional women rather than the mono-dimensional 'students' we are expected to behave as.

From our experiences, from conversations and our research into other undergraduate mature women's experiences, we find there are many common problems we all have had to deal with while in university (see Karach, 1992). Through our collective experiences as women, through our feminist readings and practices we feel that these issues, and the practice of collaborative writing as a partial solution for some of the problems we face as women undergraduates, are feminist issues. It was not until we had the opportunity through the School of Independent Studies, and the encouragement from our facilitator to collaboratively write a piece of work about 'collaborative writing', that we began 'officially' to explore the links between this method of working together and practical feminist ethics.

Continuously, we try to incorporate our new skills, experiences, academic knowledge and the knowledge gained from working together, with those we already had before we started to collaborate. Also, a fundamental part of this process is to find the links between our experiences within higher education, feminist critiques, feminist ethics, and ways forward for undergraduate women.

Conclusion

Although we had not previously recognised or acknowledged our collaborative work for written assignments and seminar discussions specifically as consciousness-raising activities, with hindsight we now see that this is exactly what they have been for us. Through the processes of working together, we can now see how they have constituted a crucial learning and survival tactic in such an alienating environment as our institution of higher education. Instead of being 'passive' learners which conventional academic teaching processes generally encourage undergraduates to be, or purely 'receivers' of knowledge, our form of collaborative learning has enabled us to become 'active' learners, definers, critics and makers/creators of knowledge, to some extent challenging conventional academic 'wisdom' and teaching/learning processes.

See Chap. 5, 10, 16

Through our informal collaborative activities, amongst ourselves and with other women, which spanned reading, thinking, discussing and arguing, to the actual physical processes of writing, we have grown in ourselves and in our confidence to challenge objectified and fragmented forms of academic knowledge and teaching/learning practices. We have learnt in new ways to come to terms with, and to understand, each of our differences and our own limitations. We have learnt the importance of working together with women for our own survival and the survival of other women in oppressive, institutional relations and practices. We have learnt new forms of interdependence in which we give and take reciprocally, and share knowledge and skills in ways beneficial to all of us concerned. It hasn't always been easy and will not always be so, and there will be times when our and the collaborations of other women will continue to be fraught with similar and different contradictions, frustrations and tensions. But as we have found through practice, struggling, learning and challenging together is more beneficial, fruitful and easier, in the long run, than struggling, learning and challenging alone is isolation. Our most positive reward from collaboration is that through the growth in ourselves and our confidence we have been enabled to challenge in myriad ways – individually and collectively – our supposedly taken-for-granted positions as *women* and as *students* within our male-centred hierarchical university.

See Chap. 18

See Chap. 5

See Chap. 19, 22

As undergraduate women students we can clearly see the positive benefits collaboration for academic assignments could have for other women students. For teachers also, we believe our method of working together, if encouraged positively for women students, would surely make teaching and learning a more interesting, stimulating and challenging two-way, spiralling process. And further, could/would pose challenges also to the presently conflict-ridden ethos and practices of higher education. These challenges then, would surely be beneficial not only for students, but also for academic teaching staff, 'formal' education and the institution of higher education, in the processes of change.

Acknowledgement

We would like to thank Roz Ivanic who made the unofficial 'official' and gave our working together a name. Thanks also the to the Teaching of Writing Research Group at Lancaster University for formal discussions about Collaborative Writing, and for sharing their own experiences of teaching and writing collaboratively with us. Again thanks to Ailbhe Smyth and Women's Studies International Forum who in a wider sense, are collaborators also.

Reference
Karach, A. (1992) The politics of dislocation: Some mature undergraduate women's experiences of higher education. *Women's Studies International Forum* 15 (2).

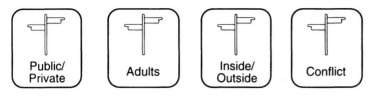

VICTOR GRENKO AND STELLA FITZPATRICK

21: Creating 'A Guide To The Monsters Of The Mind'

Introduction

This chapter is a brief look at a rather different world of literacy. The theme of our project is the strange and powerful ideas that can rule the world of the mind, and how to tell others about

> Maybe you'll recognise a bit of yourself...

them in a way that is effective and unthreatening. This is achieved in our work through pictures, with some words. We are respectively, a cartoonist who also attends adult basic education classes and a community publisher, working with writers from adult basic education. Our action research has been to develop the original ideas of one of us, Victor Grenko, and to pool our skills in order to publish a book.

Victor writes: 'Monsters of the Mind' is a book I have written about the pests (monsters) that trouble our minds, such as jealousy and sadness, worry and pride, and many more. I have illustrated the book with colourful drawings. The book is a light-hearted look at some serious ideas. I am a cartoon artist. I draw for fun, not for money. That means I am an amateur, but I know I can draw well. Using my cartoon talents I was able to create a cartoon world of pictures for my book. In the hospital where I go to do art, I drew a small black and white book of monsters. The art teachers found it amusing, so I drew some more monster books and coloured them in. Then I gave them to nurses on the wards to see what they thought. They liked the books because they mirror the hospital world and the real world. By this I mean, the 'monsters' described in my book are true for people outside the hospital as well as inside. Then my teacher at college suggested I send a book to Gatehouse, a community publishing group, who publish mainly stories about local people. I went to Gatehouse. The place was close to my house so I had no travel problems. I met Gatehouse workers John Glynn, Patricia Duffin and Andi Downs, but it was with Stella that I did all of my work.

Why Monsters of the Mind?

Why monsters of the mind? I used to live in the everyday normal world, working, signing on and so on. Then I entered the bizarre world of the mentally ill. I became ill in the mind. My whole world became abnormal, out of shape. I entered an Alice-in-Wonderland type of world, with the fear of being trapped in Franz Kafka's castle. You'll know what I mean if you're ever unfortunate enough to end up in hospital. The art in psychiatric hospitals could be called 'mad art'. You paint a prison around your own mind. Your mind is in terrible chaos and unable to escape. But on the wards, nurses and patients are drinking hot chocolate, watching a comedy show on television, laughing and relaxing. Everything is normal, safe, controlled. The chaos, fear and panic are in your mind. The doctor removes the madness out of your mind and you see everything in the world is ordinary and boring. You need the dull moments to offset the excitement and drama of illness.

The hospital contains you, keeps you out of trouble. You get a bed to sleep in, meals to eat. You get to meet other people like yourself, who often become friends. In time, it's like living with a big family. Control is held by the hospital. Good control is when you go on the ward and you see that everything is normal and safe. Bad control is when you are restricted. Some people are outraged by the lack of power they have over their lives, once they are diagnosed as mentally ill. You have your ups and downs on the ward. Your own family comes to see you. Most nurses who look after you are alright; only one or two are bad apples. You find that in all the organisations of society. You are given tranquillisers to keep you quiet. There are day schools in the hospital, pastimes, and so on. Life's not bad in hospital. They can't solve your life's problems but they can listen to you and try to clear the fog of mental illness from your mind so you can see the real world around you. One of the things to come out of all this for me is my book about monsters of the mind. I wrote it as a joke book. It's meant to be light-hearted: a rogues gallery of colourful creatures, but behind it are strong hints of this world of confusion.

The Process

(Stella writes) Working to produce 'A Guide To The Monsters Of The Mind' as a published book has been both difficult and rewarding. At the centre of the work is Victor's creation; a series of brilliantly colourful, often amusing, often bizarre cartoons and captions. These are held together by a single metaphor, the 'monsters' metaphor. It's a neat idea. Through it, the negative side of our lives is transformed into fantasy villains, like those met in the pages of comics, 'Superman' films, and so on. As well as uniting the different drawings, the monsters theme representing as it does the 'down' side of our thoughts and feelings, makes it possible to look at difficult bits of experience. Attached to the work of developing this idea for publication is the network of tasks, the discussions and workshops, the working partnership that precedes so many publications in adult basic education, and that has filled a great deal of our lives for the past two and a half years. It is this that we are trying to unpack in this piece of writing.

Consulting groups

Our joint work began in September 1988, when Gatehouse decided to publish Victor's work. The decision was based not just on enthusiasm. At Gatehouse we believe it is important to consult the readers and users of our books about materials that we are thinking of publishing. Victor's book was evaluated by tutors and students from adult basic education groups, and also by people in the field of mental health. It was recognised by Gatehouse that work on this book meant combining our primary area, adult basic education, with that of mental health. Gatehouse was interested in doing pioneering work in community publishing in the field of mental health, having begun already with another book which links the two fields: 'Listen to Me: Talking Survival', a book about child sexual abuse. The decision to publish was because of advice from people we consulted, about the usefulness of the material as a resource for a wide range of groups. These included users of mental health services, adult basic education students and tutors keen to find stimulus for writing, student nurses, and women's groups.

While the editorial process for 'A Guide To The Monsters Of The Mind' was going on, Gatehouse provided a third person to be involved in the work as support for myself, the Gatehouse editor. This had been suggested also for the work on 'Listen To Me'. My support (a series of monthly meetings with a mental health worker) helped to reduce the pressure that built during some periods of our project together. This is an important addition when a working relationship calls for increased counselling and listening and also awareness and skills in a new area.

From private to public

Victor and Stella write: Our earliest shared workshops dealt with what it's like to be published. As well as feeling rather proud to be a published author, bringing what was formerly shared with a few into a public arena can make a writer feel vulnerable. Having a book published is like a minefield. It is also a brave act, sending out your ideas for others to look at and judge. You have to live with the fact that other people's interpretation can change or modify what you intend. People can read their own things into it. One effect of this is to want to protect yourself by using a less

See
Chap. 13

controversial idea, or using more words, to establish your true motive.
Victor is an ordinary person who has suffered mental illness. Early in our
work he decided to keep a low profile during and after the publication of his
book, because there is a lot of stigma attached to being mentally ill. From the
beginning of our project, we have been aware that material which deals with
an area that many people find frightening, can trigger extreme reactions.
The notion that this joke book could give offence, that something created to
lighten and amuse could strew about it insult and anger is both irritating
and frightening. This element of risk in being published has come into many
of our discussions. We are dealing with a taboo area, though in the form of
comic creatures. Our material is challenging for some readers, because it
disturbs thoughts they hide even from themselves. During the editorial
process we have tried to remove what might be seen as adding to prejudice,
but to leave in what is made risky by being taboo.

Ideas and enthusiasms

In spite of these misgivings, about making something public that up to
then had been private, planning to have a book published filled Victor with
ideas and enthusiasms. Suggestions for its eventual format had come from
groups and individuals who looked at his work. A tape-slide version of the
cartoons, to provide a resource for health workers was one. A series of
greetings cards, or posters, based on a selection of his cartoon creations was
another. A third suggestion was for an exhibition of 'monsters' to coincide
with a play about society's attitude to mental health, which was being
staged by a local community theatre group. We took up this last suggestion,
and enjoyed the work of choosing, colouring and putting together a four-
panel exhibition. A task which demanded our separate practical skills like
this provided a 'breather' from intense discussions about the web of issues
that lie behind Victor's drawings, and again tested the water for the
forthcoming book. The other ideas, although practically possible, demanded
an investment of further time and energy, and all needed money to get them
underway. Gatehouse, a registered charity, depends on grants to enable it
to publish, having little or no capital of its own to fund ventures such as
these. For these reasons they have not been taken further.

Victor's own response to this enthusiasm was to redraw the whole book
very effectively, developing or changing some cartoons, and changing the
visual emphasis a little. The new book was an A to Z of monsters of the
mind, with cartoons organised into thematic groupings, according to the
letters of the alphabet. It was a huge organisational and creative
undertaking, accomplished in a week, at some cost to Victor himself. He
was drained and even a little high, as he worked to get it finished, but
pleased with his achievement.

CHANGE INTO

GOOD!

BAD!

RIGHT

LEFT

COME ON! MAKE YOUR MIND UP!

JEKELL AND HYDE

YOU'RE IN TWO MINDS. THIS IS KNOWN AS HAVING A SPLIT PERSONALITY. IT IS CALLED SCHIZOPHRENIA. WHEN YOUR RIGHT HAND DOESN'T KNOW WHAT THE LEFT HAND IS DOING.

CHATTER-BOX

SQUAWK! DID YOU HEAR THE ONE ABOUT...

THE TALKING PARROT

WHO WON'T STOP TALKING INSIDE YOUR HEAD. BE QUI.   BIRDBRAIN, I'M TIRED OF LISTENING TO YOUR VOICE FOREVER PARROTING ON.

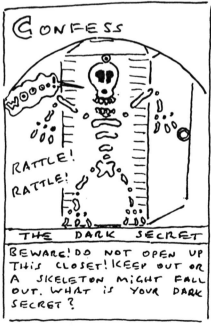

CONFESS

WOOO!

RATTLE!

RATTLE!

THE DARK SECRET

BEWARE! DO NOT OPEN UP THIS CLOSET! KEEP OUT OR A SKELETON MIGHT FALL OUT. WHAT IS YOUR DARK SECRET?

CONTEMPT

BRRR IT'S COLD!

ICE COLD TO THE TOUCH!

SCORN!

FREEZING

THE FROST MAN

YOU TURN COLD TOWARDS EVERYBODY IN THE WORLD, AND BECOME UNFEELING! YOUR EMOTIONS ARE FROZEN LIKE ICE. YOUR HEART IS RULED BY CONTEMPT.

Victor Grenko

This gave us two versions of the book: Victor's original, which Gatehouse had piloted and had agreed to work with him on developing and producing, and this second alphabet version, which was Victor's independent developing of his original idea. Victor hoped the new book would impress Gatehouse. Victor writes: I had to redraw the book to make it look more sophisticated. The original monsters were too childlike. I saw what they could become. As well as entertaining you, they could be useful to people, trying to help them with their troubles. I wanted to give them some background. This was the final version for Victor, though not for Stella, who brought a model of other editorial projects to the work on 'Monsters', as the book was affectionately called. Stella writes: Gatehouse couldn't fully accept version 2 of Victor's book. The new cartoons were wonderful but the alphabetic motif drew attention visually to the letter, carefully outlined above the cartoon and to the theme it was suggesting, with the 'monster' as a secondary image below. Gatehouse preferred the reader's attention to be only on the cartoon. It was also true that Victor had softened some of the hard edged comments in his original book, so as not to offend or hurt any readers.

Final version

Stella suggested that a working brief for Victor and herself would be to choose from each version of the book those features which were most successful and to use these in a final version. We spent seven months doing this. First of all we chose those cartoons and captions which seemed to us to work best at preserving the irony and visual humour of the original. This task called for discussion about what a particular drawing suggested or why it worked, and provided time and space for Victor to explore the origins of each cartoon for him. In each case, he deals with a host of associations, many of them urging very negative experiencing of the world, behind the jokey cartoon exterior. Victor constantly showed himself to be close to the underlying potential of the drawings, for readers. 'Monsters' is a book that comes from experience and from compassion. We chose 32 cartoons for the book, rejecting 12. Then we set out to group those cartoons which were related because of theme, for example those which were about feelings of being trapped or stifled in some way. We next turned to the look of each page in the book. Through photocopying, enlarging and reducing, cutting up and rearranging, we explored possibilities. At this stage, Stella was rejecting the four-monsters-a-page format of Victor's original version and trying to promote more space around each cartoon. It didn't work. We couldn't find a way of spacing out the cartoons which satisfied the eye. This was a tiring period of trial and error. We were enmeshed in all the choices and permutations we'd gone through. We took ourselves and our ideas off to a graphic designer working locally. He urged that it was important to preserve the comic-strip format of Victor's original. The four cartoon page was reinstated, to our mutual satisfaction, and a corner was turned. Subsequently, we added space on alternative pages to rest the eye from the impact of colour on others, developing the idea of 'quiet' left hand pages in blue, with 'speech bubbles' containing some of the things Victor had said during our workshops. These are planned to relate to each other and to provide a commentary to the underlying messages of the drawings.

Yoka Jeffrey-Moeton

Victor successfully redrew the chosen cartoons for the printer. His captions were hand-lettered by a graphic artist, so as to make them clearer, and keep the comic-strip format. Other written portions of the book were typeset. One and a half years of dedicated fund-raising raised the sum we needed to produce the book and 'A Guide To The Monsters of the Mind' was launched in April 1991.

Aftermath

Victor writes: There is a book-model in your mind of publishing from start to finish, which changes as you go along. What you set out to do and what is actually published are two different things. You need patience and luck. Doing a book is a long drawn out affair. It could take two years, working on and off (see diagram of the book cake)

You do the book for your own benefit, for the love of the work, rather than fame or money. You enjoy writing, drawing and using your skills making a book. This is an indulgence, a hobby, as well as a task. There's the joy of meeting other people. Different people give you different attitudes and outlooks. It's like having a meal. Meeting other people adds flavour to life. Also, you need to meet other people because this gives you new slants and information about your work. But having a book published is still hard work. It's been like a mountain to climb. For me it's big, like a giant in my life. I know the time and trouble I've spent and the commitment I've made. Planning it out, graphic design and so on. It's complicated to work out the format, how you want it arranged and typeset. It's a mammoth task.

When you become a published writer, it's important to keep everything in proportion. Even if you have a book published, you're still who you are. You must bring everything down to a realistic level. At first it might go to your head; you're doing this book, you might be famous, then you realise that this is unlikely. You might do the greatest book in the world, but other people might not share your enthusiasm and not buy millions of copies of your book. A trick? No! You are who you are; everything is moving in the world as before. Your friends might joke with you about being famous, but you understand the reality of the situation. You get some reviews, you feel big, but it's all just a drop in the ocean. You are not asked to meet Prince Charles, or Terry Wogan; Madonna does not want to meet you! Millions of people are not rushing to see you. In the end you're alone and lonely, but you're not too badly off. You take it easy in life; you mark a small notch on your stick, and life goes on.

Stella writes: Each editorial project has the same basic framework but there are differences because people and their writing are different. Now the book is printed, the process we've been through unfolds straight-forwardly, as things do retrospectively, and one can see who were the key people, why it was right to worry at certain points and what the realisations were, that speeded the completion of the book. In the middle of the project, it was easy to feel that we were not making progress, that the negative issues we were dealing with were sapping my strength, that our editorial work was not producing the 'best version' of Victor's work, or even that the lack of funds for a highly expensive printing process would cause it to founder completely. These difficulties were never overwhelming and were always matched by positive elements, like a belief in each other's skills, a vision of what the book could be, a mutual conscientiousness about pushing the work forward. We and our project also gained from people we met because of the work. These were many and ranged from artists working alongside creative people who've had mental illness at the START Project to Manchester Mind, who did an appraisal of Victor's work, saying it was creative, imaginative and effective. We met people from adult basic education, some of whom liked and some of whom were puzzled by the material, actors who were interpreting and dramatising mental illness, and we attended the 'Worlds of Literacy' conference, where everyone listened and many gave us helpful comments. All of these people helped us to grow as individuals and helped to develop our work in some way. 'A Guide To The Monsters Of The Mind' is selling steadily. Yet, in spite of my satisfaction about the successful outcome of the project, I'm aware of Victor's surprise and dismay at the time and work the book has cost him. I know it's important to share with writers the model in my head about getting material ready to be published. I try to do this through talking, when beginning work with a writer. It doesn't work. What works is actually going through the process. Maybe Gatehouse should develop a course to take new writers through what's involved in having a book published.

Epilogue

We are dealing with very complex problems in the book. There are large areas of our brains still unexplored, mysterious unknown parts of our minds. There are no easy answers, no magic solutions. But pictures, through their universality and openness, allow you to distance yourself or come close to your own experience in your interpretation. They also trigger

Victor Grenko

responses on many different levels. You can see in Victor's pictures colour, brightness, comic allusions, or you can see tense, emotive or even frightening situations behind them. To see the full picture, is like trying to put together a fantastic complex Chinese puzzles.

Victor writes: Problems are part of people's lives, part and parcel. You can't change the past. You are always going to live in the middle of chaos and harmony. One day you might be depressed and suicidal; another day you might be full of life and very happy. This is the reality of life. I don't know what it all means in the end. I suppose all you can do is try not to harm anybody in life. What is life? Life is a trick or a treat. A comedy of errors.

SUSAN BENTON, MARY HAMILTON & SARAH PADMORE

22: BREAKING AND REMAKING THE RULES

This piece has been put together by Susan Benton, Mary Hamilton and Sarah Padmore. We were in the group at the conference who invented this way of describing the process we go through in trying to create new worlds of literacy. Others in the group were Shirley Cornes, Peter Good, Judith Harrison, Jenny Horsman, Mary Kinane, Robert Merry and Wendy Moss.

We began with a common interest in literacy and change, literacy and power. Most of us were women and this affected the examples we gave as we talked. We are all white. We were a mixture of teachers and students from different parts of the country. Between us we held an enormous range of experience of families, parenting, changing relationships, disability, life crises, work and unemployment, expressing ourselves in words or images, feelings about language we use and the education we have had . . . . just like any other group of adults, in fact.

At the end of the session we felt we had created something worth passing on. What we had to show were two anarchic posters crammed full of words and images. We have recreated these here trying to keep the spirit of the original discussion and the many layers of ideas expressed in the posters. We did not want to force these ideas into a straitjacket of written words alone: they were made through talk and drawing more than writing.

Throughout this book we have tried to use the creative potential of different forms of literacy to help us move on, to say and think new things. It seems to fit in well, therefore, to have this final, summing up chapter reinforce its optimistic message by making use of the visual literacy conventions of the cartoon and comic strip.

The story goes like this.
Imagine a house. Who lives in it. A woman. A man. A child.
From the outside the house is much like the others in the neighbourhood.
Inside, it is a prison (perhaps the others are too?)
What makes it a prison are the bricks it is made of.

Pressures from outside make some people feel trapped and inadequate.

There are eyes all round the house, that can see through the walls.

rage . . . . dissatisfaction
hating the rules but still playing the game.
Not realising it is a game

*gradually realising its a game
and what the rules are*

*getting the confidence to break the rules, to say no, to look for a different
way of doing things.*

*The slow steps of change, what you need to do it
breaking out . . . . refusing*

*questionning
the doctor . . . .*

*asking officials to explain their
jargon & simplify their forms.*

*challenging
the teacher*

finding, over time new ways of acting,

*refusing the old ways,
making new demands.*

*putting across new
points of view. . . .*

The Opening Door .. A happy ending?

Walking off into the sunset, but with risk, challenge, awareness, hope .....

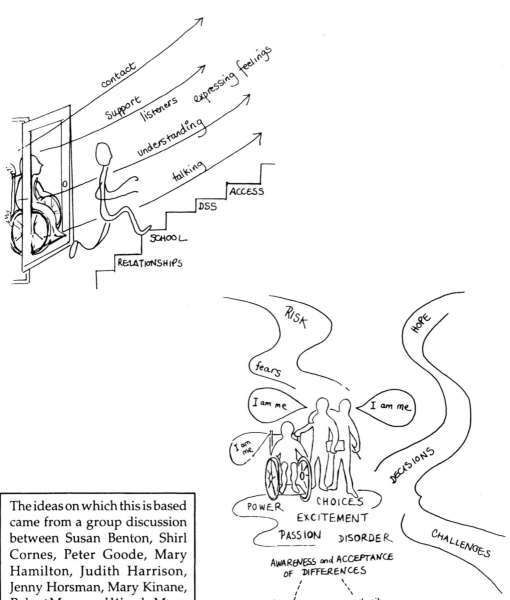

The ideas on which this is based came from a group discussion between Susan Benton, Shirl Cornes, Peter Goode, Mary Hamilton, Judith Harrison, Jenny Horsman, Mary Kinane, Robert Merry and Wendy Moss.

List of Contributors

David Barton is a lecturer in linguistics at Lancaster University. He is interested in what people read and write in their everyday lives. He co-edited *Writing in the Community*, and is one of the founders of the Research and Practice in Adult Literacy Group (RaPAL).

Nichola Benson graduated from Lancaster University in 1990 with a degree in Educational Studies and Visual Arts. Originally from Sunderland, she is now living in South Yorkshire, where she is training to teach Art and Drama.

Susan Benton completed the MA in Language Studies and Educational Linguistics at Lancaster in 1990. She has since changed direction somewhat, and is now working in Vienna as a consultant on HIV/AIDS education, and specifically issues concerning women.

Shirley Cornes graduated in 1987 from both Southampton University (Sociology Honours) and The Open University. A Londoner living in Dorset, she is an ABE, OU and Community Education tutor, part-time PhD researcher, locum hospital medical secretary and laughs a lot!

Paul Davies is a researcher at the Centre for the Study of Education and Training, Lancaster University. His main research interests are careers education and guidance. Before coming to Lancaster he worked as a careers adviser in the Midlands.

Fie van Dijk works as a lecturer at Amsterdam University (PVE: Project Adult Education), researches Women and Literacy, and is a voluntary literacy worker in her home village Breukelen (The Netherlands).

Stella Fitzpatrick works for Gatehouse Books. She develops and co-ordinates publications and training. She is a teacher and an experienced publisher and Basic Education worker.

Joe Flanagan, Gillian Frost and Peter Goode. All we got from basic education was a week at Nottingham University. At the end of the week we asked ourselves where could we get some more of the same and give other people the same chance. You might say out of that week Pecket Well College was born. Joe Flanagan, Gillian Frost and Peter Goode are founder members.

Victor Grenko overcame reading and writing difficulties. He is now a member of the Gatehouse Management Committee and a Director of Gatehouse. His latest published work is in *Telling Tales* (Gatehouse, 1992).

Sarah Gurney graduated from Lancaster University in 1990 with a degree in Educational Studies and Mathematics. Originally from Sussex, she is living in South Yorkshire and is currently training to be a pilot.

Nigel Hall is a lecturer in Education Studies at Manchester Polytechnic. He is a specialist in the writing development of young children.

Mary Hamilton works in the Department of Educational Research at Lancaster University. She is a member of the Literacy Research Group. Her main interests are in how people learn and how to link research and practice and adult basic education.

Judith Harrison graduated from Lancaster University in 1991 with a degree in Educational Studies and Linguistics. She is currently occupied with voluntary activities in her local community near Lancaster, and is hoping to continue with study or research.

Tricia Hartley works at Nelson and Colne College of FE in Lancashire, where she is leader of the ACCESS Section, the College's language and learning support unit. She completed a part-time MA in Education and Linguistics at Lancaster University in 1992.

Margaret Herrington works as the Distance Learning Organiser for the Leicestershire Adult Basic Education Service. She has worked on issues of literacy and numeracy with adult learners since 1975 and her recent work in higher education (teaching, research and development) is crucially informed by that experience.

Jenny Horsman is a community educator/researcher with a feminist perspective. Her experience in literacy includes academic research and direct programme work. Currently she works with Spiral Community Resource Group, Toronto, carrying out research, writing, training and facilitation projects.

Jean Hudson is a Senior Lecturer in Language and Literacy at Edge Hill College of Education. She is primarily involved with in-service courses for teachers and is particularly interested in the early stages of literacy development.

Roz Ivanic taught in secondary, further and adult education for 15 years and now works in the Department of Linguistics at Lancaster University. She is mainly interested in everything to do with writing: learning to write, writer identity, written language, different kinds of writing. . .

Angela Karach completed her degree in Women's Studies and Sociology in 1990. Now is a part-time worker at Lancaster University, occasional worker for Lancashire Youth and Community Service and freelance graphic artist for women's projects.

Agnes King undertook Teacher Training at Hamilton College of Education, in Scotland. Later she read Education for her BA degree with the Open University. She teaches primary aged children full-time. She is a part-time lecturer in Adult Basic Education.

Mandy McMahon was lecturer in Continuing Education at Bradford and Ilkley Community College, where she worked for 20 years. Her PhD research was on the management of Adult Basic Education. She was a founding member and central figure in RaPAL and was committed to improving access to lifelong education for all adults. She died unexpectedly in December 1990 while this book was in preparation.

Jane Mace is Senior Lecturer in Community Education at Goldsmith's College, University of London, where she teaches, writes and researches in adult literacy and writing development. She has published books on paid educational leave, literacy policy and practice, and student publishing in adult literacy, drawing on her experience of working in community education centres.

Carol Morris and Hubisi Nwenmely work together on the Patwa project in Tower Hamlets Adult Education Institute, East London, researching and teaching the Kwéyòl language.

Sarah Padmore came into literacy research via work in adult basic and bilingual education, and a school history of red biro slashes with the comment 'See me'. She is particularly interested in raising questions about education, everyday communication practices and personal writing.

Rachel Rimmershaw works as a lecturer in the Department of Educational Research at Lancaster University, teaching about language, psychology and information technology. She researches the academic literacy practices of students, teachers and researchers in higher education.

Denise Roach has completed a degree in Applied Social Science. She also works part-time for Lancashire Youth and Community Service, and enjoys spending time with close friends.

Anne Robinson is a lecturer in Education Studies at Manchester Polytechnic. She is a specialist in the writing development of young children.

Mukul Saxena works as a lecturer in the Department of Linguistics at the University College of Ripon and York, teaching about syntax and semantics of English and Hindi, and sociolinguistics. He researches bilingualism in classroom and minority community.

Irene Schwab was formerly the organiser of the Hackney Reading Centre, a community literacy project and co-edited the book *Language and Power*. She is currently a communications lecturer at City and East London College, teaching adult returners.

Brian Street is Senior Lecturer in Social Anthropology at the University of Sussex. He has written and lectured extensively on literacy practices from both a theoretical and an applied perspective. He is best known for *Literacy in Theory and Practice* (CUP), and his newest book *Cross-Cultural Approaches to Literacy*, is also published by CUP.

Index

Lightning Source UK Ltd.
Milton Keynes UK
UKOW020456051212

203191UK00002B/9/P